Personal and Family Finance
Principles and Applications

Personal and Family Finance
Principles and Applications

Margery Kabot Schiller

Allyn and Bacon, Inc.
Boston London Sydney Toronto

Library of Congress Cataloging in Publication Data

Schiller, Margery K.
    Personal and family finance.

    Includes index.
    1. Finance, Personal. I. Title.
HG179.S27   332.024   80-14896
ISBN 0-205-07095-7

Managing Editor: Robert Roen

Series Editor: David F. Pallai

Production Editor/Designer: Valerie Fraser Ruud

Printed in the United States of America

Contents

Preface vii

CHAPTER ONE   **Reflections on Money and Its Meaning to Individuals 1**
Perceptions of Money 2
Classic Models: Myth and Reality 4
Money in Real Life Relationships 9
Rational Decision Making 11
Professional Guidelines 12

CHAPTER TWO   **Financial Planning to Match Needs and Income 15**
Net Worth—A Starting Point 16
Alternate Lifestyle Needs 22
Recordkeeping Choices 24
Tips of the Trade 29
Future Trends 29
Professional Guidelines 31

CHAPTER THREE   **Paying Your Fair Share in Taxes—and No More 33**
Sharing the Burden 34
Sales Taxes 34
Property Taxes 35
Income Taxes 39
Gift and Inheritance Taxes 47
The Composite Picture 47
Professional Guidelines 48

CHAPTER FOUR   **A Place to Live 51**
Chasing the American Dream 52
Surveying the Market 56
Comparison Shopping 61
Renting Shelter 62
Buying Shelter 65
Choosing Among Alternatives 76
Professional Guidelines 77

CHAPTER FIVE   **Getting There 79**
Transportation Needs 80
Transportation Options 84
Coping Strategies 88
Purchasing Options 89
Professional Guidelines 99

CHAPTER SIX   **Credit: A Mortgage on the Future 101**
Trends in Credit Usage 102
Types of Credit Available 105
Basic Sources of Credit 107
Unique Credit Arrangements 109
Cost Comparisons 111
Applying for Credit 113

The Credit Contract 120
Post-Transaction Activities 130
Professional Guidelines 133

CHAPTER SEVEN A New Definition of Debt and Its Implications 135
Exploring Attitudes Toward Debt 136
Examining Danger Signals 137
Assessing the Situation 138
Collecting Past-due Accounts 141
Choosing Among Debt Management Alternatives 149
Professional Guidelines 163

CHAPTER EIGHT Options for Protection Against Financial Disasters 165
General Principles 166
Property Insurance 172
Medical Insurance 178
Disability Income Protection Insurance 187
Life Insurance 190
Switching Policies 203
Professional Guidelines 203

CHAPTER NINE Cash Substitutes and Storage Facilities 205
Types of Banking Institutions 206
Safety Precautions 208
Services Available 210
Professional Guidelines 221

CHAPTER TEN Putting Your Assets to Work 223
Investment Readiness 224
Investment Variables 228
General Types of Investments 229
Selection Criteria 240
Guidelines for Decision Making 247
Consumer Protection 254
Professional Guidelines 256

CHAPTER ELEVEN Lifestyle Adaptations for Retirement and
Estate Planning 259
Lifestyle Adjustments 260
Costs of Living in Retirement 261
Sources of Retirement Income 263
Estate Planning 271
Professional Guidelines 276

CHAPTER TWELVE A Word in Closing 277
Ideologies Challenged 278
Realities Perceived 278

Glossary 281

Index 293

Preface

This book presents important theories of personal finance along with a variety of opportunities for field testing the implementation of those theories. You will have the opportunity to draw on past experiences for this application, a multitude of case studies, and some dialogues with people in order to learn in the manner most appropriate for you.

Learning by doing has long proven to be an effective teaching technique for adult learners. Personal experiences in living become a resource for evaluating the relevance of theory and its practical application to the real world.

Yet to afford the instructor maximum discretion in using the experiential learning tools, they have generally been presented in the instructor's manual only. In this way, each teacher has full freedom to choose when and how these various assignments may be useful for each particular class of students.

In order to maintain continuity, the major topics for experiential learning are subtly woven into the design of the student text. This allows project work to complement textbook readings and vice versa for a more unified approach that hopefully will enhance the learning environment. Accordingly, some references in the textbook case histories may seem a bit vague. This has been done purposely to provide a connecting link to the activities developed for the instructor's manual. None of these references are critical to understanding chapter content, yet all are reasonable points of inquiry for related class discussion or research if pursued individually.

Acknowledgments

Although a great number of people assisted with and influenced the development of this text, special thanks are given to:

Ted Christiansen, C.L.U., Coordinated Financial Planning, Inc., Farmington, Connecticut

Robert W. Eddy, Account Executive, Dean Witter Reynolds, Inc., Burlington, Vermont

E. David Smith, President, Butler Insurance Office, Inc., East Hampton, Connecticut.

Doris Morse and Ann Marie Beloin are gratefully acknowledged for the invaluable service of typing this manuscript.

Also, much appreciation is offered to Gene and Jonathan Schiller, whose cooperation and understanding made completion of this book possible.

Personal and Family Finance
Principles and Applications

ONE

Reflections on Money and Its Meaning to Individuals and Families Today

It was awkward to go back to college at forty-three, but Jessica Winthrop needed the graduate degree in order to enter administrative work at her social service agency. So she began pounding the pavement of her hometown, asking the residents questions about their spending habits—prying into their personal business! Why? Because she needed the money. Participating in this replication of the Consumer Expenditure Survey was the best paying job available. Aside from some limited savings, her earnings from the survey work were now her only source of income, and she had to eat.

Her assignment was to conduct twenty face-to-face interviews with people living in a one-block area to study the design and effectiveness of this questionnaire. Jessie felt the task was simple, but embarrassing. Talking to people about money always made her uncomfortable. She couldn't wait for the interviewing to be over so she could get into the more challenging work of evaluating the data.

Money does tend to evoke an emotional response in most people in virtually any context. Although the denotation of the word is "medium

1

of exchange," the connotations are far more diverse. Because they deal with psychological meanings, the connotations of money have grown to reveal more about its real value to people in contemporary society than the denotation.

PERCEPTIONS OF MONEY

By definition, money has traditionally been a vehicle of convenience for obtaining desired or necessary goods and services. Instead of trying to trade three chickens for a shirt, money allows us to obtain currency for the chickens which we may then use to purchase the shirt. While this latter method involves a third exchange, it actually simplifies the transaction. In the first system of trading, called bartering, the owner of the chickens could not obtain her or his desired merchandise until the owner of an appropriate shirt would accept the chickens in exchange. The time and energy involved in matching buyer to seller could be great.

In the money economy where currency is an acceptable medium of exchange, the owner of the chickens need never find an owner of a shirt who wanted to trade. Their common bond is currency. It is easily portable, and it can help negotiate a trade without buyer and seller ever meeting. Hence, money became the liaison in facilitating market transactions. Its value became decided by supply and demand as well as people's attitudes. Paper money today, while legal tender in the United States, has no actual worth. Its value is based on the good faith of our country's citizenry to assign a hypothetical value to that paper and treat it equal to any item of that inherent worth.

MICRO IMPACT

As a medium of exchange, money is realistically only a means to an end—and that is precisely how it is viewed by normal, healthy individuals. It eases the development of coping skills required to deal with our world. Often a person who learns how to earn money and spend it wisely can avoid studying other skills to build her or his own self-sufficiency.

Problems begin to arise when people view money as an end in itself rather than a means to an end.[1] Their motivation may become the accumulation of currency alone. Somehow the process of exchanging money for goods and services gets distorted, and these individuals attempt to use money to purchase power, respect, affection, and companionship. Accordingly, these people may feel compelled to hoard currency, using it as a weapon to demand selected emotional responses from family members, coworkers, or friends.

In reverse, other people spend blindly and carelessly in a cry for attention and/or a substitute for lost love, as a rebellion from responsibility, a weapon for inflicting suffering on others, a tool for demonstrating command of power, a compensation for loneliness, or other voids in life's bounties. The list goes on and on. Its common thread is the purpose for which the money is used—a purpose dominated by emotion rather than logic and activated by psychic desires despite survival needs and related coping mechanisms.

An awareness of this fact and a recognition of some cues to the way people use money to meet emotional needs can alert you to potential problems in your own use of money and that of significant others in your life. This may eliminate the problem before it begins, particularly in developing interpersonal relationships. If you recognize the fact that a certain individual uses money to command power, you may not choose this person as a spouse if you prefer egalitarian relationships. This same insight can also aid in sustaining positive permanent relationships among family members or others who have very different perceptions of money.

Professionally, persons employed in the human services must also be keenly aware of people's perceptions and uses for money. Money management practices reveal a lot about people's basic value systems and their abilities and willingness to cope with reality.[2] Observing and/or discussing these management practices can reveal facts about an individual's self-respect, ability to work with others, and adeptness in dealing with stress. It may help explain that he or she has a problem adjusting to the world around them, although money seldom explains why that is so. In reverse, wise money management practices can indicate emotional maturity and strong coping skills despite crisis situations. Whether your chosen profession is personnel administration, credit granting, social service work, financial counseling, or psychology, an awareness of people's attitudes toward money can prove invaluable in providing relevant assistance to your clients.

In a broader sense, people's attitudes toward money have been proven to affect the functioning of our national economy. In the early 1960s, research done at the University of Michigan showed that in our affluent society consumers' willingness to buy was as important as their ability to buy in affecting economic trends.[3] Many Americans at this time could afford to buy more than the basic necessities of life. Yet their decision to save or spend discretionary income was related to their perceptions of the future. When they felt financially secure and anticipated continued employment and rising incomes, they spent their extra money on nonessential goods and services. Many even mortgaged future income through the growing use of in-

MACRO IMPACT

stallment buying. Yet, when perception of future prosperity grew dim, even though nothing had actually changed in their ability to buy, these same people generally preferred to save in anticipation of future shortages.[4]

CLASSIC MODELS: MYTH AND REALITY

In reviewing the history of our nation, the sociology of its people and their stages of personal development, we can also find insights into American money management attitudes and practices. Some of the traditional models find less application with the diversity of lifestyles today and the government regulation of economic functions. But they still serve to increase our understanding of why people use money in some of the ways they do.

SOCIETAL AND
TECHNOLOGICAL
INFLUENCES

In the history of America, our agrarian forefathers were able to produce most of the goods and services they needed to live comfortably in their times. Therefore, money had limited usefulness or importance. Yet, as we moved into an industrialized and urbanized society, the specialization of labor increased our dependency on money because of its convenience as a medium of exchange. Even children switched from being an economic asset on the farm to an economic liability in the city, especially after the child labor laws restricted their ability to help the family earn.

While wars brought hard times for all, they greatly reduced unemployment and limited consumer ability to buy. So, when wars ended, the civilian economy boomed, at least for a few years. When speculation grew too rampant and the economic upturn collapsed, we reverted to meeting basic survival needs through bartering or money income, depending on availability—especially during the Great Depression.

Spurred by a major need to revitalize the peacetime economy, Congress acted to build Uncle Sam's image of "parent protector" to the masses by instituting select government controls on economic behavior. Social insurance programs were also implemented and expanded in an effort to use government spending to counteract the Depression and increase the economic security of Americans. And when all of these good intentions weren't quite enough to produce economic recovery, we entered another war, which coincidentally helped to bring us back into a growth spiral. Even so, the sudden severity and duration of hard times had an indelible effect on many Americans who would forever anticipate a recurrence of economic stress so frightening in their earlier years.

The post-World War II economy produced another basic change in American values and an image of never-ending affluence for the next generation. Prosperity grew at all income levels. Jobs were plentiful and credit buying offered a new way to mortgage your future because it was always going to be financially secure. While the optimism seemed never ending, perceptions of reality were somewhat distorted as evidenced by ever-increasing rates of personal bankruptcy despite the boom.

Then hard times began again in the 1970s with more people than jobs and scarcities of all kinds. They never reached the tragedy of the 1930s, but many older people perceived the same problems to recur. Younger generations who grew up in the age of affluence disagreed and looked to Big Government to protect them from starvation. Social insurance programs were expected to provide total care, preserving existing levels of living despite unemployment unless Uncle Sam produced jobs for everyone who wanted them. Yet, reality still wasn't quite the same as it was perceived. After slowing down in the early 1970s, personal bankruptcy rates soared to new heights and debt was now redefined as "falling behind in payments, not simply owing money."[4]

Future predictions vary with the philosophy on which they are based and the distance which they project. The 1980s are generally perceived as a more reality-oriented era with an abundance of U.S. workers competing for fewer jobs due to the reduced needs of smaller families and the more limited resources of people accepting earlier retirement. Many young adults will discover they cannot achieve the prosperity they grew up with during the early 1960s. Faced with the necessity of conservation of natural resources, we will all be pushed toward accepting a lifestyle in tune with new realities. This may prove paradoxical for some since incomes are expected to rise. More discretionary money may prevail, yet its uses could be limited by scarcities of energy, etc. Spending may move toward the purchase of more services for some, while others struggle to meet survival needs among an ever-increasing maze of choices. The question of a more or less materialistic America remains in debate except in the mind of one author who perceives the future as a post-industrial, noneconomic society where the household is more dominant than the marketplace and money is replaced by time as the measure of economic functioning.[5]

History and futurology confirm the dilemma of contemporary living where economic theories and conditions demand continuous adaptation to change. The task is not an easy one, nor has it taken priority in our skills training for adulthood. We have long encouraged our youth to learn about work and develop the required skills to earn. Yet educators have only recently begun to complement this effort with the related need to learn how to spend wisely in light of current economic considerations. The challenge remains to focus on coping with the reality and stress of modern existence.

Unless or until money becomes meaningless, that challenge focuses largely on personal resource management where time, energy, money, and talent are effectively combined to meet individual life goals.

THE PERSONAL FINANCIAL LIFE CYCLE

A look at classic models of the role of money in personal development can also offer some insight into its meaning for individuals. Research in this field is far from extensive, but even the stereotypes generated can provide help in finding clues to why people spend and save as they do and how these money management decisions relate to lifestyle choices and coping behavior.

Early Childhood. Very young children have no clear understanding of money and its uses. Money becomes magical in its abilities to be transformed into food, toys, or other more desirable objects. It is not until age five or later that a child learns the different values of various coins and how they can be used in the marketplace.

Money attitudes in children are a reflection of their parents. Children learn quickly by observation and mimicry. That's why the child whose behavior has been manipulated by money rewards will probably grow into an adult who focuses on wealth as the primary source of satisfaction in life. Bribing a child with money can produce an adult who will only function well when money is offered in advance of completing a required task. Rewarding a child with money will produce a job well done before the money is received—but only if it is promised in advance. While the latter is more in keeping with societal norms, neither takes into account the work required as your fair share of family responsibility or your contribution to community betterment where the rewards are completely intangible.

It is quite possible that Jessica Winthrop's discomfort with discussing money matters may stem from her own childhood training. If she grew up in a home where children were never included in family spending decisions or where grown-ups talked in hushed whispers about these matters, Jessie would have to make conscious efforts to overcome adopting this same reaction pattern in her own life. Even working with her clients' money problems may not change Jessie's attitude if she sees the discussion of money as a necessity only for select groups to which she does not belong. Her role model in these matters remains her family and peers.

Teen Years. Teenagers have already formed their basic attitudes about money. Now its role begins to center on the dollar's ability to provide them with that desperately desired independence in decision making. Earning can be more closely tied to spending in addition to or in lieu of the traditional allowance because the options are more realistic. Learning to carefully evaluate alternatives and make decisions based upon *your* values becomes a priority. Cooperation as part of the family team must find a balance with individual achievement. The concept of credit may also be effectively introduced while under the watchful eye of parental guidance.

Early Adulthood. Traditionally, single adulthood is characterized by hedonistic spending. Enjoying life becomes the prevailing mode. Savings is considered less important because there are usually no dependents to protect. The start of a full-time job may mean the first time a person has enough money to spend freely. This is also perceived as the only chance to enjoy luxury before settling down to the serious business of raising a family. The one trend unique to recent years is that luxury may be viewed as freedom from work and pleasure equated with aesthetic fulfillment, not money freely spent. Settling down demands a job and financial security—not independent adult living.

The Couple.   When two people marry, they enter the next stage of the life cycle and begin to redirect their priorities. Family needs and goals take priority over those of each individual and protection begins to be more important than enjoyment. Instant gratification becomes common among couples who hurry to meet their parents' level of living on incomes far too modest to make these goals realistic. They want much more than they can comfortably afford, willingly mortgaging future earning to meet today's desires.

Dual income families make living this dream more feasible until unemployment hits or job transfer or pregnancy. When the family is reduced to one income, they may no longer be able to stretch their dollars in all of the previous directions. Adjustments in spending become critical, but the results may still be staggering if fixed expenses take too large a chunk of income.

While free spending may have worked successfully for the same people as singles, the interdependence of married life generally demands a restructuring of management practices to provide more security against future emergencies and more careful planning to reach longer-range goals.

Young Families.   When children join the couple, the expanding family is likely to consciously increase their level of indebtedness. Children cost money for today's necessities of life and tomorrow's education. Savings are important, but family income is relatively low because the young worker has not yet reached peak earning capacity. One spouse may also be out of the job market to accept responsibility for child rearing. Or, if both parents work, a large portion of their earnings may be used for child care. Space for living becomes a growing need, so housing costs may further plunge the young family into debt.

As the children grow quickly towards adulthood, the family situation reverses somewhat. Income rises toward its peak with help from a spouse's return to work and/or teenage children contributing to family earnings. Savings for the children's education takes priority and related child-launching rituals like weddings use up many accumulated resources.

College Years. The following empty nest stage, when the children have gained financial independence, is marked by a return to the pleasure-oriented lifestyle of bygone years. Yet the desire for enjoyment while still young enough to appreciate it is coupled with increased savings for retirement and a concerted effort toward debt repayment before income is sharply reduced by retirement.

Retirement. Retirement and the aging process may bring a return to childhood dependency for physical or financial reasons. Inflation rapidly eats away at the fixed income of pensions while medical science extends life beyond imaginable limits for some people. The combination can yield inadequate financial resources to maintain independent living. Forgetfulness or medical problems can also change spending roles, bill-paying habits, and investment decisions until it is just plain easier for someone else to trouble themselves with all of these money matters.

Other Views. This classic model of the financial life cycle has recently been compounded and intriguingly altered by the introduction of a new way of looking at stages of adult life. Most popularly received in Gail Sheahy's *Passages,* that author looks at adult life as a series of crises that must be faced and resolved sequentially if we are to grow to true maturity. These crises are considered predictable, nonparallel in men and women, often signaled by societal demands in competition with instincts and a plausible reason why adult life does not proceed as smoothly as just explained.

Physical or mental illness, unemployment, separation, divorce, death of a spouse, etc., can all change the classic model of the family financial life cycle into a far less simple way of following people's money management practices. Very often two or more stages of the life cycle overlap or never materialize. The adult who chooses to remain single throughout life is more prevalent than ever, as is the single parent and childless couple. While any of these people may fixate at their entry stage of the life cycle, they can just as readily proceed through all stages like the traditional two-parent family will do under ordinary circumstances. While generalizations can effectively stimulate thinking about a particular issue or trend, they cannot be accepted as the only way of doing things.

MONEY IN REAL LIFE RELATIONSHIPS

Since the meaning of money varies with the life experiences of individuals, it becomes vitally important to recognize and deal with these differences in our interpersonal relationships. This requires an awareness of similarities and differences in any two or more value systems and a plan for effective interactions. Keeping money in perspective as a means to an end rather than a symbol of power can go a long way in helping to attain this goal.

INDIVIDUAL VERSUS GROUP NEEDS

When you are the only person using a specified sum of money, you are the only person who needs to be involved in making decisions about that money, unless you choose to solicit the advice and opinions of others. When that sum of money is to be used for the support of a group of individuals, then all members of that group should be allowed to help in deciding how that money will be used. In a traditional family, if the children are expected to curb recreational spending because the parents want to buy a new house, then the parents must also find a way to help the children reach their financial goals. Otherwise, there is no clear understanding of why the group is together and interdependent rather than serving one or more leaders exclusively.

Flexibility is an important ingredient, coupled with an allowance for human error and some impulsive behavior. While it would be unrealistic for most groups to allow half of their income to be used without planning and purpose, it can be very wise to allow each group member a few dollars regularly to meet their whims and wishes. By so doing, primary attention can be given to working toward group goals because the escape valve is always there for a small splurge to satisfy an impulse. It is equally wise to set aside some form of emergency fund to compensate for the miscalculations of costs, or unplanned events that eventually crop up and demand attention. Even on the most limited of spending plans, people must have some options from which to choose at least occasionally in order to feel in control of their funds and master of the situation. Of course, the key to flexibility is effective communication to acknowledge these needs and accommodate them with the allocation of money and other resources.

The sense of feeling in control of your finances is often a major step in reaching your goals—and that sense of feeling in control can have a marked impact on your general attitude toward money matters. Jessica Winthrop, from the introductory case study, might feel more comfortable discussing money matters if she were more confident about her abilities to live within her presently reduced income. Right now the stress of her personal adaptation needs are being transferred to her work situation so that she doesn't quite feel in command in either role.

POTENTIAL
PROBLEMS

Some people have problems managing money because they have never been taught how to do so. Their parents never bothered, the topic never came up in school, and they were always too embarrassed to ask. These skills were assumed to be something acquired with adulthood and a source of income.

Others use money management difficulties to symbolize deeper emotional conflicts inherent in personality development or interpersonal relationships. While it is often unclear which is the cause or the effect, the existence of the difficulty is a cry for help to unravel the whole mystery. It may require professional counseling to truly resolve the dilemma, but even that can only be accomplished when the counselor understands wise money management as well as personality development.

Often problems of this nature remain hidden until a change in lifestyle emphasizes them. This is likely to occur with a sudden change of income, either up or down, because both require adjustments to reality. Similarly, the problem may be exemplified when someone refuses to accept responsibility for their own financial management or their share of a group's management. The single adult who regularly "forgets" to pay bills when they are due may do so to gain attention, declare a need for dependence, or otherwise ignore the reality of an independent lifestyle that he or she really does not enjoy. The spouse who frequently charges luxury items without concern for the family's ability to pay off the debts may be daring her or his partner to limit these purchases as a demonstration of real love or rebellion against extreme dominance in other forms of decision making.

While extremes of this type of behavior in dealing with money can signify serious problems in personal identity or interpersonal communication, we all fall victim to these manipulations upon occasion. The environment in which we live perpetuates some of these manipulative games to the point that even healthy individuals will try them out. Television, movies, and novels simulate reality for entertainment value. They are not intended to be accepted as fact, but often these stories follow the vicarious lives of real people. So if money can buy happiness on TV, why wouldn't we expect someone to try out the same philosophy in real life? The experiment is only natural. People are always trying to manipulate the behavior of others to meet their own desires. That is not likely to change, nor is it likely to pose insurmountable problems as long as it is done consciously. When it becomes

an obsession, or takes precedence over the bonds of friendship and cooperation among individuals, look out! Inappropriate uses of money could then
be the first sign in breakdown of the reality function of the individual.[6]

RATIONAL DECISION MAKING

There is no pat formula to using money wisely. Like so many other things,
your choices about money reflect your personality. They are different for
everyone, although some guidelines may prove helpful in realistic decision
making.

Above all else, you must know yourself in order to use money to help reach
your goals. You must decide what is really important to you now and for
the future. Look carefully at the way you live, including the way you spend
and save. Does it reflect your basic values? Does it tell the story of you as a
person that you choose to share with the world? Are your priorities evident?
Are you comfortable with and confident in continuing this lifestyle? Is it
realistic in light of present economic conditions, family responsibilities,
health, etc?

    If you answer yes to these questions, you've got a good start on using
your money as a means to an end. Your goals are clearly in sight and you
are obviously striving toward them. That is precisely the way money was intended to be used, so keep up the good work!

    A negative reply to one or more questions tells you it's time to restruc-
ture your financial management in line with reality. Most people can
accomplish this on their own by examining existing spending and savings
patterns. Finding the money leaks will provide clues about your real values
to help you make conscious choices about priorities. If you say appearance
is of little importance in your life, yet you spend 25 percent of your income
on clothing, there seems to be a conflict in values that must be resolved for
realistic spending to be planned and implemented. Can you reduce or eliminate the leaks to stay within your stated values? Or are the leaks really an
unconscious signal that your values are changing and that you had better re-
think your goals?

**PERSONAL
GUIDELINES**

To succeed in money management you must have enough discipline to
handle your money as a true reflection of your values and goals as an individual and an active member of the group to which you belong. Group
membership may require adjustments in your uses of money in order to preserve the importance of the group. Whether you live in a nuclear family or

**GROUP
CONSIDERATIONS**

commune, if group needs take priority over those of the individual, compromises may be in order.

Financial responsibility in any group involves sharing and cooperation. Mutual respect and commitment to group goals also help, especially in long-term relationships like marriage and family. Talking out values and goals before finalizing the bonds is an important step in realistic planning. Also important are joint decision making and open channels of communication. Flexibility makes the whole idea workable, as does the Golden Rule: *You Rule the Money: It Doesn't Rule You.*

PROFESSIONAL GUIDELINES

The same basic ideas apply when your job includes responsibility for helping others learn to manage their money wisely. Listen carefully to what they say and do about money management to determine if perceptions and reality match. Do all members of the group reflect similar values and goals? Is money used as a means to an end—a goal that is clearly defined and attainable? Or are there barriers to communication, money leaks, power struggles, or other clues to management problems? Do the problems reflect deep-seated emotional conflicts that require psychological counseling? Or are they the frustrations of limited coping skills that can be resolved with training and guidance?

Do you have the expertise to deal with these problems? If not, can you make a referral to another professional who can offer specific assistance to your client or customer? It is to your advantage to develop and maintain contacts with helping agency personnel, from government assistance workers to mental health counselors. The team approach is most effective when helping troubled persons and families. The positive feedback and cooperation generated can only enhance your abilities.

But the key to success in your own work and your referrals is that you (1) know your business well, and (2) work within the values system of the person requesting help. Attempting to impose your values on others is a sure road to failure in professional helping relationships. It must be avoided if help is to be accepted and implemented.

Essentially the guidelines for rational financial decision making are the simple and logical first steps to wise money management. The specifics will be detailed and expanded throughout this book, although the principles will remain unchanging for as long as our money economy prevails. Techniques for developing a workable spending and savings plan will be explored next as an immediate aid in applying the principles just discussed.

ENDNOTES

1. James Knight, *For the Love of Money* (Philadelphia: J. B. Lippincott, 1968), p. 12.
2. Herb Goldberg and Robert T. Lewis, *Money Madness: The Psychology of Saving, Spending, Loving and Hating Money* (New York: William Morrow, 1978), p. 52.
3. George Katona, *The Mass Consumption Society* (New York: McGraw Hill, 1964), p. 3.
4. Yankelovich, Skelley, and White, Inc., *The General Mills American Family Report 1974–75* (Minneapolis: General Mills, Inc., 1975), p. 91.
5. Scott Burns, *The Household Economy: Its Shape, Origins and Future* (Boston: Beacon Press, 1975), pp. 245–246.
6. Knight, *For the Love of Money,* p. 73.

TWO

Financial Planning
to Match Needs and Income

#8 Congress Street. Residents: Jeanne Martin, widow, age 28, and her son Jerome, age 7. Their participation in the expenditure survey confirmed all the theories of financial planning that Jessica had ever studied. Motivation toward goal attainment really could help people live realistically within their income. Although her Social Security survivor's benefits plus the proceeds of a small life insurance policy were her only sources of income, Ms. Martin managed to keep her family fed, clothed, and sheltered adequately with some resources left over to have fun. Sure, sometimes fun meant a game of hide and seek at the city park, but she and Jerry would be together sharing the sunshine. That was all that counted.

In contrast, the residents at #2 Congress Street had three times the income and half the organization. David and Maria Welch lived in a charming older home they purchased to renovate into the castle of their dreams. A dual career couple with a combined income of $25,000 annually, the Welches felt their money was unlimited and spent accordingly. The mortgage plus other debt repayment ate up Maria's whole salary. Their spending records were incomplete and inaccurate. Neither partner really cared about what it cost to live as long as the money kept coming in at its present rate. While they claimed the house was important to them both, most discretionary spending seemed to be for clothes, travel, and cars.

In the case study introduced earlier, Jeanne Martin has obviously realized the value of planning and its subsequent implementation. She is aware that money is her most limited resource right now and that she must learn to use it wisely if it is to meet all of her basic needs. By taking on two full-time jobs plus the responsibilities of housekeeping and home remodeling, the Welches are feeling more pressure for time than money. So while they carefully plan how to spend each nonworking hour, they carelessly ignore the value of total resource management in which time, energy, money, and talent are balanced to meet their goals.

NET WORTH—A STARTING POINT

To plan wisely and well for the full utilization of your resources, you must first determine what your resources really are. Some are very limited; others are quite flexible. There are only twenty-four hours in a day, so time is bound by that limit for us all. The question, then, remains how many uncommitted hours do I have each day—not for work, sleep, eating, or commuting, but for other things? What is the quality of this remaining time? Is it fifteen minutes here and forty-five minutes there—or blocks of two- to three-hour periods that I can purposely devote to an important use. And is that time of sufficient quality for me to use any way I choose? If you don't fully wake up until noon, the hours between 6:00 and 8:00 A.M. may not be the best to devote to a high concentration activity.

Relate the same concepts to your energy and talent resources. While these are less easy to quantify, your perceptions of their bounty or scarcity can offer strong clues to their real worth. If your occupation is physically and/or emotionally draining, the energy you have at the end of a workday may be more limiting than the time. Or if your mechanical aptitude tests out well below average, all the time and energy in the world may not be enough to develop your desired skills in cabinetmaking or car repairs.

If your awareness of these resources is somewhat vague, keep a record for one week or longer of how you spend these resources. Be specific enough to easily recall the events of each day and honest enough with yourself to make the task meaningful.

Put aside your records on this type of resource review. Supplement this survey with a list of all the time, energy, and talent you *think* you have. Later we'll match the list against your records to see if your perceptions are in keeping with reality.

To complete the picture of your available resources, it is important to include a survey and inventory of your money wealth and spending practices. The clearest way to do this is through the aid of a basic accounting tool called the *net worth statement*. This is a mathematical summary of where you stand financially. It is defined as the difference between all you own (your assets) and all you owe (your liabilities). All calculations are made in terms of current dollars to provide a clear picture of where you are now.

Liquid assets are those things you own that can easily be converted into cash. Finding out today's market value is fairly simple. For stocks and many bonds, their selling price today is listed in most daily newspapers. The way to compute the present value of life insurance policies and other bonds may be attached to each one. If not, a phone call to the salesperson from whom you purchased this investment will quickly answer your questions. These liquid assets are your cushion against emergencies or unexpected expenses, so it is always wise to know where and how to liquidate them properly—and if a fee is involved to do so or any penalties charged.

The cash value of employee benefits is generally available when you leave the company. The employee benefits officer or someone else in the personnel office should have access to this information. It is a common inquiry that may take some time to calculate, but it is certainly a reasonable request.

Determining the fair market value of real estate is more likely to be a realistic estimate although a real estate agent or appraiser can provide an educated guess for this purpose. The same technique will have to be used on evaluating personal property, too. However, well-kept real estate often appreciates in value as the years go by. Personal property seldom does. In fact, the value of used goods is often much lower than the owner would like to believe. To be fair in evaluation, comparison shop among the second-hand stores for furnishings that resemble yours, and estimate on that basis. When in doubt, use the lower value figure, except for antiques and collectables that have an established and rising value determined by market demand.

When you have listed all assets, total them up and subtract the sum of your liabilities. Include all of your debts—from yesterday's doctor bill to the balance due on your home mortgage. Your home and other installment purchases are actually figured on the asset and liability lists. The current market value is listed as an asset while the balance due remains a liability. The difference is the present value of that purchase. The total of all these differences between assets and liabilities is your net worth.

Ideally, assets will be greater than liabilities to show some degree of real wealth. But that's not always the case. A negative net worth is common during certain stages of the life cycle. As explained in Chapter One, this can almost be anticipated. Self-supporting college students who must borrow to pay for their education will generally run a negative net worth; so will the young person or family embarking on a new career or buying a first home. Future income at these stages can usually be safely planned for use to reverse this net worth position gradually but steadily.

In reviewing the introductory case studies, the Martins and the Welches may be in a negative net worth position, especially if both families are paying off home mortgages. The depth of indebtedness each carries will be different, as are their respective abilities and willingness to reduce it. It is quite realistic to speculate that Jeanne will consciously work toward regularly reducing her negative net worth, even if progress in that direction is very slow. The Welches, on the other hand, don't seem too concerned about this "big picture" as long as their income continues to expand to cover all of their expenses. Because youth is in their favor, both families can probably proceed in their present manner without harm, unless or until a crisis arises. The one major difference implied about these two families is that the Martins seem to be in a more liquid position and more closely approaching their financial goals than the Welches.

Regular reductions in a negative net worth and steady growth in a positive net worth show movement toward attaining financial goals. To make this determination you must find your net worth annually and compare it to last year's record. If you find a "no growth" position, maybe it's time to make changes again. Even when growth is obvious, you must look at it in light of your goals to see if they run parallel.

THE SPENDING PLAN—A FLEXIBLE GUIDE

If changes are desired in your net worth, they can often be accomplished by adjusting your cash flow for on-going expenses incurred against your regular income.

Save receipts or keep records of all purchases made during one full pay period or one month. Concentrate on being accurate and avoid including duplicate receipts on any purchases. (It is quite common to be given the cash register receipt along with your credit card slip, etc.) Label every receipt with a note about what was purchased. Then set this accumulation of receipts aside with your other survey and inventory data on resources until you complete one more very important step.

VALUES AND
GOALS

By this time you have gathered a vast amount of vital data about the way you live. These facts can reveal a great deal about you. But they serve a more important function than you may first realize. The way you spend your resources tells the world what is important to you. It is a direct reflection of your values and goals—although some of this reflection may be determined in your subconscious.

In order to match your perceptions against reality, make a list of what you feel are your values and goals. Be specific. Include long- and short-range goals, the big things in life that count and the little ones that matter, too. Take enough time to be clear and complete in presenting your real feelings. When you're satisfied that this list represents everything that is important to you, pull out the rest of your survey and inventory data for comparative analysis. If your goals do not match your actions, it is time to make some important changes.

Common sense says that spending plans are easier to alter than values and goals. If you agree, then your changes will be made in spending. On the other hand, if this exploration of "the real you" awakens an awareness that your values and/or goals have taken new direction, it may be easier for you to accept new priorities than change present practices. The decision is a very personal one that only you can make.

A WORKABLE PLAN

For most people it's a small miracle if income matches expenses perfectly on the first try. If you are lucky enough to be one of those people, your spending plan is all done—provided it also reflects your goals. If income exceeds expenses, you have money left over to spend as you deem most meaningful in light of your priorities. Or if the reverse is true, and your spending exceeds your income, it's time to make some changes.

You have two basic alternatives in curbing overspending. You can increase your income to match your expenditures or you cut expenses to match the more limited income. The decision is highly individualized, although it is also directly affected by economic considerations, time, energy, and talent resources.

While it often sounds simple to increase your income, it may be a lot easier said than done. You can certainly try to find a higher paying job, moonlight, or send other group members to work. Finding extra work takes time—time during which you run deeper into debt unless spending adjustments are used to compensate in the interim. To really increase your income, you must also look at the net results of the additional work. To do so, check the relevant state and federal income tax tables to see if the added income raises your tax bracket, and, if so, how much of the new income do you really get to keep? Also, what additional costs of commuting, uniforms, meals away from home, child care, and related expenses are directly attributable to the new job? What time, energy, and talent resources that you normally contribute to the household will now have to be purchased because of the additional time spent at work? Subtract all of these costs from the minimum anticipated additional income. Look at the bottom line. Do you really meet the additional income demands of your original spending plan? If the answer is "yes," you've accomplished this goal and can move on to recordkeeping tasks.

If you can't increase your income enough to meet your spending then you need to seriously review spending to see where and how it can be curtailed to match your income and goals. To begin, divide your expenses into two categories: fixed and flexible. Fixed expenses are those that remain stable for relatively long periods of time. They include all installment obligations (including the home mortgage), insurance costs, taxes, and housing. Flexible expenses are those that fluctuate continuously. Included in this category are food, clothing, recreation, transportation, gifts, etc. Depending on the demands of your chosen lifestyle, you may argue that some of these expenses belong in the opposite category. That is fine as long as you follow the guideline that flexible expenses can be adjusted quickly when required, while fixed expenses have greater time restrictions on implementing a change. Both types of spending can be vital for survival, so that is not an issue here.

Obviously, based on these definitions, you would look first at flexible expenses for adjusting your spending plan. Look at each category and re-examine the expenditures made.

To make effective changes, you must know yourself, and the group with whom you live and spend, to determine which sacrifices you can make and stick to until financial circumstances improve. A clue can often be found by looking back at your list of goals in relation to expenses. Obviously those expenses that don't make the "top 10" of your priorities list are the ones that can be cut most easily. Often these are money leaks for which the sum of your spending is greater than you planned in the first place. The loose change in your pocket or purse that goes for incidentals like candy, cigarettes, fresh flowers, or an ice cream cone can add up. Even ten dollars a week slipping through your fingers totals a fair sum by the end of a month or a year.

When the situation is serious, you will also want to look for ways to reduce your fixed expenses as well. Sometimes the total of these are unknowingly costly because many of them occur only once or twice a year. To avoid a surprise attack, figure your monthly spending plan to include a regular amount to be set aside toward meeting these expenses. The simplest way to do this is to review last year's check stubs and list all annual or less than monthly costs that recur consistently. Property taxes, life, health, auto, and homeowners insurance premiums are some examples to consider. Add up the sum of all these expenses at a present day level of costs that reflects anticipated changes from last year and divide by twelve. Open a savings account or interest-bearing checking account to be a depository exclusively for accumulating the funds to meet these costs. Then deposit that one-twelfth sum into the account each month. Draw against the account for payment of these obligations. In this way, you have a revolving fund readily available to meet planned expenses, plus the added benefit of earned interest as a hedge against inflation.

If, after all this, your income still does not match expenses, you may need professional help in developing a realistic spending plan. In addition to classroom teachers in the field, two generally reliable sources of help that are widely available include Cooperative Extension Service home economists, and professional money management counselors.

PROFESSIONAL HELP

The Cooperative Extension Service is a public outreach educational program funded through the U.S. Department of Agriculture in conjunction with state and county governments. It is paid for by your tax dollars and is located in all fifty states and most counties in those states. The agency maintains a staff of home economists whose primary task is to educate the taxpaying public in the ways in which they can improve the quality of life and learn to better cope with the changing world around us. If for any reason the scope of the money management problems are beyond their level of proficiency, each home economist is generally equipped to refer you to the most appropriate local helping agency for further guidance.

Professional money management counselors vary in expertise, experience, time, and dedication. There are currently no national requirements for working in this field, although some are under development at this time. Therefore, the only way to find capable counseling is trial and error, or referral. If the counselor listens to your needs and attempts to work within the framework of your values and goals, that person is beginning at a realistic level.

Throughout the years, the federal government and a number of other industries and agencies have attempted to devise a formula for spending to help simplify the task of matching income to expenses. While these formulas were once used extensively for this intended purpose, they have proven to be unworkable for three basic reasons.

STATISTICAL AIDS

1. They are based on mathematical averages or other statistical abstractions that don't think, feel, or react like real people—nor do they even exist in this hypothetical format in which they are presented as a model.
2. Existing attempts to reduce the effects of the previously listed inaccuracies have also failed because of the inability to define a typical American family to use as a more realistic model. For example, the Bureau of Labor Statistics' most publicized spending plan is

figured for a two-parent family, living together with two school-age children and one wage earner. Yet recent figures from the same department indicate that only seven out of one hundred families in America fit this description.[1]

3. No allowance is included for reflecting individual differences in values and goals in relation to spending as a mirror image of these priorities.

That means statistics, formulas, and pie graphs describing the way Americans spend should be used with discretion in developing any realistic spending plan—whether these tools are used by you or a professional counselor. They should only be used to satisfy curiosity about how your spending compares to that of others or, perhaps, when you need a starting point to develop your first spending plan at a drastically different level of income.

The one possible exception that may prove of some routine value to lay people and professionals is the Consumer Price Index (CPI) calculation. The CPI measures the change in price of a constant market basket of goods and services. One use, therefore, is an index of price change including effects of inflation. In this way, it serves as an economic indicator. For personal budgeting, it may help explain why overspending in certain categories seems to be habitual. The CPI may also act as a guide for projecting those areas which inflation may continue to hit hardest so you can adjust your spending accordingly. However, the CPI has several limitations when used in this manner because it fails to account for changes in consumer shopping habits made in adjustment to relative prices found in the market. Therefore, it is not really a cost-of-living index, although it is often perceived as such.

ALTERNATE LIFESTYLE NEEDS

To bring the concept of financial planning fully into the twentieth century and beyond, it is important to examine the implications for various lifestyle choices. The techniques for developing spending plans are the same for everyone, the variables to consider and the complexity of planning are different.

SINGLE
INDIVIDUALS AND
CHILDLESS
COUPLES

These two groups of people will usually have the easiest time in developing realistic spending plans, provided they attempt the task honestly and are motivated to follow through. Generally, the financial burdens on these groups are the lowest because they have the smallest number of people to share in decision making and the fewest dependents, since they are one- and two-person households. Their decisions for spending become more complex if this lifestyle stage is anticipated to be temporary, or if they are financially responsible for aged parents or other adult dependents.

Even childless couples like the Welches must be careful in planning expenditures based on two incomes since one or both partners can lose their jobs. Unemployment hits all levels of professional endeavor because of lack of work, product obsolescence, environmental problems, etc. Or one person may be asked to transfer to a new geographic location. It may take time for the partner to find work in the new location, if he or she chooses to go along. If the couple prefers to try a week-end marriage for the sake of their respective careers, housing, travel, and telephone costs are liable to exceed salary increments. The added strain on interpersonal relationships may also be reflected in revised spending habits.

SINGLE-PARENT FAMILIES

Here the priorities in financial planning are more likely than anything else to differ from the first group, especially in relation to child care for a single working parent with young children.

If Jeanne Martin needs time to herself outside of her son's regular school hours, she must be prepared to pay for child care since she is solely responsible for her son. In the average two-parent family, that burden of child care is shared and therefore reduced.

TWO-PARENT FAMILIES WITH CHILDREN

In one- and two-breadwinner families, decision-making with children requires extra effort to include the children's values and prove that their input in this process is vital to family cohesion and goal attainment. The task gets more difficult with two breadwinners who bring home enough money to ease the family's economic strain, but may run short of time and energy to meet other family needs.

In a recent study by Cornell University, researchers found that the number of children in the family and the age of the youngest child at all socioeconomic levels were more closely related to time use than employment of both spouses.[2] While husbands and teenage children helped around the house more when the wife worked, their increased time commitment could be as low as six additional minutes per day on meal preparation, house care, and after-meal clean up.[3] Yet the same study found that employed wives spend an average of two and one-half hours per day less total time on household work than their unemployed counterparts.[4] This clearly indicates a substitution of resources to meet remaining household work demands or a change in the standards for these activities when both spouses are employed.

Therefore, a thorough cost benefit analysis becomes essential in realistic decision making on the number of breadwinners for the family and the division of their work and home responsibilities. A commitment to dual careers and other priorities established with the formation of modern families may sharply alter household time use among family members. Fewer children added to the family in somewhat later years of marriage can mean the availability of greater financial resources to relieve the stress of limited time for some families—so will simpler lifestyles with easy care homes or the return to city living that frees endless hours from commuting.

COMMUNES

Many individuals and families living together may ease or complicate their financial management depending on the rules of the group. If all income is pooled and all household tasks shared equally by group members, the number of people in the group and the commonality or diversity of their goals will be the determining factor. With unity of purpose and sufficient income and ingenuity, this version of the extended family can easily succeed in their chosen lifestyle. Because it includes a greater number of adult members than in the average nuclear family, the commune can use a greater specialization of labor to increase productive capacity and streamline consumption activities. Some members can work outside the home to earn income that is literally spent for them by other members whose primary responsibility is to feed, clothe, and shelter the group. While a general spending plan is essential to match income with outgo, this task may become the responsibility of one individual who functions as an accountant and clearinghouse for all spending.

In contrast, other styles of communes also exist in modified versions of shared multiple household units. Sometimes resources are shared only for select activities like housing, child care, and some meal preparation and clean up. Other resources will be handled by individual member units of the commune. This necessitates financial planning at two levels. But it can still offer some specialization of labor to increase efficiency of operation and conserve limited resources.

RECORDKEEPING CHOICES

After considering all the variables relevant to your financial lifestyle, you will certainly have been able to revise your original spending plan as needed to be realistic. While that much alone may encourage you to feel a strong sense of accomplishment, you have only reached the halfway point toward the objective of wise financial planning. Now that the plan is developed, how will you test it for accuracy? The answer is to establish and implement a recordkeeping system to check your actual spending against your planned spending.

Like the spending plan, your recordkeeping system must reflect your lifestyle and personality needs. It should help you to realistically meet your goals, and guide you gently in your chosen direction for spending. When the plan and the recordkeeping are viewed positively as a vehicle for goal achievement, they will both be followed more devoutly until their use becomes automatic and routine behavior.

When income is above minimum survival needs and flexibility in spending is important, the rubber budget principle may come closest to meeting your recordkeeping needs. With this method, your spending plan is reviewed monthly with actual expenses matched against planned expenses and the differences carried over to the next month's plan. Both plus and minus balances are carried forward. So if you allocate $35 per month toward recreation and spend $50 in January, you carry a $15 deficit into February. You must then decide to either reduce spending in this category to $20 for that month to get "out of the red" or continue the deficit longer because it will be more easily adjusted during warm weather months when your costs in this category go down. During the same time you may be running a $30 surplus in the clothing category because your winter wardrobe is in good shape. The surplus then offsets the deficit to balance income against outgo in the reconciliation. (See Figure 2–1.)

Figure 2–1
Rubber Budget

CATEGORIES SPENDING PLAN	Recreation	Clothing	Insurance	Food
	35	35	40	130
	10	3		50
	15	2		14
	3			36
	12			30
	10			
TOTAL SPENT	50	5	0	130
CARRY OVER	– 15	+ 30	+ 40	—

This recordkeeping system only sends hints about overspending. The system does not have to restrict it. When enough dollars are available, the system freely allows you to knowingly violate the spending plan. Therefore, the secret to living comfortably within this system is the addition of a slush fund (unaccounted money) to pick up the deficits that occur if or when actual spending exceeds planned spending.

If you can't afford the slush fund, but you would like to try this style of recordkeeping, a few adjustments in your spending plan may solve the problem. For this first year, revise the amount set aside for all annual expenses to meet the full amount needed by the due date. Then change your plan to reflect a full twelve-month budget for the following year. For example, this would mean a monthly amount set aside for auto insurance from January to July of $35 per month, dropping to $20 each for August and each month thereafter until the premium changes. Of course, adding $15 to this category for seven months will mean subtracting $15 from flexible expenses unless you can increase your income instead. Since most annual expenses are fixed costs, it is important to plan realistically to meet these demands as they come due because they cannot be adjusted easily.

To use this recordkeeping system, you will need a simple account book, self-made or purchased, plus a place to keep your purchase receipts for the month until the day of reckoning arrives, and you match actual spending to the plan. The nature of this recordkeeping system allows cash, check, or credit card purchases or any combination of them all, provided you keep receipts of some form on all spending. It is a somewhat sophisticated method that offers substantial freedom in spending, provided you can expediently deal with the consequences of that freedom when it reflects deviation from your plan.

THE ENVELOPE
METHOD

A recordkeeping system for cash-oriented spending that works quite simply is the old-fashioned envelope system. You establish the system by marking an envelope for each spending plan category with the amount to be spent on the category. Then on payday or at the interval you prefer, you put cash in each envelope equal to the amount allocated for that category. Your spending for each category is then limited to the money in that envelope. There is no need to collect receipts because all spending is confined to cash available in each envelope. To write a check or make a credit card purchase, you must remove the cash from the envelope and deposit it into the checking account first. Then you can write the check for the purchase or pay the credit card bill when it comes due.

Obviously, there is also limited flexibility in the system. Other drawbacks include storing cash at home or carrying large sums of money with you, difficulty in locating exact change for all purchases and the confusion of returning change to the proper envelope, especially when there is more than one spender using the system simultaneously.

A modified envelope method can be developed through the use of a checking account. All paychecks and other income will be deposited into that account. At the start of each pay period or each month, checks will be written corresponding to anticipated needs for each spending plan category. These checks will then be cashed as needed for spending in that category or mailed in payment for bills in that category on the dates required. Any uncommitted funds in the checking account will build an emergency fund until needed.

CHECKING ACCOUNT

   Or, if you prefer, advance checks can be written for fixed expenses only and the remainder used as needed for flexible expenses. However, if this choice is preferred, a separate bank account should be used to hold reserves for annual expenses to avoid overspending these sums.

   Last, spending can be done at will from the checking account under the rubber budget principle. In this case, the checks merely serve as uniform receipts for all purposes.

The advantages of these various methods can be combined in a very precise recordkeeping system functional for the most strict budget needs yet flexible enough for less rigid financial planning. While it may take an extra hour or two to develop, it requires less time each month in subsequent recordkeeping until a change is required. To develop the plan, you need a calendar for the next twelve months with which you begin by circling each payday. If the calendar is large enough, you need then to write down the income to be received on that day and the required expenditures to come out of that paycheck. To do this accurately, you must take into account the due date of all monthly and annual bills.

THE CALENDAR OR PAYDAY CHART

   It is easier to begin by listing fixed expenses on the calendar, then flexible. Sometimes you will need to make adjustments later or decisions based on your lifestyle. For example, if you bring home a weekly paycheck of $175 and owe a monthly rent of $225, you may set aside the rent money in four equal installments of $56.25 or any other combination that better meets your needs, provided it gives you the lump sum required by the first of the month.

   With the calendar in front of you, it will be easier to figure out when you receive an extra check because that month has an extra payday for weekly or bi-weekly payroll plans. Since all months technically contain four and one-third weeks, this type of long-range planning can allow you to more carefully use your full income to best meet your needs. These "extra" checks may arrive just in time to help meet certain annual expenses, pay for a vacation, or add substantially to your savings—but their use will be planned to meet your intended purpose.

Once you work out the details, it may be easier to draw a simple spending chart that lists each payday per month and the expenses to be met with that income. (See Figure 2–2.) Then you can apply the same spending habits to the first check for each month, the second, etc. Keep the chart and the calendar together to double check your plans. Then you can use cash, check, or credit card purchasing within the limits of spending for that pay period. You may even supplement the plan with envelopes for predominantly cash spending, a checking account for monthly bill paying, and a savings account for building reserves toward meeting annual expenses. Credit card purchases can be offset by a check written against income but held for mailing to the credit card company until after the bill arrives.

Figure 2–2
Calendar Paychart

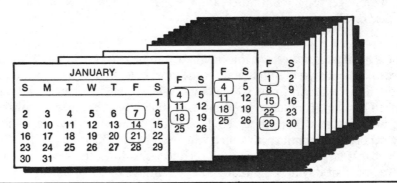

1st paycheck $250.
100 - rent
35 - food
40 - insurance
20 - recreation
15 - personal
40 - transportation

2nd paycheck $250.
100 - rent
35 - food
40 - insurance
20 - recreation
15 - personal
40 - transportation

3rd paycheck (3 times a year) $250.
35 - food
40 - transportation
180 - vacation!!!

TIPS OF THE TRADE

There is no one right spending plan or recordkeeping system that works for everybody. Individual differences in goals and lifestyles require that you experiment until you find the one that works for you. It may have been described here or perhaps it is a totally new and unique concept. As long as it helps you to direct your spending to meet your goals, it has served the intended purpose well.

Self-discipline will help you achieve your goals. If the temptation to spend is too great, then do not carry extra cash or credit cards when you don't need them. Avoid shopping as recreation. Go to the stores only when you really need to buy something. Pay your bills first each month and the savings account next so these sums can't get misdirected. Put up a picture of your dream home, car, vacation, college, etc., as a stimulus to keep you working toward the financial goals that will bring this dream into reality. Think carefully about all major purchases so you are not caught up in the spirit of the moment only to regret it later.

In group-living situations, establish a rule that all members must decide together on those purchases of a set minimum cost which will be shared by all. When at all possible, allow for some freedom of financial expression by providing each group member with a personal allowance. This money can be used for any bit of foolishness, impulse, or planned expenditures, provided the individual stays within the limits of that allowance. In that way, everyone has an escape valve—no matter how small—from the existing structure in which to rebel if they choose or compensate for frivolities. That makes for more realistic planning and a greater likelihood of follow through on the implementation of the plan.

FUTURE TRENDS

Of course, if the cashless, checkless society perceived by the futurists comes into being during our lifetime, financial planning decisions and tools may change by necessity. In recent years computer technology has begun to introduce new electronic funds transfer systems (EFTS) to our economy.

The goal is to eliminate the paperwork of check and credit card transfers of funds as we now know them as well as the safety problems and clumsiness of cash usage. The substitute methodology will transfer funds via electronic impulse from the purchaser's bank account to the seller's account—without real money being handled by human hands or paper transactions.

The impact of this new technology on financial planning can be both positive and negative. On the plus side, EFTS may simplify and speed up the majority of our financial transactions. The current balance of your checking account will always be up to date since withdrawals and deposits will always be handled immediately upon electronic presentation. The possibility of errors in transfer of transactions should be lessened with computer technology. The availability of credit may become more widespread because the creditors have easier access to the borrowers' funds for repayment. Automated bill paying may be expanded to the point that your bills are submitted electronically to your bank for payment with no need to involve the U.S. Postal Service in handling the transfer. In sum, that could mean EFTS frees consumers from the task of writing checks, balancing checkbooks, verifying credit card charges, or even depositing wages. EFTS takes care of all this for you.

But this same system can also complicate financial planning by limiting consumer decision making in controlling her or his own funds. EFTS can automatically process full payment on all bills, even if you only want to make a partial payment. It can also lend you money to pay all of the resultant overdrafts at the going rate of interest for the financial institution controlling the EFTS system. Billing errors will be hard to acknowledge without receipts at point of sale and a monthly statement summary of transactions. In short, the freedom to follow or deviate from your spending plan may be out of your control under EFTS because it will require conformity with predetermined expenditure patterns developed to meet the needs of the majority of users.

While that picture seems bleak, it represents the extreme implementation of a new idea. Industry and government efforts are continuously being made to improve the system to better meet human needs and consumer demands. It now appears quite probable that the forthcoming EFTS programs will insure individual rights of privacy. Receipts will be given in writing for all point of sale transactions so they can be compared with periodic statements on the status of your banking account. Some flexibility for financial decision making will also be added in keeping with the American ideal of individual freedom of choice.

Then, when the transfer to electronic funds processing is complete, the net result for financial planning will be easier money management through increased efficiency. This can mean substantial savings in personal time spent in recordkeeping, bill paying, and waiting in line to add or subtract money from a bank account in order to spend the dollars you have accumulated to date. That alone can be a positive benefit for a society in which time is becoming our most limited resource.

PROFESSIONAL GUIDELINES

From the bank's loan officer to the community action coordinator, anyone employed in the helping professions will at some point be confronted with client requests for assistance in determining their ability to pay for something. That determination must be reasonably accurate to aid in decision making, and it must focus on the relationship of this new cost to present spending.

You begin to assist the clients by reviewing their spending plan in accordance with the guidelines just discussed. Your professional responsibility is to ask appropriate questions to help the clients develop a better awareness of their economic position. Oftentimes clients follow your recommendations without further review. That can spell trouble if you miscalculate their ability to pay through haste or the application of inappropriate statistics.

Be careful and realistic in your approach to this important matter—and learn the limits of your own expertise in this area. If the financial affairs of certain clients are so tangled that you cannot make a realistic assessment of their ability to pay for the product or service under consideration, make a referral to the nearest local agency that can offer assistance. Then invite the clients to return to you when their financial situation is clear enough to realistically ascertain their ability to pay.

Try to never reject clients on financial grounds without offering some hope for resolving the dilemma. Since the discussion of money and budgeting still holds negative connotations for many people, it is important that helping agency professionals work to dispel these notions to avoid future perpetuation of these attitudes which only hinder the development of good money management skills.

ENDNOTES

1. "Family 'Model' is Obsolete," *The Hartford Courant,* March 10, 1977.
2. Kathryn E. Walker and Margaret E. Woods, *Time Use: A Measure of Household Production of Family Goods and Services* (Washington, D.C.: American Home Economics Assoc. Center for the Family, 1976), p. 247.
3. Ibid., p. 257.
4. Ibid., p. 251.

THREE

Paying Your Fair Share in Taxes— and No More

Mrs. Cranmore, age 82, lives at #23 Congress Street in a small but tidy first floor apartment. She made a strong impression on Jessica during her recent interview. Alert and organized, Mrs. Cranmore easily answered Jessie's questions on spending habits. Savings didn't really exist—except, of course, as another addition to her modest income. Social Security benefits plus a small pension from her late husband's employer composed her entire income. She could manage on that since the sum was slight enough to avoid income taxes. But taxes had been a real source of hardship for her in recent years. She had to sell her home a few years ago because she could no longer afford to pay the property taxes—and those ever-increasing sales taxes really reduced the buying power of her dollars.

Her next-door neighbors, the Stones, also felt overpowered with tax liabilities, but for very different reasons. With four children as dependents and the purchase of their first home, the Stones expected a sharp reduction in this year's income tax costs. But when Mrs. Stone went back to work to help pay the new mortgage, they wound up paying more taxes of all kinds, yet they also became more sharply aware of the benefits these tax dollars can provide. They moved to our town because of the plentiful public recreation facilities, good schools, and efficient government operation. That costs money—so does the luxury of eight rooms and a spacious lawn. Their disillusionment with taxes related primarily to the system's inequities, especially the "marriage penalty."

SHARING THE BURDEN

Government spending is a method by which the common needs of large groups of citizens are met with reasonable efficiency and little duplication of efforts. Instead of asking all Americans to build their own roads, or pay road tolls to private entrepreneurs, the government has accepted this responsibility for providing passable roadways between key travel points. The same concept applies when government supports public schools for all American children with no direct out-of-pocket cost to their parents. These and other goals for the common good are funded through federal, state, and local taxes to government as each individual's contribution toward meeting these common needs. Hopefully, government operation of these facilities reduces their cost by eliminating the profit needs of private enterprise. It also simplifies access to these facilities by centralizing the financial recordkeeping in government tax departments. That reduces the time and energy of individuals required to buy all of these services separately. At least in theory, that is how our tax system is supposed to work.

While reality does not quite match this theoretical framework, paying taxes is a virtually inescapable part of life. So the best coping mechanism is to learn to understand and use the tax system to your best advantage.

SALES TAXES

Paying for something a little bit at a time sometimes makes the true cost of that item seem lower—or at least more tolerable. Sales taxes generally follow that philosophy of payments toward your share of government operations. They are levied as a small percentage of the purchase price of certain goods and services. The taxes are even gathered by the merchant making the sale; hence, the collection of sales taxes appears less obvious and more convenient.

Sometimes sales taxes are only charged against goods and services classified as luxuries—like restaurant meals, amusements, etc. It seems at first glance then that the persons with a higher income and greater ability to pay carry a larger burden in sales tax payments than those individuals living at a subsistence level. More commonly, however, these taxes are also levied on many necessities of life—from clothing to utilities, household goods, and gasoline. In these cases, the sales tax becomes regressive because it takes a greater percentage of the income of low income families than it does of higher income families.

Sales or excise taxes are also used to penalize certain types of behavior that the government claims not to support. Some examples are the taxes levied on the purchase of cigarettes and liquor. In reverse, you will note there is no sales tax on the purchase of a home or land.

In addition, because most sales taxes are levied by state, county, or municipal governments, the amount of sales tax you will pay at a constant income level can vary greatly across the country. According to 1979 statistics by the Internal Revenue Service, a reasonable estimate of sales taxes paid by a family of four earning $10,000 annually will range from a low $55 in Vermont to a high $227 in Mississippi[1] (not including the sales tax paid on the purchase of a motor vehicle or other major item during that year).

That is a substantial difference in local rates of taxation. A logical conclusion, therefore, is that where you live and where you spend will affect the amount of sales tax you will pay. This is, indeed, a true statement. But, before everyone rushes to Vermont to save tax dollars, you must remember to look at the *total* tax picture. When property and income taxes are added to the sales taxes levied Vermont is not so inexpensive nor Mississippi so costly.[2]

PROPERTY TAXES

Another type of common tax levied on things is the property tax. This tax is levied on select items that you own. Unlike the sales tax, property taxes are levied annually on the present value of these items. Therefore, if the fair market value of the property goes up, so, too, does the tax unless the tax rate changes.

Property taxes generally fall into two categories of possessions: (1) real property, which includes land and the buildings constructed upon it; and (2) personal property, which includes individual articles of nonreal property that are determined to hold sufficient worth and evidence of ownership that they can be taxed fairly (motor vehicles, boats, etc.).

ASSESSMENTS

Fair market value means the price at which you could sell a piece of property today without taking advantage of buyer or seller. Generally, an employee or appointed official(s) of the community called a lister or assessor has the responsibility, as prescribed by state statutes, of determining fair market value for tax purposes. Because uniformity is critical for treating all citizens fairly in making tax assessments, this job is very complex.

The assessor must first develop a list of all taxable properties within the community. Once this information is collected, it is then organized in a manner usable for easy reference. After this list is complete, the assessor must determine the fair market value for each piece of property. For motor vehicles the determination is quite simple because the assessor can use "blue book" value. This is a monthly publication detailing the depreciated value of all cars and trucks on the road today. The values are developed by the automotive industry as a guide for the sale of used cars. Since these schedules are intended to be fair to buyer and seller, they are generally acceptable for tax assessments as well.

Determining the value of real property is more difficult. More factors must be taken into consideration, including additional allowances for individual differences among the prices of real estate being assessed. The present sale price of similar properties offers some idea of present market value, but it may not be the fairest value. However, the assessor can use the price of several comparable pieces of property, making allowances for differences in location, etc. Condition of the property is also important. Moreover, this method of assessing is most fair when all comparable properties have been bought and sold frequently. It is a difficult method to use if there is only one geodesic dome or round house in the community.

Therefore, the alternative basis for assessments is generally the cost approach. Theoretically, this method requires a detailed analysis of the construction methods and materials used to build the structure originally, plus a depreciation factor to provide a common denominator for assessing buildings of varying age and condition. To assess in such detail is very time consuming. As a shortcut, many assessors use construction cost tables which are developed to help them determine the cost per square or cubic foot of building space. Often the assessor compiles this manual personally to be sure it is consistent with unique local costs and conditions.

Of course, the assessor cannot apply this cost method to determining the value of land. So for household purposes the only valid method of assessment is the market value determination. However, some assessors will assess income-producing property like apartment buildings (including the land on which they stand) on the basis of the income that is or could be produced by that property. However, this determination becomes unreliable when owners are not required to reveal actual income and expenses for the property. While estimates are available from the real estate industry, they are generally far from accurate—or equitable—when some assessments are based on real income.

TAX RATES

Fairness and uniformity of assessment are the most important considerations in levying and living with property taxes. A big step in this direction was taken years ago when local governments decided to tax all residents of the community at the same rate. Owners of a house assessed at $10,000 pay the same rate of taxes as the owners of a $100,000 house in the same community, although these rates can vary greatly across town lines.

Tax rates are generally expressed in "mills" or "dollars per hundred or per thousand of assessed value." A mill is equal to one-thousandth of a dollar. A 50-mill rate then is equal to 5 cents per dollar of assessed value. A house assessed at $10,000 in a community with a 50-mill rate would cost the owner $500 in property taxes annually. This would be equivalent to a tax rate of $50 per thousand.

In order to motivate citizens to pay taxes promptly, some communities (as enabling state statutes permit) have chosen to levy taxes on the basis of a designated percentage of fair market value. Therefore, a $10,000 house may be assessed at 50 percent of full value or $5,000. That may sound like a real bargain to the owner who knows his or her property is worth much more. But to compensate for the loss in revenues from this reduced valuation, the community raises the tax rate to 100 mills or $100 per thousand. The net result in taxes levied is the same, but many homeowners, thinking they got a bargain because of the lower assessment, more readily pay their taxes.

Therefore, to determine the true cost of property taxes in a community you must find:

1. the assessed value of the property
2. percent of assessed value used to determine the "Grand List," or official tax roll for the community
3. the tax rate.

Even then, your work is not done if you want to be sure that property taxes are levied fairly in your community. It was noted earlier that tax rates are generally stable throughout a community, although assessment may vary by neighborhood. Sometimes they even have ceiling limits imposed by state law or subject to voter approval for greater increases. Therefore, tax rates are relatively clear cut although they can be levied somewhat piecemeal with separate billings for school use, general fund, or multiple taxing jurisdictions in which you reside.

UNIFORMITY

Because tax rates are public and uniform, some communities camouflage increases in taxes by various alterations to property assessments. If they treat all taxpayers equally, the technique is perfectly legitimate. For example, a community may decide to raise the percentage of assessed value on which it levies taxes. The result would be higher taxes collected from everyone although the tax rate remains unchanged.

Problems can arise, though, when the community chooses more latent ways of reassessing property. A common but unacceptable practice is the reassessment of property each time a new buyer takes possession. This is discriminatory because it assesses property bought and sold regularly at a higher rate than property that remains in the hands of the long-term owner. The discrimination is against newcomers to the community and in favor of natives who remain in the family homestead.

TAX APPEALS

Obviously, then, it pays to check out community practices on property assessments before you make a final decision on a place of residence. To begin, go to the hall of records in your community and speak with the assessor. Ask about the method by which the Grand List is determined, when the last community-wide reassessment was done, and when it will be repeated. Find out if there are any legal limits on the tax rate and when, if ever, it is voted upon by the residents.

Check the assessment of your property to see if the description of the property is accurate. If that is correct, then go on to compare your assessment to similar properties that you have located around the community. When the assessed values vary greatly, ask the assessor why this is so. If the explanation does not seem to comply with uniformity in tax levying, protect yourself against an unfair tax burden.

Legally, you have the right to appeal what seems to you to be an unfair property tax assessment. In fact, an official mechanism is already established in each community to guide you in this effort. There are certain deadline dates, which vary locally, that you must meet in order to file an appeal during the current tax year. In addition, you must be able to prove your case very convincingly to win the appeal.

After determining the deadline for filing the appeal, complete the proper forms and begin to gather records to prove your case. Take pictures of your own property and that of comparable others. Point out the differences in construction, location, etc., that could affect the true value. Show proof of any inaccuracies on the file records about your property. In other words, deal with the facts of the case and begin with an appeal to the local property tax review board.

While the duties and responsibilities of this board may vary locally, they are the first logical step in the appeals process. You may hire an attorney to represent you before this board, although it is not required. Your reason for appealing to them is that your tax levy is "arbitrary and capricious" and should be revised based on the facts you will provide that show a need for greater uniformity in assessments. A well documented and carefully organized presentation may mean a more equitable assessment on your property. If the appeal is denied, you can take the case to a regional or state review board, or finally to the courts. But most cases are resolved at the local level, so a concerted effort at appealing your case here may be well worth the effort.

When you examine the equity of tax levies in the community, also take a good look around to see what these property taxes actually provide for citizens. What is the quality and condition of public facilities, schools, parks, and local roadways? How efficient are local government operations? Are individual problems handled fairly and quickly by municipal staff—or does politics encourage favoritism in services as well as taxes?

Mrs. Cranmore sold her home because she could no longer afford to pay the property taxes on it. Ironically, though, her fixed retirement income could someday be stretched beyond capacity as a renter for the same reason—unless she can find residence in a government-owned public housing project that is exempt from paying these taxes. Even then, she may not escape this dilemma completely if she owns certain other types of taxable personal property.

In those municipalities that levy a personal property tax on motor vehicles, residence can also make a difference in the tax rate charged. Neighboring towns may have comparable rental housing units, with convenient access to work, friends, and schools. But the personal property tax rate may be quite different, thereby affecting your total living cost in that area. In addition, the date residence begins in the community may affect whether you are taxed this year on personal property or if the tax levy is postponed in whole or in part until next year.

INCOME TAXES

In addition to taxing things that you buy or own, various levels of American government also choose to tax money that you earn as another way of diversifying the tax basis. This income tax is levied by the federal government, most state governments, and some localities. It is intended to be a progressive tax, thereby placing a higher burden on persons with a greater ability to pay. However, complexities and inequities of the income tax law mean that the intent of the law does not always coincide with the reality of it.

The way income tax rules have been drafted, there are a number of loopholes that can substantially affect who pays these taxes and how much they pay. For example, a person who earns $10,000 from wages will pay more income tax than a person who earns $10,000 from the sale of her or his home, even if all other factors are equal. A married couple will generally pay higher taxes than each of these two people would pay on their respective half of that income if they were unmarried.

There is no clear cut, logical explanation for this type of tax policy. But as of now, it still exists and is upheld by law and tax courts. In effect, the income tax has been used as a means by which our government has chosen to reward certain types of preferred behavior for its citizens. Those persons who follow the ideal lifestyle as implied by the Internal Revenue Service will generally pay lower income taxes than their conventional counterparts.

FILING
REQUIREMENTS

All aspects of income tax law are subject to continuous congressional revision. This can serve as a reminder that current tax requirements presented in this book are only a guide for key points to check against future changes that may affect individual and family income tax liabilities.

As of 1979, all U.S. citizens or residents of this country for one full year must pay federal income taxes if their gross income exceeds (1) $3300 for an individual, or (2) $5400 for a married couple filing jointly, with larger exemptions for persons over sixty-five.

Some persons must file to get a refund rather than to pay taxes because the government has already collected tax dollars that these persons do not owe. The annual sum of income taxes due per household is so great in comparison to other tax levies that our governments have chosen to assure payments by withholding a portion of each citizen's wages and salary toward the payment of these taxes. Employers all over the country accommodate the income tax authorities by handling the paperwork on income tax withholding and turning appropriate receipts over to the relevant tax agency. Although employees have some choice in the amount of withholding taken from each paycheck, this is limited to an adjustment for each dependent supported by that employee. Often a variety of circumstances will reduce that employee's annual tax liability below the government's tax estimate. In those cases, the employee must file an income tax return to get a refund for overpayment of income taxes.

Basic government philosophy on income taxes is that citizens must pay their fair share and no more. However, the government only hires staff to verify that everyone pays enough taxes. They do not purposely seek out persons who overpay. This becomes the sole responsibility of each taxpayer, although the taxing authorities have provided vehicles for reporting tax liabilities that allow taxpayers to request a refund as easily as making additional payments. This is evidenced on the routine personal income tax forms (1040) and the special form (1040X) for filing an amended tax return which is used to correct past errors.

FILING STATUS

All individuals are not treated equally in determining income tax liabilities. Marital status affects the dollar amount of taxes due. For example, the tax liability for a person earning a taxable income of $14,800 would be lowest if that person was "married filing jointly." That implies that married couples living together follow the chosen lifestyle of tax authorities, so they reap the tax benefits. True, these are the only persons eligible to pool their income and file one tax return. In fact, these couples actually have a choice of filing a joint return or two separate ones—although the rate of taxation differs in these two columns. That is the real clue to a major inequity of the system.

Joint tax returns benefit single breadwinner married couples and those with major differences in total earnings of the two spouses. This is rationalized as a compensation for the spouse that does household work, which is not recognized as labor force participation or a contribution to the GNP. It therefore serves as an incentive to reduce the number of paid workers in an economy that has more workers than jobs.

The tax advantages of marriage backfire when spouses have comparable earnings. If each spouse in the previously cited example had taxable earnings of $7,400 in 1979 annually, they would owe $1,340 as single people, $1,582 as married filing separately, or $1,588 as married filing jointly. In effect, being married costs them $248 more in taxes each year—and that gap multiples as the individual incomes of these spouses rise.

While they are probably affected by this marriage penalty no matter how they file, the Stone family in our case study should compute their tax liabilities under both options each year. As income varies for each partner, they may sometimes discover that filing jointly is to their advantage, although in other years "married filing separately" may be more economical espccially when individual earnings of the couple put them in different tax brackets. Only single breadwinner families can be assured that filing jointly will always be to their advantage.

TAXABLE INCOME

An individual's income from wages and salary forms the basis for estimating income taxes due. However, many persons also earn money from tips, interest on savings, dividends on investments, rent and royaltics, pensions and annuities, alimony, child support, commissions, hobbies, prizes, awards, gambling winnings, scholarships, and employee fringe benefits. Therefore, to be fair, the federal taxing authority (Internal Revenue Service) and its state counterparts (which generally follow IRS guidelines) have determined that all income you receive in the form of moncy, property, and services is taxable unless specifically exempt from tax.

Some types of income exempt from taxation include:

1. proceeds from accident, health, life, and casualty insurance
2. disability and death payments
3. gifts, bequests, and inheritances
4. scholarship and fellowship grants
5. social security payments
6. unemployment compensation (sometimes)
7. veterans' compensation
8. workers' compensation and similar payments
9. state or local government welfare payments.

Persons receiving income from any of these sources should check specific IRS rules to be certain they qualify for this type of income exemption. Often there are detailed guidelines for making this determination in questionable cases; for example, when it is unclear if a graduate assistantship is scholarship aid or a form of paid employment.

DEPENDENTS

Income tax liabilities also vary with the number of persons you support on your present income. Because this tax was developed on the principle of ability to pay, a small portion of each taxpayer's income is exempt from taxation because it is assumed to be used to meet basic survival needs. As of 1979 that sum is equal to $1000 per person.

In addition to claiming one $1000 exemption for yourself, you may claim a second $1000 if you are sixty-five years of age or more, and a third exemption if you are blind. When married couples file a joint return, each is allowed to claim a $1000 exemption. You may also claim a $1000 exemption for each child living with you and certain other individuals if you can meet the IRS specified tests of dependency.

ADJUSTMENTS
TO INCOME

In addition, some types of income get special treatment for income tax purposes. Instead of taxing people at a rate comparable to a percentage of their gross (or total) income, the IRS allows adjustments to gross income under certain circumstances which may reduce your taxable income.

For example, if you move your household for the purpose of accepting a new job, the IRS wants to know about this. Then, if the move is more than thirty-five miles from your old residence to your new place of work, you may deduct from your taxable income up to $3,000 in moving expenses that you pay out of your own pocket. Employee travel and gift and entertainment expenses that are not reimbursed by the employer can also be deducted from your taxable income; overpayments on these reimbursements must be reported as additional income. As with moving expenses, you must be able to provide records to verify these deductions and reimbursements.

Small amounts do add up. So it always pays to check IRS rules when preparing your tax statement. For example, if you are reimbursed at 12 cents a mile for driving your car 10,000 miles this year for business, the IRS says you can claim an additional travel expense deduction. Since the IRS figures business travel in 1979 at the rate of 18 1/2 cents per mile and you are reimbursed at 12 cents per mile, you may claim the 6 1/2-cent difference as an adjustment to your taxable income.

Another allowable deduction that should be given careful consideration is the employee educational expense deduction, which allows deductions for travel, transportation, meals, and lodging expenses under certain circumstances. Eligibility for this deduction is given if the training (1) is required by your employer, legal authorities, or regulatory agencies to keep your present job; or (2) maintains or improves your skills required in performing the duties of your present employment or other trade or business.

However, if the education qualifies you for a new trade or business, the educational expenses are *not* deductible, even if you have no intention of entering that trade or business.

Self-employed persons are allowed to deduct business expenses from their gross income in order to determine their appropriate taxable income. These calculations are done on Form 1040 Schedule C for the IRS. Allowable deductions are similar to nonreimbursed business expenses, except for the addition of deductions for paying salaries and benefits to others and equipment expenditures. When the self-employment is an extra source of income—like for the college teacher who writes a published textbook—the expenses of earning this income may exceed the dollars earned in one year. That loss is then deductible against other earnings for that year, further reducing taxable income.

There is another instance when losses of earnings are also deductible from your taxable income. This occurs when you lose money on various types of property owned, called *capital assets*. These include any property you own or use for personal use, pleasure, or investment. Examples include stocks or bonds held in your personal account, a dwelling owned and occupied by you and your family, household furnishings, or an automobile used for pleasure and commuting.

Any profit or gain that you receive from the sale or exchange of a capital asset is taxable. However, losses from the sale or exchange of such property are not deductible unless they are the result of casualties or thefts—except for investment properties. The sale or exchange of stocks and/or bonds, real property, etc., can produce a capital gain or loss, which can translate into specific tax advantages.

Capital gains and losses are divided into two categories for tax purpose. Short-term gains are calculated on capital assets held for *less* than one year. Long-term gains are calculated on all capital assets held *more* than one year. The total net gain or loss is then found by adding the net short-term gain or loss with the net long-term gain or loss.

A net short-term gain is added to your taxable income at 100 percent of its dollar value. A net long-term capital gain, however, is added to taxable income at less than half of that rate or 40 percent of its dollar value (due to a 60-percent deduction). That tax advantage is increased by the fact that net short-term capital gains may be reduced by net long-term capital losses within certain limits.

Since the federal government supports a belief in home ownership, taxpayers may go one step further and defer payment of income tax on all or part of the capital gain received from the sale of a principal residence. If you buy and occupy a new house within eighteen months to two years (depending on whether you build or buy an existing house) before or after the sale of your old residence for a price that equals or exceeds the price of the old house, you may postpone payment of capital gains taxes. This postponement can carry through the ownership of any number of subsequent homes until you finally sell the home without replacing it within the appropriate time limits. Then capital gains taxes become due and payable.

Another recent addition to the list of adjustments to income is an allowance for contributions to an Individual Retirement Account or Keough Plan (to be discussed more fully in Chapter 11). By law, contributions to this plan are tax-exempt. However, withholding tax is generally taken out of your paycheck on wages used for this contribution. So to get your refund on taxes paid on these contributions you must list these contributions, thereby lowering your total taxable income.

As of 1977, payments for alimony are also deductible in this category of adjustments to income.

STANDARD
VERSUS ITEMIZED
DEDUCTION

Some expenses for ordinary and necessary living are also deductible from your taxable income. These include various medical expenses, interest paid on loans, contributions to charity, other taxes paid, etc. To simplify tax computations, the IRS has developed a standard formula for estimating these expenses at various incomes. This is called the zero bracket amount and it may be used by all taxpayers without showing proof of these expenditures.

As of 1979, the zero bracket amount is $3400 for married couples filing jointly, $2300 for a single person or unmarried head of household, and $1700 for married couples filing separately. (Please note the "marriage penalty" applies here again to a sum of $1,200 difference between benefits given to single and married persons.)

If you have kept tax records during the year that show proof that your actual expenses exceed those allowed under the zero bracket amount, you may itemize your actual expenses and deduct the actual amount you spent on these items. This would be done in lieu of deducting the zero bracket amount since you can't do both.

Itemizing deductions is generally advantageous to persons who (1) paid interest and taxes on a home they own, (2) had unusually large uninsured medical and dental expenses during the year, (3) made large contributions to qualified charities, or (4) suffered major uninsured casualty losses.

Ideally, each taxpayer should compute her or his tax liabilities using all alternative methods allowed in order to figure the lowest taxes due. Some years itemizing may help reduce taxes, while other years the zero bracket amount will be more favorable. The one caution that must be observed besides accurate recordkeeping is that married couples filing separately must both elect the same method of claiming deductions for that year.

In an attempt to treat all taxpayers more equally, the IRS has developed a seemingly endless list of regulations on what deductions can be itemized and how these calculations should be done. This book will only attempt to highlight key areas of concern. More details can be obtained directly from the IRS.

Medical expenses for yourself, your spouse, and your dependents can be itemized including *uninsured* doctor and hospital fees, special equipment (from wheelchairs to contact lenses), and medicines and drugs (including special foods prescribed for treatment of an illness). In addition you may deduct all costs of transportation for and essential to medical care and some expenses for medical insurance. However, the total of all medical and dental deductions are limited to those in excess of 3 percent of your adjusted gross income.

Taxes imposed upon you and paid by you are also deductible here if they fall into one of the following classes: (1) Income tax (state, local, or foreign); (2) Real property tax (state, local, or foreign); (3) Personal property tax (state or local); or (4) General sales tax (state or local).

You may also deduct cash and property contributions to qualified organizations such as: a state or local government if made for public purposes; an organization operated exclusively for charitable, religious, educational, scientific, or literary purposes or for the prevention of cruelty to children or animals; a war veterans organization; a nonprofit volunteer fire company; a civil defense organization; and a nonprofit cemetery company. Deductions here are equal to the full value of your dollar contribution minus any personal benefit received.

Interest payments paid for the following purpose can also be deducted when you itemize: (1) Mortgage interest, (2) Points (if you are a buyer), (3) Mortgage prepayment penalties, (4) Finance charges separately stated, (5) Bank credit card plan interest, and (6) Note discount interest.

Certain miscellaneous other deductions are also allowed if you itemize. These include certain employee related costs including employment agency fees; tuition, books, and lab fees for employment related education; dues to professional societies; physical exams required by your employer; the portion of your home used for work; small tools and supplies; subscriptions to professional journals; uniforms not adaptable to general use; and union dues and expenses. In addition you may deduct certain interest and legal fees, clerical help and office rent in caring for investments, expenses of an income-producing hobby, gambling losses (to the extent of winnings), and safe deposit box rental if box is used to keep investment related papers and documents. You may also deduct tax counsel and assistance fees paid to prepare your income tax and up to $100 of cash contributions to political campaigns.

TAX CREDITS

All of the sums discussed so far are deducted in some manner from your income before taxes are figured. The net effect of these deductions is equivalent to a savings equal to your tax bracket. However, some reductions to taxes due are made in the form of tax credits which are subtracted directly from the amount of taxes you owe or have paid.

While there are a long list of tax credits, we will focus here on a few more widely used credits. The most generally applicable tax credits are those given to all taxpayers who have had taxes withheld from their pay during the year which are to be applied to their income taxes. The same is true for self-employed persons and others required to file quarterly payments of estimated taxes.

The next most common credit is a credit for the overpayment of FICA or Social Security taxes. Since these are also withheld from wages, persons who hold more than one job or change jobs during the year earning a total gross income in excess of $22,900, have overpaid their Social Security tax. The overpayment may be claimed as a tax credit.

A tax credit of $400 for one dependent and $800 for two or more dependents is also allowed for child care and similar expenses without regard to income limits. Eligible taxpayers now include two full-time working spouses and families with one full-time and one part-time worker or one full-time student as well as divorced and separated parents who have custody of a child. Payments for these child care services are now available to the child's relatives as well.

If you are sixty-five years of age or older, or if you are under sixty-five and receive a pension or annuity from a public retirement system, you may receive a tax credit equal to 15 percent of your income.

GAMESMANSHIP

It has already been explained that income tax levies have certain built-in biases that can only be changed through tax reform legislation. You can help by actively participating in the reform movement.

In the meantime, you can also protect yourself by developing a thorough understanding of present income tax legislation. While the time involved in good quality recordkeeping and tax studies can become the equivalent of moonlighting, the benefits can parallel these extra earnings, too.

Also know your rights and responsibilities if the IRS or other income tax authority at the local level audits your tax return. The procedures of how an audit is handled and steps throughout this process are public information. Become familiar with the procedure before your turn comes to have your tax records checked for accuracy. Then exercise your rights to assure yourself of fair treatment during the audit.

GIFT AND INHERITANCE TAXES

Gifts, bequests, or inheritances you receive are not income. But if the property you receive in this manner later produces taxable income, that interest or dividend income is taxable to you.

Gifts are sometimes taxed to the giver rather than the recipient in an attempt to reduce the sums people will give away in anticipation of death in order to avoid estate and inheritance taxes. These death taxes are also levied against the person leaving the estate or inheritance. All taxes must be paid to the appropriate state or federal government before the proceeds are handed over to the beneficiary.

While the intent of these taxes was to limit concentrations of wealth, these taxes are sometimes considered underutilized.[3] While that philosophy has considerable merit, considering that the transfer of these funds is often an accident of heritage rather than a reflection of abilities, the federal government doesn't necessarily agree. In 1977, they reduced federal estate taxes by changing the tax exemption to a tax credit. The net result of this change, new marital deductions, and changes in gifts to spouses, will mean that by 1981 a person who dies may leave her or his spouse an untaxed inheritance of $475,625. That substantially exempts thousands of middle income taxpayers who would formerly have been responsible for death taxes on estates of over $120,000. (For more details see Chapter 11.)

THE COMPOSITE PICTURE

Looking back through this chapter, it is easy to understand why taxes are such a vast and complex concern in personal money management. As inflation continues to grow, so do tax liabilities because they parallel rising incomes and property values. The cycle is self-perpetuating and inescapable. But a thorough knowledge of the system, including your rights and responsibilities under tax laws, can help equalize your contribution. Time and energy resources may need to be spent abundantly to reduce tax dollar costs. But the choice is yours alone to make because you, alone, are responsible for determining that your payments are a fair share and *no more* of our joint tax burden assessed to meet ever growing community needs.

PROFESSIONAL GUIDELINES

While the information presented in this chapter will by no means make you a tax expert, it should show you tax considerations to explore, as well as help you know when to send a client to see an expert. To do so, you will need to locate the various sources of tax help available in your locality. Tax departments at all levels of government are prepared to offer taxpayer assistance. However, access to that help may be limited to certain hours of the day or days of the week, etc. In addition, some people are more thorough and more accurate in their analysis than others. This holds true for tax department personnel and private accountants. Therefore, it will be most helpful to your clients if you can make necessary referrals to specific people in these various agencies that you know are capable of handling the problem.

If you still sense that the problem is not being resolved satisfactorily, talk to the client to determine if she or he is clearly giving all relevant facts to the tax expert. Or volunteer to intervene on the client's behalf if your own employer allows this. Another alternative would be to send the client to a different expert for a second opinion. Mistakes are only human, but they can be costly to your client.

Tax considerations apply to persons of all income levels. It is not just the affluent that need to weigh this factor in financial decision making. Low income clients need to be sure they are taking full advantage of tax benefit programs developed for them. Sometimes this varies by state or community. If Mrs. Cranmore lived in a community that provided property tax relief for the elderly, she might still be a homeowner—or her net income could be increased if her state of residence gave an income tax break comparable to the federal low income allowance. Checking out eligibility for these benefits can sometimes prove financially beneficial even to persons who would otherwise pay no taxes. Their sole responsibility may be to complete the required forms to collect their refund.

Middle income clients have more complex tax-related decisions concerning when they may be able to afford the choice of home ownership versus renting or savings versus investment choices. Tax considerations can substantially affect the net profit or loss from these alternatives. Therefore, these factors should be explored to make fully informed decisions in any or all of these areas. Because middle income people often feel their potential savings are too small to compensate for the fees of a private tax consultant, they often erroneously rely on the opinions of family and friends on these matters—and lose money because of it. Some basic education in this area and/or referral to the relevant taxing authorities for assistance may yield some surprising results (to be discussed at greater length later in this book).

Affluent clients may have similar problems especially if their wealth is recently acquired. Others may be in a reverse situation whereby tax considerations take such a high priority in decision making, that other life goals are not being met to the client's satisfaction. This is especially true if a conflict in values exists between the tax advisor and the client or if circumstances change and the advisor is uninformed.

Therefore, it is to everyone's benefit to learn the basic elements of financial planning in relation to taxation and to apply these principles in decision making. As a professional in a money related career, it is your responsibility to stimulate this awareness among clients and steer them to relevant sources of help that are meaningful in relation to their needs.

ENDNOTES

1. *1979 Federal Income Tax, Forms,* Dept. of the Treasury, Internal Revenue Service, 1979, pp. 44–45.
2. *Ibid.,* pp. 31–38.
3. Robert M. Brandon; Jonathan Rowe; and Thomas Stanton, *Tax Politics: How They Make You Pay and What You Can Do About It* (New York: Pantheon, 1976), p. 28.

FOUR

A Place to Live

"Siamese twins. That's what it reminds me of!" thought Jessica as she approached 92–94 Congress Street. A split level duplex, this structure was a very unusual component of the neighborhood. Most amazingly, the occupant families also looked like mirror images—until you got to know them.

Roger McFetters, his wife Joyce, and their two sons lived on one side. They owned the building and took great pride in the wisdom of this purchase, both for family comfort and investment reasons. The McFetters really didn't enjoy "puttering" around a house or cleaning seldom-used rooms. So, two bedrooms plus a den were ample space for them to share. The tax advantages that make repairs and upkeep of a rented apartment deductible expenses help Roger justify hiring local workers to help with maintenance of the property. The rent payments from the other side also help to reduce the McFetters' costs for shelter.

In addition, this family is confident in knowing that the next time they choose to move for career advancement they have more options to preserve their investment. If the duplex doesn't sell easily, they can rent both sides and wait until they get a realistic price for sale of the property. Yet the tenants would also get a reasonable rent for the space provided.

When they moved here from Seattle, they had to sell a single-family home. The process was slow. Roger had to leave his family behind in order to start work on time at the new job. The separation added unwanted stress to the adjustments of relocating. Most infuriating was the fact that they made no profit on the sale. Oh sure, they sold that house for $4_,000 and only paid $38,900 for it three years earlier. But after figuring the costs of paint, wallpaper, and a little remodeling plus closing costs and the fee for the real estate broker, they certainly weren't ahead financially on that investment!

Bill Daniels, his wife Sharon, and their two boys rent the other half of the duplex. While they conceded to being reasonably comfortable with these living quarters, they still dream of owning their own single family home. Sharon went back to work solely for the purpose of saving for this goal. It would be a grand house, set out in the country surrounded by trees, and maybe a brook with plenty of privacy and lots of space to move about. The boys would have separate bedrooms. There would even be a real guest room decorated with ruffles and soft colors. That way when Bill's daughters came to visit they would have a room of their own instead of sharing the sofa bed in the den. While their second marriage was, indeed, a happy one, a little more space for privacy and quiet times would be welcome by all.

More than that even, Sharon would finally feel complete if they had a house of their own. Then she could put her creativity to work building a unique home environment that doesn't have to be dismantled because the rent went up or the neighbors were noisy. In fact, she and Bill were now seriously exploring the purchase of a double-wide mobile home set on an acre of land about thirty miles outside of town. While it wasn't their dream home, it was a step in the right direction!

CHASING THE AMERICAN DREAM

Shelter is an necessity of life. There is no way around it. The size and type of shelter needed to sustain life and promote some realistic degree of creature comforts is far more controversial. The nature of that controversy stems from a composite of life experiences and future goals.

When adequate choice is available, the selection of dwelling space is a direct reflection of the occupants' values and goals. The reasons for selecting one option above others often also reveals the occupants' insight into an objective understanding of housing costs.

Without a doubt, the majority of Americans agree that their preference for shelter is owning a single-family detached home. The size, shape, design, location, and price of that home will run the gamut of conceivable possibilities. But it must be an owner-occupied dwelling with some land around it—a home that the occupants can use or alter in almost any way they choose.

This is, indeed, a realistic choice for some Americans. The fulfillment of this dream can build a near environment for the occupants that best strengthens their abilities to cope with the pressures of modern life. It can offer an oasis in the desert of anonymity, an opportunity for tension-relieving physical activity, creative expression, the luxury of true privacy, and the added bonus of a reasonable hedge against inflation. But that only holds true under select circumstances. Under other conditions that same single-family detached house can build unnecessary stress into the lives of its occupants, breaking down their coping skills, and deteriorating the interpersonal relationships among the occupants.

Home ownership has always been so much a part of the American dream that the federal government publicly fosters this ideal despite changing lifestyles. Our federal income tax system offers incentives to home owners not shared with renters (see Chapter 3). The government also provides a variety of direct subsidy and lending guarantee programs to further encourage people of all income levels to purchase housing. Ironically, though, other segments of the federal government claim that single-family housing is no longer realistic in terms of energy costs, land use, pollution, etc.[1]

Moreover, the costs of home ownership and/or the time commitments required for proper upkeep are often beyond the scope of many Americans. Statistics show that an ever-increasing percentage of homeowners are dual income households.[2] While that lifestyle choice often permits the financial commitment to home ownership, it may not provide sufficient extra funds to purchase home maintenance services. The possible result is "house slaves"—owners whose total leisure time is devoted to cleaning, painting, remodeling, landscaping, etc. When these activities are enjoyable as well as emotionally and financially rewarding, the choice of shelter was appropriate. But if these house maintenance activities are considered drudgery, depriving the owners of precious time to spend on the beach, golf course, tennis court, etc., some changes may be needed to better match shelter choices with lifestyle.

Housing costs for American families have taken a steadily increasing percentage of income according to the last Consumer Expenditure Survey of 1972–1973.[3] Since that time the trend has continued to the point that housing and transportation combined can take 60 percent of disposable personal income.

That means housing mistakes can be costly. Financially, the costs of moving can alone dent the average bank account. When housing is purchased to provide shelter plus investment, the dollar losses can be multiplied many fold if any number of circumstances require selling the house below cost. There is also the emotional stress of relocation to consider as well as the time involved in reestablishing the household routines and the energy for packing and unpacking all of those cartons!

ANALYZE YOUR
NEEDS

The key to accurately interpreting the type of housing best suited to each household is to know basic needs and priorities. Work toward finding housing to accommodate these personal preferences despite what those around you are doing. In other words, break with tradition if necessary to find dwelling space that enhances your lifestyle.

Begin by listing all of the purposes to be served by the dwelling in which you live. Eating, sleeping, and personal grooming will be on everyone's list, but the space and equipment necessary to perform these functions can vary dramatically—so can preferences in climate control, laundry facilities, storage, entertaining capabilities, guest accommodations, and hobby areas. Write down these spatial needs for all household members. Then use your list as a guide to evaluate available housing in relation to your real needs.

Carry this list with you as you shop for shelter. Use it as your link to objectivity (along with financial considerations to be discussed next). Too often people let their emotions rule housing choices out of the desperation to get relocated or the desire to achieve a higher status in the community. They need closer ties to reality to avoid this type of impulsiveness. While a list of needs can easily be discarded under emotional stress, it may also help the shopper balance the housing owners' enthusiasm to find a new occupant for the dwelling whether it fits properly or not.

Now look again at the American dream. Does it approach the requirements of your needs assessment? If it does, what sacrifices are you prepared to make to reach this goal? How hard will you work to get it? Do all household members agree about the priority of the goal? If so, your next step is to raise the necessary money to make your dream come true, just as the Daniels are doing.

For many Americans this dream falls far short of meeting their housing needs. Then the question becomes, "Can you break with tradition and live with yourself?" Do you feel compelled to buy a house because everyone tells you it's a good investment or better for the children? Can you live comfortably with the lower status ascribed to renters in most regions of the country? Would you feel cheated if you purchased an apartment in the city, and your colleague spent the same money to buy five acres of country property plus a house?

You must be able to answer these questions honestly in order to objectively appraise your finances and move on to the shopping trip. The relative importance of your housing choices has to become part of your master spending plan. Its position in that plan will often determine the funds available to devote to other lifestyle preferences.

It is commonly recommended that the prudent consumer should spend no more than 25 percent of his or her income on housing—or about one week's take-home pay. That figure can be stretched to one and one-third week's pay when utilities, maintenance, and commuting costs are added. If your take-home pay is $200 per week, that means you can afford to spend from $200 to $267 on housing. A single person or small household might be able to find suitable housing within that price range in many areas of the country. A family of eight might not.

This determination can be more accurately made by reviewing your spending plan (as discussed in Chapter 2). Total all of your fixed and essential flexible expenses excluding those related to shelter. Subtract this sum from your net income. The result is the *maximum* amount of money you can spend on shelter including household operation (without major changes in your lifestyle). It would be wiser, though, to spend somewhat less than this sum to allow some discretionary money for unanticipated needs, inflation, etc.

Some households must, out of necessity, spend a larger than average amount of their income on shelter due to family size or special needs. Their options are limited by these constraints, so they must either follow a strict survival needs spending plan, go into debt, or find subsidized housing. Other households commit an equally large percentage of their income to housing despite the number of options available. This is risky business for many people. Often the prize dwelling is taken for granted too soon, and spending demands in other areas strain even the high income budget.

Spending up to or beyond the maximum available amount for housing should be avoided whenever possible. It can, however, be justified more easily when there are ample savings to cover an emergency; job security with good potential for regular salary increases; few, if any, debts; and limited nonhousing demands that could divert spending. While the temptations of occupying that perfect dwelling may encourage you to consider foregoing new clothes and recreation spending now, how long will it last? As a fixed expense, the cost of shelter cannot usually be changed quickly to compensate for spending in other areas. Therefore, a hasty spending decision here can turn that dream residence into a nightmare!

A generous emergency fund can reduce or eliminate this dilemma until income rises to more easily meet these housing costs. Accordingly, a substantial amount of savings usable for housing can also increase the options available in the shelter market.

In order to afford rental housing, the potential occupant needs cash on hand equivalent to one month's rent. In addition, he or she may be asked to pay one or two additional months' rent as a "security deposit" or set aside in the event of tenant damages to the premises. (The security deposit is refundable, minus damages, when you move out of the rental housing.)

In contrast, a potential housing buyer may be required to have as much as 25 percent of the cost of the dwelling available immediately as a down payment. On a $40,000 home, that means having $10,000 cash on hand just to enter the market.

Therefore, when reviewing your finances, it is also important to determine the sum of your assets that can be devoted to housing—or the lack of assets that, coupled with a modest income, could help you qualify for a government subsidy program to purchase housing.

SURVEYING THE MARKET

After you determine your housing needs and budget, it's time to locate alternative dwellings that may serve your purposes well. There are two basic types of dwellings to consider—single family or multi-family. The diversity within each group allows a wide range of housing styles, sizes, and costs. The primary difference is that one household occupies a single-family home while two or more households share a multi-family home. Either type of dwelling can be rented or purchased.

Upon careful examination, it becomes evident that each of these housing types meets the needs of certain groups of people at various stages of the life cycle. Since the average American moves several times during his or her lifetime, a different housing style may be appropriate at each relocation.

MULTIPLE-FAMILY DWELLINGS

Rooming Houses.   People first establishing a household independent of their family often have limited income and comparatively few worldly possessions. Yet because of a desire for independence or necessity of relocation they leave home. Sometimes this first move is into an institutional setting like the college dormitory, military service, or a job where housing is provided (camp counselor, farm hand, etc.).

Under these circumstances few options may be available for housing. Even the one room assigned to you could be shared with one to several others. Your choices may be limited to one bed in the room. But comfort in or, at least, adaptability to a dwelling space can affect your coping skills in that new job, etc. So be sure to take a good look at what's available and decide if it meets *your minimum* standards for survival. If there is any doubt that the structure meets minimum health and safety standards, check with the local community's housing inspectors before you agree to live there.

When some choice is available, review your priorities carefully. Sometimes you discover that a certain lifestyle is inappropriate for you only after you have experienced it. However, it would be helpful to review your priorities and your previous requirements for comfort. The student who has a private room at his or her parents' home and insists upon total quiet for studying plus nine hours of uninterrupted sleep each night needs to find a realistic counterpart environment on campus—or learn to be very flexible. The gregarious student who studies with the radio blaring and who can sleep through anything needs a different type of dwelling space. When these two personalities have to share a room, compromises are in order!

As a consumer of housing space in any multiple-family dwelling, you deserve minimum rights of privacy and enjoyment of common facilities. You should find out the rules of the house and how strictly they are enforced in order to appraise your willingness to live there. If you cannot or will not adapt to the surroundings, look elsewhere for housing.

If you feel you can adapt to this housing situation, analyze the costs in relation to your budget to see if you can afford to live there. Most rooming houses and institutions supply basic furniture, window treatments, etc., for their occupants. Cooking facilities are generally lacking in rooming houses, and bathrooms are often shared. Ask what items are included with the room to determine your costs to move in. What additional things, if any, will you have to purchase to live in moderate comfort? If these additions are realistically within your budget, you are all set, provided you accept the contractual arrangements offered for you to occupy this space (which will be discussed in detail later in this chapter).

Apartments.   If you prefer more space and/or your own kitchen and bathroom facilities, an apartment may be a more appropriate choice of housing. This dwelling can still be as small as one room (called an "efficiency") and completely furnished, or it can be many rooms that you furnish and decorate yourself. Generally, when comparing costs of a room to an apartment of comparable quality, you will find the apartment to be more expensive. However, the savings in food costs by home preparation of meals may offset the total cost of living in the apartment.

In selecting an apartment you must determine your minimal needs and optional items. Can you supply your own furniture and appliances? Do you need laundry facilities in the same building? A parking space? Extra storage space? A pleasant view? Security doors? Recreational facilities? How far are you willing to travel to get to work, school, shopping, etc.?

If the price is too high for the apartment you want, are you willing to share it to reduce costs? Do contractual agreements for occupancy allow roommates? If so, do you know someone who would be interested in sharing? Are you willing to advertise for a roommate and live with a stranger?

Do you have enough savings to handle the housing costs alone when you are between roommates? How many others do you need to share the apartment with in order to afford to live there? Is it realistic to find that number of compatible people?

The types of apartments available in your locality can vary from space provided in an older home to units of six to ten apartments in a building or over one hundred units of a high-rise multi-unit development. The housing features will also vary as will proximity to community services, etc. All of these will affect the price as well as the supply and demand in the local market. When demand is high, compromises may be in order because the range of choices is limited.

When searching for an apartment to meet your unique housing purposes, regional difference may directly affect your success or failure. This is especially true when your household is large or has special needs. Three-bedroom apartments may be very common in the urban area where you presently reside and virtually nonexistent at the same level of quality in a small town fifty miles away. Furnished apartments may come in a wide array of sizes and styles in areas of highly mobile populations. But trying to find comparable choices in a New England mill town could result in a rude awakening.

When relocating to a new community, it is wise to investigate the availability of apartments to determine if this is a realistic housing alternative to meet your household needs and geographic preferences. Some areas of the country have an overabundance of apartments, so costs are reasonable and choices among them are plentiful. Other regions have an apartment shortage due to rapid growth or limited zoning, etc. If you assume your preferred style of apartment exists without checking, you may be disappointed. Moving costs money, especially as your collection of worldly possessions grows. So be sure to consider this element of housing costs if you decide to settle for far less than the ideal dwelling "for the time being."

Townhouses.   Also called "row houses," this type of dwelling offers a compromise between single-family and multiple-unit dwellings. A townhouse has one or more private entrances per household and two or more stories of dwelling space. It can have a private basement for each occupant household and some private outdoor space designated by fencing to parcel out the backyard, etc. However, each townhouse is connected to the next by a common wall, therefore reducing construction costs and land acquisition. The common walls can also reduce privacy and increase noise transfer unless proper soundproofing is provided.

Townhouses can be purchased or rented. Although they were most commonly a city dwelling used to save land, townhouses can now also be found in suburban and rural areas. Today they are often built to sell as comdominiums, a form of owner-occupied multi-family dwellings that attempts to combine the advantages of renting and home ownership. They are also a popular type of rental housing because of their separation of sleeping quarters and living areas and the ample total space generally provided.

Mobile Homes.   Constructed on a factory assembly line and trucked to the site on which they will be located, mobile homes can be a low-cost version of a single-family detached house—the American dream come true. Sizes and styles of mobile homes offer a wide range of design options for this single-story dwelling. Although the typical mobile home is 12 × 60 feet, double wides are growing in popularity. Expandable rooms are also available to change the shape of the dwelling and add greater interior living space. Furniture and appliances are generally included in the purchase or rental price to complete the housing package and incorporate all of these costs into one financing arrangement (which is not necessarily to the buyer's advantage).

    Although this description makes the mobile home sound like an excellent choice for people in early stages of household formation and/or retirement years, that is not always true. Mobile homes have the potential to achieve this goal because of the lower costs of mass production. But shoddy workmanship, inadequate safety standards, and expensive financing arrangements discourage many potential mobile home dwellers from considering this type of residence.

    In recent years industry and government have tried to change some of these drawbacks. By 1972, forty-six states required all mobile homes to be built in accordance with a series of minimum construction and safety standards developed by the American National Standards Institute and the National Fire Protection Association. Proof of manufacturer's compliance was exhibited by a seal of approval placed near the entrance door of the home. Congress then passed the National Mobile Home Construction and State Safety Standards Act of 1974 to offer minimal uniform protection nationwide to the occupants of *new* mobile homes. Although the federal standards are more stringent than those developed by private industry, they incorporate most of the ANSI/NFPA code. In addition, this law makes enforcement a responsibility of all states. Ironically, though, it is still possible despite all of these programs that a particular mobile home may never be inspected by anyone other than the factory foreman because all of the aforementioned programs require only spot-checks for compliance.[4]

    This situation is compounded by the fact that mobile homes are classified as vehicles in most states even though few are truly portable anymore.

SINGLE-FAMILY
DETACHED
DWELLINGS

However, this classification exempts mobiles from the requirements of most local building codes. That throws the entire responsibility for determining safe construction onto the prospective occupant of this dwelling, especially when the unit under consideration was built prior to the early 1970s.

Classification as a vehicle also affects other aspects of mobile home ownership although they have less direct impact on mobile home renters. First of all, financing arrangements are similar to automobile loans rather than home mortgages. That difference can substantially affect costs since the rate of interest charged is higher for mobile homes and the length of the loan shorter. Like cars, mobile homes also depreciate with age—as much as 20 percent after one year.[5] (Conventional homes usually appreciate in value when properly maintained.) So while there is some resale value to the mobile, it is generally less than the purchase price.

Local zoning ordinances often limit the location of mobile homes because they are frequently accused of lowering nearby real estate values. Therefore, most mobile homes are located in parks established specifically for them. Because demand for space in these parks generally exceeds supply, entrance requirements and ground rules can be reminiscent of some unappealing apartment complexes or worse. In addition, a fee is required for renting park space and using water and sewage facilities, etc. When added to rent or purchase costs, this can substantially increase housing fees.

While mobile homes are truly single-family detached housing, they must be selected with careful scrutiny to assure safety as well as comfort. However, according to at least one financial expert, "If a mobile home meets your space needs and financial limits, it is the best buy you will find."[6]

Modular Housing.   Also factory constructed and trucked to the site, modular homes are permanently placed dwellings, virtually identical to conventionally built homes after completion. Mass production affords some cost controls here. Factory construction also reduces some building delays due to inclement weather. Construction standards vary somewhat with the producer, although all modular homes must meet local building codes. Producers of these dwellings claim they are even stronger than conventionally built homes because of the impact they must absorb during transport.

Until recently the classic modular has been a single-story ranch home. However, increased demand has created the development of two-story modular designs using stacked components. Alternatively, some builders are using a modular first floor and a conventionally constructed second story to offer Cape Cod and Saltbox designs, etc.

When shopping for a modular home it is important to investigate the reputation of both the factory and the local dealer/builder, both of whom will have significant input into the completion of this home.

Financing arrangements are the same as other permanently sited homes. Although built in a factory like mobile homes, modular houses are otherwise treated like conventionally constructed dwellings.

Site-Built Houses.   Conventionally constructed houses are built by craftspeople on the site where they will be permanently located. Lumber and other materials are cut to size at that time as the pieces of the house are added one at a time. These houses can be custom designed by or for the future owner, built from commercially reproduced blueprints purchased for this purpose, or constructed in tracts or developments where one to several styles are available to prospective purchasers.

They may also vary in size, shape, and design features more than factory-built housing. Accordingly, they will vary in cost and quality of construction, materials used, craftsmanship, etc. These are presently the most common type of single-family homes.

COMPARISON SHOPPING

Since this chapter is devoted to meeting household shelter needs, it is important to concentrate the focus on this priority. (Home ownership from an investment perspective will be analyzed in greater depth in Chapter 10.) Shelter needs must begin with safety, followed by efficient space utilization for comfort and economy.

Energy costs take such a substantial portion of today's shelter dollars that they must be given careful scrutiny by everyone, although their rank among priorities may change. Even affluent households must evaluate shelter alternatives in light of future energy sources and their availability at any price if they want the security of knowing that their present residence will be adaptable to any predictable energy shortage.

Primary energy concerns will focus on the type and amount of fuel used for heating and cooling, as well as how fuel usage can be reduced with proper insulation, site planning, construction standards, and lifestyle adaptations. Accordingly, fuel considerations must include use for commuting to work or school. One analyst found that living four instead of twenty miles away from work allows you to afford $13,000 more house (with a bonus for the related income tax advantages) because of lower commuting costs—and the probability of increased resale value as energy costs rise.[7]

The variables involved in choosing shelter are numerous and diverse. They are so highly individualized that it is difficult to generalize the various components into practical guidelines for decision making. An exploration of the financial as well as spatial and ecological considerations will help in this regard, although the weight of these various factors in decision making rests with each household. However, as a book in money management, the focus herein will be financial considerations in relation to lifestyle needs—or renting versus owning and the ramifications of these shelter choices.

RENTING SHELTER

PROS AND CONS

Someone just beginning to explore housing options will generally choose to rent dwelling space for two reasons. Renting requires less commitment (financial and otherwise) to the shelter choice. That minimal cash outlay can be very important to people just entering the working world or unsettled about finding appropriate dwelling space.

Rent payments are most commonly due one month in advance. In addition, many landlords require a security deposit equal to one month's rent or slightly more. This security deposit is held by the landlord as a fund upon which to draw if any damage other than normal wear and tear is done to the rented premises. If the dwelling is undamaged when tenancy ends, the security deposit is refunded to the tenant. State laws can regulate this transaction. Generally, when drafted, these laws limit the size of the security deposit; determine how much, if any, interest will be paid to the renter on these funds; and when they will be returned to the tenant.

It is also easier to calculate the total housing costs related to rented dwelling space since many housing costs are included in the basic rental fee. Property taxes and building maintenance are two housing necessities that are included in the monthly rent payment. In some cases, water, sewer, natural gas, and/or electric utilities are also incorporated in the basic rental fee. For some tenants, the only additional housing costs are telephone, commuting to work, etc. Although the majority of renters pay their own utility bills for fuel, lights, etc., as well, the mathematics involved in determining true housing costs are simple and easily mastered.

In addition, renting offers great flexibility to follow a highly mobile lifestyle. The commitment between landlord and tenant can be changed at any time by their mutual consent. Hence, renting is a logical choice for persons preferring to explore a variety of housing types and geographic regions before settling down. That flexibility is further enhanced by the limited responsibilities that accompany renting since building maintenance, remodelling, etc., remain the landlord's decisions.

Renters must also realize the disadvantages of this shelter decision. First, there is no return on the dollars paid as rent (other than the security deposit). In other words, rental dollars do not carry any built-in savings or investment feature. They buy pure shelter only—although renting may free other funds to be used for various investment purposes.

Second, restrictions on lifestyle within a rented dwelling can be greater than in a purchased single- or multiple-family dwelling. Renting adds another layer of authority between the tenant and the community laws. That extra authority is the landlord or building owner who has the legal right to establish "rules of the house," more restrictive than local laws and zoning ordinances, etc.

Last, the renter usually has less prestige in the community because success, according to the American dream, includes home ownership. Although lack of prestige is intangible, unlike the other disadvantages of renting, it is still highly relevant to status-conscious households like the Daniels family, and it must be considered when making a shelter decision.

By paying rent for a dwelling, you enter into a legal contract or lease for that shelter if the landlord, in turn, gives you possession of the dwelling in exchange. This agreement can be oral or written.

LEGAL CONTRACTS

When a lease is made, it can be for a specific time period or "tenancy at will"—as long as the renter and landlord agree to maintain this relationship. Under "tenancy at will," the lease continues indefinitely or until one of the parties involved wants to change it. From the tenant's standpoint this type of tenancy is advantageous when flexibility in housing is important. Although most states require thirty to sixty days written notice to break this agreement, that is a short waiting period in which to terminate a real estate transaction.

Despite the increased tenant mobility this type of legal arrangement provides, it has two serious drawbacks. The landlord can raise the rent with the same thirty to sixty days written notice (depending on state law). He or she can also change the rules of occupancy. Therefore, the tradeoff for flexibility becomes the potential for fluctuating rent and rules.

Many landlords and tenants prefer to rent for specified time periods to guarantee the payment of a mutually agreeable rent for a longer minimum period. Called "tenancy for a fixed period," this rental agreement is generally completed in writing since oral leases are usually only valid for short periods of less than one year. The following points should be included in the rental agreement:

1. Name and address of landlord and tenant(s).
2. Rent for the space to be leased.
3. A description of the space to be leased including use of common areas such as hallways, etc.
4. The terms and time period for which the property will be leased.
5. The purpose for which the space will be leased.
6. The signature of landlord and tenant acknowledging acceptance of the lease terms.

The terms of the lease can go so far as to specify the hours during which laundry equipment can be operated, the length and frequency of guest visits, etc. It is, therefore, important to read and accept each clause in order to comply with the rules of occupancy. If a particular term is unacceptable to the tenant and unenforced by the landlord, it should be stricken from the lease and initialed prior to signing. Otherwise, the landlord may use this violation of the lease terms as a reason for terminating the rental agreement prior to the fixed period for which it was drafted. Or the tenant may use the clause as a means to violate the lease in order to terminate it early.

In addition to expiration of the lease and violation of it, tenancy can be ended prior to the fixed period for several other reasons. These include (1) mutual agreement between landlord and tenant; (2) eviction due to damage to the premises, failure to pay rent, or creating a nuisance; (3) condemnation of the building; or (4) "operation of lease" which results from bankruptcy or death of the landlord or tenant (under specific circumstances).

When renting shelter it is imperative to consider your alternatives in the event the landlord fails to properly maintain the rented property or your "quiet enjoyment" of it, which is essentially the only legally binding promise made to every tenant. Possible actions include (1) moving out, (2) instituting legal action through a private lawsuit or intervention by a public authority depending upon the nature of the dispute, (3) paying for necessary repairs yourself (in the case of improper maintenance), or (4) organizing with other tenants to strengthen your bargaining power in an attempt to encourage the landlord to voluntarily comply with your demands. Unfortunately, all of these alternatives drain some tenant resources of either time, energy, or money to effect them.

Because of the need for greater equality under landlord-tenant law, some state legislatures have instituted legal reforms in this area. In 1972 the National Conference of Commissioners on Uniform State Laws drafted and recommended nationwide enactment of the Uniform Residential Landlord and Tenant Act (URLTA). The major benefit of this act is to deny the traditional separation of a tenant's obligation to pay rent from a landlord's obligation to maintain the property since it is this separation that so greatly writes lease terms in favor of the landlord. Under this model law, adopted in some form by a growing number of states, it becomes mandatory for all landlords to maintain the building for occupant health and safety.

Additional provisions include limitations on the size of security deposits as well as conditions under which they must be returned to the tenant. Guidelines are also provided under this law for legal actions to encourage landlords to make necessary building repairs and prohibit retaliatory actions when a tenant complains to a government agency or joins a tenant organization in an attempt to improve residential living conditions.

BUYING SHELTER

The alternative to renting shelter is buying it—in any size, shape, or location you select to meet household needs and financing arrangements. In most cases to consider this option, the household needs more cash on hand than for renting. The minimum cost to any purchaser includes a series of fees for professional services needed in the legal and financing arrangements as well as ownership transfer (including proportionate shares of property taxes, stored fuel, etc.). Called "closing costs," these fees can easily total $1,000 or more depending on the circumstances. That figure alone can deter many people from considering the purchase of shelter.

When this minimum investment can be met, the advantages of home ownership can appear very attractive. First, there is an ultimate return on your housing dollar. Even when shelter is purchased for credit (i.e., with a mortgage), there is a growth of equity as ownership continues. Part of every mortgage payment includes a reduction in the principal, thereby increasing the return potentially available upon sale of the dwelling. It is a form of forced savings like other types of credit buying. Yet, while the value of most used items declines in value with age, housing usually grows in value. So the potential return on the purchase can be greater than refund of the principal paid.

This growth of equity and appreciation of the value make housing a good investment for many households. Government subsidy to all home-owners adds to this motivation for buying shelter. As explained in Chapter 3, some closing costs plus all interest payments and property taxes paid on a dwelling can be used to reduce federal and most state income tax liabilities of the owner. In addition, the sale of the dwelling when made above cost can be deferred for years if the profits are properly reinvested in another dwelling. Then when the last dwelling is sold without reinvestment, total profits on home ownership throughout the years can be treated as a long-term capital gain, taxed at 40 percent of its value, or exempted from taxes entirely if the seller meets federal guidelines.

While the actual dollars saved in taxes is greater for more affluent people in higher income tax brackets, even the lower income homeowner enjoys the opportunity to find any legal means to reduce tax liabilities. Tax liabilities are even further reduced by the allowable deductions for depreciation, etc., when the purchased housing is a multi-family dwelling since it then qualifies for special tax treatment as a business investment. That is why the McFetters can better rationalize ownership of an apartment house instead of a single-family dwelling. Their priority in housing is the investment potential.

Another common reason for home ownership is prestige. The American dream has been fulfilled. To people like Sharon Daniels, that is a very important reason for buying shelter—no matter how hard you have to work to do so. Home ownership is often the first sign of rising status within the community. Upgrading that home is also the overt sign of continued success.

The freedom to use or divide dwelling space as you choose also entices many people to own shelter. There are no longer the classic rental restrictions of white paint on the walls and no permanent structural changes to the dwelling. Now the only limits are community ordinances and personal finances. The effect on resale value is also a very valid consideration, but its priority varies with reasons for ownership.

Despite the pleasures of personalizing a dwelling, when it comes time to move, owning shelter can be a drawback, particularly from an investment standpoint. If the owner is anxious to sell because he or she needs the equity to purchase another dwelling or to accommodate a job transfer, etc., the price accepted for the sale may not hold the anticipated profit. This is especially true when a home has been designed and remodeled to exceed the value of surrounding dwellings. It also happens when this investment must be liquidated despite economic circumstances which reduce demand.

In addition, the costs of selling shelter are usually greater than breaking a rental lease. Contracting for professional services of a real estate agent and attorney can be costly although they are often essential to properly execute the sale. When present funds are tied up in one dwelling and you wish to purchase another one immediately, interim financing arrangements must be sought and paid for. Sometimes, when occupational reasons prompt a geographic relocation, household shelter must simultaneously be provided in two places for at least part of each week. That adds to total housing cost as does the transportation cost, etc., to reunite household members on weekends until they can once again live under one roof.

More people are also tempted to overspend on shelter when it is being purchased to maximize the advantages of ownership. They also anticipate stable housing costs for the term of the loan since these mortgage payments usually remain constant during that period. Unfortunately, housing maintenance costs do not remain constant. Rising taxes, utilities, maintenance and repair costs, and inflation can make a once affordable dwelling beyond the limits of the household income.

In addition, there is usually a greater time and energy commitment required with home ownership. If repairs are required, the owner must learn to fix these malfunctions or locate reputable service people to do it. There is no call to the landlord to accomplish this task. The homeowner who selects a single-family detached dwelling after renting space in a multi-family unit will also find new maintenance demands for exterior upkeep and the costs of supplying necessary equipment or service people to do the job. Even routine cleaning can be more costly if purchased space is substantially larger than that which was rented. In total, that makes home maintenance advance to take a higher percentage of the dollar and time budgets of household members.

Fairly recent advances in the expansion of housing options in the American marketplace have led to a variety of purchase alternatives that can help interested homeowners find suitable dwelling space from an apartment in a multi-family complex to a single-family detached home. Some of these purchase arrangements even limit maintenance commitments and other burdens of home ownership depending on the type of housing selected.

PURCHASE
OPTIONS

Purchased apartments generally fall into two categories: *condominiums* and *cooperatives*. Condominium owners purchase a single apartment within a larger multi-family dwelling plus a share of all common areas held for the use of the occupants. Cooperative owners buy shares in a stock corporation that owns the building. The shares of building space purchased by the cooperative owner is equal to the amount of private living space assigned to that shareholder plus an equivalent percentage of common areas. The nature of these purchase agreements determines some lifestyle and housing decisions for the occupants.

The condominium buyer pays for his or her apartment the same as the purchaser of a single-family home. Interior maintenance is the sole responsibility of both types of housing owners as well. However, the condominium owner pays only a proportionate share of the maintenance and/or development of common areas from parking areas to lawn care or recreational facilities. Each condominium owner contracts for these services for common areas as part of the purchase agreement for the dwelling. Fees for these services may vary with time, but they remain equal to all owners, unless some services can be optionally contracted. This arrangement also means any changes made to common areas must be done only with majority rule of the owners. Decisions about interior changes are the sole responsibility of the individual owner. Even the sale of the dwelling is the owner's responsibility, including establishing a marketable price and finding a buyer. The only legally allowable intervention in this sale process is dictated by state law, which may give the condominium owners' association right of first refusal to purchase the dwelling when it goes up for sale.

In contrast, the cooperative purchaser must defer to majority rule more frequently in everything from subletting to acceptable purchasers upon resale of the unit. If the cooperative is a profit corporation, any money made on the resale of the dwelling belongs to the shareholder. In a nonprofit cooperative, all shares must be offered first to the corporation which generally reimburses the shareholder only for the original price. While that eliminates the need for the shareholder to find his or her own replacement, it eliminates the investment potential of this dwelling choice. In addition, if one occupant-owner of a cooperative fails to meet his or her payments as contracted, the other shareholders must take over since they jointly own the whole building and share responsibility to repay that mortgage. From a tax standpoint, the cooperative can provide some advantages. The shareholder can sometimes get income tax deductions on the mortgage used to buy shares in the dwelling plus a portion of the mortgage on the total building as well as property taxes, etc.

Obviously, then, it becomes imperative for persons shopping to buy housing to carefully study the rules of the game. In addition to quality construction, they must also investigate financing arrangements and legal contracts (including purchase agreements). This should be done long before the shopping trip has narrowed down the choices, or the emotional aspects of decision making may override logic and economy.

CONSTRUCTION STANDARDS

The same signs of quality home construction apply to rental or purchased dwellings in relation to safety, durability, and comfort. The difference is often the priority placed on these standards to meet occupant needs. When maintenance is the landlord's responsibility, many people prefer to seek out a responsible party to rent from—or a short-term lease—if building construction is less than ideal. Moving to another rental is still one of the most common coping behaviors of most renters who become uncomfortable in their present dwelling.

When dwelling maintenance becomes the owner's responsibility, quality construction becomes more important for two new reasons: (1) to preserve the resale value of the property, and (2) to minimize housing maintenance costs (in dollars and time) for the present owner. It is considerably more expensive to frequently buy and sell dwellings in order to avoid major maintenance needs than it is to change rental units, even if the cost of transporting household possessions remained constant. The reason for this is closing costs and possible realtor fees. In addition, few dwellings are left in "move-in" conditions for a new buyer. Most need at least a fresh coat of interior paint or new wallpaper. It is, however, possible to find many rental units already painted and ready for occupancy.

While almost anyone can paint interior walls with relative ease, other maintenance requirements can require far greater technical knowledge and skills training. Even the ability to recognize quality construction and assess its true value must be learned. This is also true for determining the durability and life span of various structural components. People interested in buying dwellings must then learn to judge construction quality to estimate the total costs of home ownership—or they must shop in areas where they can purchase qualified professional home inspection services.

Because so many housing buyers lack the ability to accurately assess the quality of construction in dwellings, housing inspection services have emerged in most densely populated areas of our country. Their primary role is to act as an impartial third party to inform buyer and seller about the condition of the dwelling and anticipated structural or major equipment flaws that could result in costly repairs. These services can be purchased by buyer, seller, or real estate broker for single-family detached homes, condominiums, and cooperatives. The dwellings can be new or used.

Many of these services offer assistance beyond just housing inspection. In addition, they will warranty the house from one to ten years against specified structural defects. Generally, the warranty protects only against defects of structure and/or equipment that are sound at the time of the inspection. Those determined to be faulty during inspection are *excluded* from the warranty. To further protect home buyers, some of these housing inspection programs offer insurance against defects rather than warranties alone. Their sponsors claim the protection is greater because insurance sales are regulated by state agencies while warranty programs are not.

Numerous warranty programs exist. To determine the quality of comparable warranties, learn to comparison shop and weigh the alternatives carefully. Be sure to read the specifics covered by the program and how to make a claim. Also know your rights of recourse by law against the builder, realtor, or seller, if you purchase a dwelling without warranty coverage.

While none of these programs promise to make home maintenance carefree, they offer a way to control expenditures in this regard on warranteed items. They usually offer sufficient lead time on detecting defects that many households can organize an appropriate emergency fund to meet this need when it arises.

LEGAL CONTRACTS

All real estate purchase and sale transactions must be completed in writing to be enforceable by law. That makes oral agreements worthless in the purchase and sale of real estate. It also means any written agreement made in negotiating the purchase or sale of real estate may be a legally binding contract. Therefore, all real estate agreements should be very carefully drafted and signed only when thoroughly understood and mutually agreeable to the parties involved. Logically, this also means any real estate agreement should be reviewed by an attorney for the buyer and a separate attorney for the seller to be sure that agreement expresses the intent of both parties.

Legal representation on real estate agreements is probably more important than on many other types of contracts because of the doctrine of "specific performance." Under ordinary contract law, if the agreement is breached or broken by one party, the other party can sue for actual money damages equal to the losses resulting from the broken contract. In real estate transactions, if one party breaches the contract, the other can sue to uphold the original contract as signed. Money damages cannot be substituted for the purchase or sale of a dwelling!

The basic legal contract used in real estate transactions is the purchase or sales agreement. This is the written promise of buyer to seller and vice versa in order to exchange ownership of the dwelling. The agreement can be handwritten by the parties involved, completed on a standard purchase agreement form, or drafted by an attorney for the particular transaction. While the last of these alternatives is the safest, any purchase agreement should include the following points plus any additional ones warranted by individual circumstances:

1. The names of buyer and seller.
2. A description of the property to be sold including its location.
3. The price for which the property will be sold.
4. The closing date—or when (and where) the transfer of ownership will take place.
5. How ownership will be transferred (the type of deed to be given).
6. The right to free and clear title or acceptable encumbrances to it.
7. The amount of cash payment to be given by the buyer as deposit.
8. The manner of financing the amount owed beyond the cash payment—plus a refund of the earnest money deposit if this financing cannot be obtained.
9. An identifying list of removable personal property to be included in the sale.
10. The terms under which this agreement is voided.

If this sounds like a lot of detail to clarify, purchasing a condominium is even more complex! In the purchase agreements for condominiums, ownership must be established to differentiate private units from common areas. For example, does the condominium owner have possession of half a door since one side is within the apartment and the other in a common hallway?

A document called the "Enabling Declaration" contains the legal rights and responsibilities of condominium owners in regard to common areas, policy-making powers, etc. Therefore, this document plus association bylaws, operating budget, and management contract should be carefully studied before a purchase agreement is signed. Comprehension of the facts provided in these documents is the only way to evaluate the quality of shelter provided for the price and its coincidence or contradiction with your lifestyle.

Cooperative housing also has legal documents to scrutinize before signing a purchase agreement. But in this case the purchase agreement is to buy shares in a nonprofit corporation. There is no division between private and common ownership of the building as in a condominium, so the legalese may be simpler. But there may be greater lifestyle restrictions because of common ownership of the total dwellings.

A real estate purchase agreement becomes legally binding only after it is signed by both the buyer and the seller. In fact, until such time as the seller signs this document in acceptance of the offer, the buyer retains the right to withdraw it at will. After it is signed by the seller, the agreement cannot be broken except for the reasons mutually agreed to in this document.

The other legal contract in all real estate transactions is the transfer of title or ownership of the dwelling (and/or land). This is done through a contract to *deed* the property, or give title to it. This contract to deed should be drawn by an attorney. It describes the property and the dollars to be exchanged for it as well as when the transaction will take place and who is to make the exchange.

There are two types of deeds. A *warranty deed* is given by the seller who guarantees that she or he legally owns the property and has the right to dispose of it because no one else has any claim to it. The seller who offers a warranty deed is so sure of his or her ownership rights that he or she will agree to defend the buyer against anyone else's claim to the property. A *quit-claim deed* is also legal in some cases. It merely states that the seller agrees to give up any interest he or she has in the property—not anyone else.

Common and usual practice in your locality often dictates the type of deed used in residential real estate transactions. To help assure proper ownership rights to the buyer, it is also possible and advisable to do a title search to be sure that historically clear title has always been granted from one owner to the next. While this generally only involves reviewing old public records of deeds, it may be more thorough when handled by an attorney knowledgeable of real estate practices.

Better still, a buyer can usually purchase title insurance to protect his or her rights of ownership. This insurance defends your ownership if it is questioned. A number of seemingly minor issues can affect legal ownership of real estate. Therefore, it is important to ascertain a clear record of title with a realistic assurance that the title is marketable in preparation for resale of the property. Title insurance can help in this regard since the insurance is not granted until a search for ownership has been completed.

Two other legal contracts may also become part of this real estate transaction. These are a brokerage agreement and a credit contract. Real estate brokers and salespeople are frequent third parties to the purchase of a home. They act as a liaison between buyer and seller and earn their fee for this service as a commission of each sale (generally 6 percent of the selling price). However, because they are agents of the seller, real estate brokers contract *only* with the seller even though the buyer may wind up paying 6 percent more for the dwelling to compensate for the realtor's fee. The sum may prove worthwhile if the services provided in locating the dwelling were helpful.

A credit contract is the other legal contract that may become part of the total real estate transaction. Most buyers cannot afford to pay cash for a dwelling. Instead they give a down payment equal to a specified percentage of the purchase price and pay the rest through a long-term installment loan called a mortgage. Other buyers who could afford to pay cash for the dwelling may also prefer to mortgage the property for tax and/or investment advantages. A variety of types and sizes of mortgages are available to meet the diverse needs of home buyers.

FINANCING
OPTIONS

Most housing is financed with a mortgage, or loan made on real estate with the dwelling (and land) used as security for the loan. The mortgage is a long-term installment loan, similar in many ways to the credit contracts used to purchase a car, appliances, etc. Both types of loans are written for a specified period of time, at a stated rate of interest that remains constant throughout the length of the loan which is repaid in equal monthly payments during this period. Mortgages, like other closed-end credit contracts, generally require a down payment. This is a portion of the cash price to be paid when the loan is made in order to secure the borrower's commitment to repayment.

Essentially, the same laws apply to all types of credit granting (as explained in Chapter 6). However, state laws on maximum interest rates charged on home mortgages may be independent of maximum consumer credit interest rates.

Loan payments on mortgages are amortized so that you pay interest only on the outstanding balance of the loan. But monthly payments remain constant for the term of the mortgage. That means the portion of each monthly payment used to repay interest and principal will vary, with higher interest payments made during the earlier years of the loan. In other consumer credit transactions, the percentage of each monthly payment assigned to repayment of interest and principal usually remains constant since interest is often computed on the total borrowed. Amortization results in a lower cost for borrowing, although the actual dollar cost of home financing can be staggering due to the size and length of the loan.

The size of a home mortgage and the interest rate charged for it varies with characteristics of the property to be purchased, size of the down payment, ability of the buyer to repay, and general economic conditions including the availability of funds for this purpose. Mortgage rates may vary among lenders in the same community or across the country. Within certain government limitations, each mortgage lender sets individual guidelines for granting home mortgages and establishing a rate for those loans. Some customers can get preferential treatment because of other business dealings at the same financial institution, clout from their employers who are influential in the community, eligibility for preconstruction financing agreements made by the housing builder, or eligibility for various government insurance programs. In other words, it pays to comparison shop very carefully for the best available mortgage terms.

A small difference in the mortgage rate or length of the loan can substantially affect the monthly payment. For example, a $30,000 loan for thirty years at 8 percent requires a monthly payment of $220.20. The same mortgage at 9 percent raises the monthly payment to $241.50—an increase of $21.30. For some households, that is enough to throw the budget out of balance. That is especially true since housing costs are more than mortgage repayment alone. They also include taxes, utilities, property insurance, maintenance, and repairs.

Recently, several innovations have been explored to increase the financing options available to potential home owners to encourage the purchase of shelter. Called "alternative mortgage instruments," the most popular innovations are the *graduated payment mortgage* and the *variable rate mortgage.* Under the graduated payment plan, borrowers can make interest-only payments on the mortgage at the beginning of the loan with periodic increases in the monthly payment through the years until the unpaid principal is repaid. Then the monthly payment levels off to remain constant for the remainder of the term. The rate of interest charged on the loan never changes. This is advantageous to many borrowers who anticipate rising incomes but cannot presently afford to purchase shelter (or a particular dwelling). Variable rate mortgages offer flexible interest rates modified on a predetermined schedule based on market fluctuations. They can go up or down as contracted, thus affecting the size of monthly payments and total interest paid on the outstanding loan. These mortgages are appealing to home buyers who feel locked into high mortgage rates by market conditions at the time of their purchase.

Reverse annuity mortgages are also growing in availability to meet a very different lifestyle need. Geared to older persons, this mortgage arrangement allows qualified homeowners to borrow the equity accumulated in their homes without selling the dwelling. Instead, they pay interest only at conventional mortgage rates while drawing on monthly reduction of the principal to meet basic living costs. Although the terms of this loan can be limited to ten years or less, it has merit for many retired people. While the owners draw upon their equity, the home may continue to grow in value prior to its sale and repayment of this reverse mortgage.

Mortgages are available from a variety of financial institutions under different terms. The possible options are also expanded by private and government mortgage insurance programs. Savings and loan associations, savings banks, commercial banks, life insurance companies, and other private lenders offer long-term home mortgage loans—so does the Farmers Home Administration of the U.S. Department of Agriculture. Eligibility varies with each lending institution. In all cases, the house or apartment to be purchased with the mortgage becomes collateral or security on the loan. If the borrower defaults or fails to make payments as agreed, he or she can lose ownership of the dwelling through a process called foreclosure.

The conventional mortgage is offered by private financial institutions. Eligibility requirements include a good credit rating (see Chapter 6 for details), the required down payment, and enough income to meet the monthly payments. Generally, this type of mortgage is written for about 75 percent of the selling price, although it can be as high as 95 percent. The borrower has to pay the remainder in the down payment. The length of the loan is usually twenty-five to thirty years, although forty-year mortgages are gaining popularity. The longer repayment period will reduce the size of monthly payments, but add substantially to the total interest cost. The interest rate charged will vary with market conditions, etc. There is virtually no waiting period to find out if your application has been approved since the necessary credit investigation can be handled within a day or two. Costs of processing the loan vary with the procedures of each lender. Many conventional mortgage contracts will carry a prepayment penalty clause. This clause tells how much of the loan you can pay ahead of schedule without being charged extra for this privilege. This penalty is charged by the lender to cover expenses incurred when you change the original terms of the loan. It usually only applies to refinancing the house rather than sale to another party.

Farmers Home Administration mortgages are granted by this agency of the federal government to low and medium income rural families who need housing but fail to meet the eligibility requirements of conventional lenders. The interest rate charged can be 2 to 3 percent below conventional rates for a maximum repayment period of thirty-three years. No down payment is required for this loan, nor is there a prepayment penalty. In fact, the loan contract provides for refinancing through a commercial lender when the financial position of the borrower improves to meet eligibility standards to do so. The FaHA loan can be used for an existing structure or to build a new home adequate for household needs as determined by this government agency.

When a borrower chooses to purchase a particular home for which she or he does not have sufficient down payment, the purchase of mortgage insurance can often help. Both private and government insurance programs exist to help people buy homes. Conventional mortgage lenders will extend higher percentage loans to qualified applicants who carry this specific insurance coverage that protects the lender against default, at least in part. Qualified applicants can sometimes obtain a 95 percent insured mortgage. The fee for this insurance is about 1/2 percent of the mortgage in the first year and 1/4 percent thereafter. Borrowers who qualify for mortgage insurance are generally household breadwinners with a promising financial future who are presently short of the down payment needed to obtain the mortgage.

The Federal Housing Administration is a government agency that insures loans and guarantees the commercial lender that it will pay losses resulting from foreclosure. The buyer is sometimes charged a lower interest rate than on conventional mortgages because of the lower risk to the lender. However, lenders do not enjoy losing money because of a reduced interest rate. So, they instead may charge *points* on the loan. One point equals one percent of the mortgage charged as a one-time fee payable when the loan is finalized. FHA allows the buyer to be charged only one point. However, some lenders charge additional points to the seller to avoid losing money by granting this loan. FHA appraises homes it is asked to insure. The results of the appraisal are given to the lender and available to the buyer. It can help determine if the selling price is in line with the market value. Because of this and other details of the FHA application, it may take a month or more before the mortgage is approved. Down payments may be as low as 5 to 10 percent per year without penalty. There are limits of the maximum size of the mortgage but no restrictions on the location of the home, etc.

The Veteran's Administration is another government agency that guarantees mortgage loans. This is done as a benefit for any veteran who served at least six month's active duty in the Armed Forces. Each qualified veteran is limited to one VA mortgage loan in his or her lifetime. Usually no down payment is required, there is no prepayment penalty, nor is there a charge for mortgage insurance. The buyer can be charged a "one-time origination fee" up to 1 percent of the mortgage (or one point). The repayment period is thirty years. The inability to qualify for conventional mortgaging financing is not relevant to obtaining a VA mortgage since this is a benefit program for the Armed Forces.

Sometimes a housing buyer can afford to make this purchase most easily by taking over an existing mortgage. If the seller has owned the house for many years, it is likely that the existing mortgage was taken out when interest rates were much lower; and it would be advantageous to "assume" that mortgage rather than get a new one at higher interest. However, to do this requires a large amount of cash for the down payment—the difference between the purchase price and the balance due on the mortgage. Because a large amount of the existing mortgage has probably been paid off by the owner of an older home, and the property is likely to have appreciated considerably in recent years, the difference might amount to a large sum of money. Not all lenders will allow a new buyer to assume an existing mortgage because they can make a greater profit if the buyer takes out a new higher rate mortgage.

Sometimes a seller will help a perspective buyer to finance the purchase by carrying the mortgage personally or through land contract. Under a land contract, the seller keeps the existing mortgage on the home but only acts as an intermediary, forwarding mortgage payments for the buyer to the mortgage holder. When the mortgage is fully repaid, ownership is transferred to the buyer according to a written agreement signed when the land contract was initiated and legally binding on buyer and seller.

Shopping for home financing is serious business. The size and length of this loan mean a major financial commitment, so extra care should be taken to find suitable terms for your lifestyle. You can save money by finding the lowest interest rate. But you must also compare mortgage processing and closing costs to finalize this sale. Points and other charges can affect the total cost of buying shelter.

To help home buyers in comparison shopping, the Real Estate Settlement Procedures Act (RESPA) was passed in 1975 and amended in 1976. It requires that lenders give all mortgage applicants an estimate of settlement costs within three business days after they apply for the loan, with the right to inspect actual settlement costs one business day prior to the closing or transfer of ownership. When the loan is approved, the lender must also give the buyer a statement showing the true annual percentage rate of the loan computed on the annual interest plus other finance charges like points.

CHOOSING AMONG ALTERNATIVES

Although innumerable lifestyle factors enter into making decisions about shelter, it is important to be aware that the application of simple arithmetic computations can clarify the economics of various shelter choices. Because of the potentially long-term residency and/or ownership of the chosen shelter, these calculations are at best careful estimates of the cost comparison. They do, however, accurately point out the various factors contributing to economic gains or losses related to the choice.

The most comprehensive analysis of this kind for layperson's use can be found in a U.S. Department of Labor Bulletin 1823 entitled, *Rent or Buy? Evaluating Alternatives in the Shelter Market.* A mini-workbook, it guides the reader through specific calculations (based on individual lifestyle choices) for comparing the costs of owning versus renting a dwelling. Although these investment criteria will be discussed more thoroughly in Chapter 10, the following key point is implied: *Buying a dwelling is not always a good investment for all households!*

Factors such as mobility, local housing costs for purchase and rental, and the return on alternate investments can greatly affect the profitability of purchased shelter. In fact, one well-known authority on personal finance proved that certain strategies can actually make the net cost of owning versus renting come out exactly equal.[8]

That conclusion should only serve to emphasize the importance of values in decision making and reinforce the need for thorough analysis among choices to find the best alternative for your unique household needs. It should also point out that as times change so do shelter needs and their investment value. The economy is not stagnant, so any and all financial choices must be periodically reviewed to determine if they remain economically advantageous or otherwise worthwhile to maintain.

PROFESSONAL GUIDELINES

Since shelter is a necessity, some people make their choice of housing without careful consideration of its total cost or ability to meet their needs. The role of the helping agency professional, therefore, must begin by clarifying household values and actual housing costs including commuting.

Some people falsely believe they are economizing by adhering to one shelter choice only because they never stopped to calculate its real cost. Others are unaware of the scope of options possible in housing or are frustrated by external pressures to follow tradition. So breaking the stereotypes can also help some clients to choose shelter more rationally.

Because housing is a fixed expense, it takes time to make changes even if they better meet the client's lifestyle. The cost of moving and reestablishing the household can also outweigh the advantages of making this change under some circumstances. Yet many housing decisions are made on emotion without regard for economics. While one cannot be totally separated from the other, a capable professional working in personal finance will help clients recognize this dual magnet affecting their decision making and help bring both sides into perspective.

ADDENDUM

While this chapter deals exclusively with housing selection, food and clothing are basic necessities of comparable importance that should also be given careful consideration when allocating household resources. They are not specifically included in this book because food and clothing consumption are commonly key components of other home economics courses in the required curriculum or whole courses unto themselves.

However, for nonmatriculating students and professionals using this book, relevant information on buying food and clothing can be obtained at little or no cost from the local Cooperative Extension Service Office, Government Printing Office bookstores in urban areas across the country, or the federal Consumer Information Center, Pueblo, Colorado.

ENDNOTES

1. Mary Winter and Earl W. Morris, "The Housing We Would Like," *Journal of Home Economics* (May 1977): 7.
2. Marshall A. Kaplan, "Outlook for Housing and Mortgage Markets," *Family Economics Review* (Winter 1977): 11.
3. *The Kiplinger Washington Letter,* September 9, 1977, p. 2.
4. "How to Pick a Really Good Mobile Home," *Changing Times* (March 1975): 20.
5. Center for Auto Safety, *Mobile Homes: the Low Cost Housing* (Hoax, N.Y.: Grossman), 1975, p. 28.
6. Sylvia Porter, "Can Mobile Homes Be Considered a Bargain?" *The Burlington Free Press,* March 17, 1975.
7. Merle Dowd, "Increasing Commuting Costs Should Figure in Housing Plans," *The Hartford Courant,* April 4, 1979.
8. Robert Rosefsky, *The Money Book* (Chicago: Follett Publishing, 1975), pp. 60–61.

FIVE

Getting There

Working during school holidays was never Jessica's preferred way to spend free time. But in this case it afforded the opportunity to talk with young adult residents of the community who were otherwise away at school. Such was the case with the households visited today. Coincidentally, college students at her own alma mater were among those with whom she spoke.

Gwen Evans was a freshman who commuted forty-five miles daily to the state university. For high school graduation Gwen's parents bought her a brand new car with the agreement that she then take full responsibility for operating costs, including insurance, and all repairs. That seemed most reasonable—so did the offer of free room and board if Gwen chose to live at home for her college years. Surely a part-time job plus her savings would raise enough money for tuition, books, the car, and incidentals.

Now more than half way through the first term, Gwen is not so sure she chose the most economical method of attending the state university. Car costs were rapidly eroding her college funds with no end in sight! The costs of commuting were much higher than she had hoped. Her inconvenient class schedule made carpooling difficult. Traffic jams and parking problems sapped her energy for studying, as did the long hours of driving.

The physical strains, tension, and costs made Gwen almost resent the car that her parents were so pleased to buy for her. For their generation, owning a car was a dream come true—a goal every young person gave great priority. Not only was it the symbol of independence, but gas was cheap! How could Gwen explain the hassles it was causing her when a car was such a valued possession for them?

Doreen Eliott lives next door to Gwen and attends the same university, but as a resident student. Sometimes she rides home with Gwen for the weekend or vacation. At first she was envious of Gwen's "wheels," but Doreen soon realized that in many ways, her life was easier with freedom from car ownership. Her living costs were a bit more predictable.

When she first arrived on campus, Doreen felt very confined without access to a car. Although her food and shelter needs were taken care of by the school, it was a closed-in feeling not to be able to get off campus and return on your own schedule. Bus transportation to the school was minimal—only two trips daily—and then only to the nearest city. Even taxies were nonexistent. Bicycling was popular but so was bike stealing. When she lost a ten speed bike from her own dormitory storage rack, Doreen decided not to replace the vehicle.

Now that she has adapted to a pavement-pounding life-style, it's begun to grow on her. Her physical fitness has improved noticeably and so has her disposition (at least on sunny days). The new problem is graduation and the pending job hunt. Will she ever be able to find an engineering job where she can walk to work? Will she be able to locate housing where laundry facilities and grocery stores are close enough to make the car unnecessary for transporting goods? While it's always possible to rent a car for a weekend away, that's not practical for everyday activities, so public transportation must be adequate for her needs as well as pedestrian safety for walking home alone. Well, it's a goal to strive toward at least!

TRANSPORTATION NEEDS

In order to effectively choose among existing transportation alternatives, each household must first assess its basic transportation needs. Once these purposes for transportation are clear, it is easier to objectively evaluate community transportation systems to select appropriate modes of travel for various trips. The specific transportation needs of each household are unique because of individual interests, obligations, and other lifestyle choices. However, the following general purposes should be at least minimal considerations in transportation decision making.

MOVING PEOPLE
AND THINGS

The first logical purpose of any mode of transportation is to move people and things from one place to another in accord with lifestyle demands and time schedules. Where, when, and how these people and things will move varies greatly. A top priority is to move people between their home and work sites. In addition, transportation is necessary to provide those necessities of life that are not generally delivered to the home. Specifically, these essentials include food, medical care, clothing (purchase and upkeep), personal grooming needs, some equipment repairs, and general shopping needs. In addition, most people need transportation to actively participate in some types of recreation, entertainment, and/or education.

The deciding factors in this transportation decision begin with who or what must be moved over a specific distance. If two household breadwinners must commute to work daily, one with two thirty-pound sample cases and the other with a brown bag lunch, their selection among transportation alternatives may be different. On-the-job transportation requirements after arrival at work and physical limitations, if any, of these individuals will also need consideration. If both people were of comparable stature and health, the worker carrying only a lunch would find it easier to walk 1/4 mile to work or to bicycle.

Yet individual and household values play an important role in determining whether or not that worker will even consider walking or bicycling as viable transportation alternatives. Assuming the actual commuting distance is 1/4 mile, these would seem to be realistic alternatives. However, they provide low status in most communities. In addition, safety factors in some inner-city areas may limit the wisdom of these choices as will climatic conditions for some people. More realistically, it may be impossible to find adequate housing, etc., that distance from work. So when the travel distance increases, acceptable transportation alternatives may also change.

In effect, then, transportation decision making is very closely tied to other lifestyle choices. It is particularly relevant to housing and occupation or education since 25 to 40 percent of all home-based trips are for work purposes.[1] Alternatives available for these trips are directly affected by housing location in relation to work site. Shelter and transportation choices may need to be reviewed simultaneously in order to maximize resources and reach household goals. For example, the household that wants a single-family home in the country may have to sacrifice many long hours for commuting in order to reach an urban work site, or seek alternative employment closer to the dream home, unless the job takes greater priority and the dream home is deferred until retirement or used as a vacation retreat.

The manner of transportation selected can also affect the comfort in which people and things will move from one place to the next. The person who prefers not to feel rain, snow, or wind directly while enroute to a destination may choose to travel by car from one garage to another connected to home or office, etc. A tall person may choose a large car for the leg room. A large

COMFORT AND CONVENIENCE

family may select a station wagon. A frequent traveler may opt for an air-conditioned vehicle in order to make the task of getting from place to place more pleasant.

Accordingly, many Americans may drive cars simply because it is the most dependable form of wheeled transportation available in their community. Buses may run on ever-changing schedules or routes despite the need of some residents to seek reliable public transportation to and from work. Other Americans may opt for bicycle transportation because it can actually be faster than auto travel in highly congested areas. The bike is also far more easily stored than the auto upon arrival at the destination.

Essentially, the level of comfort and convenience required in selecting transportation reflects the priority of these values in the household lifestyles and the commitment of resources to meet this goal. How much money will you spend to travel in comfort? What sacrifices will you make? Will you spend more dollars on auto travel to provide the leg space you want for commuting? Or would you be more willing to stand on an overcrowded bus as long as someone else is driving through the rush hour traffic?

Comfort can be physical and/or mental. It can include peace of mind as well as padded seating. It is also truly different for individuals of distinct sizes, ages, and past experiences.

SAFETY

Although less frequently acknowledged than comfort and convenience, safety is or should be a priority consideration in selecting transportation. Research indicates that transportation-associated accidents account for 50 percent of accident fatalities.[2] That alone makes it important for travelers to investigate the safety of all types of transportation being used and do their best to maximize its safety. For privately owned vehicles, careful selection, use, and care will help improve safety. Although this is more difficult to ascertain for public transportation, research is available on the topic. In addition, emergency procedures are generally outlined for protection of passenger safety. Learn to follow these guidelines and encourage others to do so as well.

Even walking can be dangerous for the person improperly dressed for environmental conditions or wandering aimlessly across unsafe neighborhoods. Cyclists must follow weather conditions for safe operation and seek other modes of transportation during icy weather. Some weather conditions can be so adverse that automobiles and their drivers should stay at home to preserve the safety of all concerned.

COSTS

The total cost of transportation must be calculated in more than dollars of direct expenditure alone. In addition to the actual dollars spent on this category of need, there are many indirect costs associated with it. For privately owned vehicles an obvious indirect cost is depreciation, or decreasing value, of the equipment used. Taxes and replacement costs must also be considered.

In addition, for all modes of transportation, it is imperative to consider the opportunity costs associated with transportation—or the sacrifices that must be made because a certain amount of your limited resources are being used for transportation. In other words, what are you willing to give up to spend $100 a month for transportation or two hours a day commuting, etc.? Since all resources are limited, these choices reduce your opportunity to spend the same resources on other items of interest or need.

ENERGY USAGE

Although energy usage is a direct and indirect cost of transportation, it is listed separately here as a point of emphasis. U.S. government figures indicate that 40 percent of all direct household energy use is devoted to automobiles.[3] Total transportation services use 60 percent of all petroleum produced in the United States and 30 percent of all the energy used.[4] At a time when energy costs are skyrocketing, this may bring the actual and opportunity cost of autos beyond the reach of more Americans. Then the question becomes how much personal energy and other resources will be substituted for the dollars needed to drive a car? Carpooling is a possibility to cut energy costs. Other suggestions include using public transportation, walking, bicycling, or moving closer to work.

Ironically, many people who are willing to expend more personal time and energy to spare environmental draining, will meet only frustration. While mass transit can help resolve this dilemma, it remains underfunded and inadequate to compete effectively with the idolized American automobile. Projections further indicate that this dilemma will continue at least through the mid-1980s with 85 percent of commuters driving private cars.[5]

Despite these facts, the basic hope for development of less energy expensive modes of transportation will be consumer demand. Only then can the cost/benefit analysis of more creative energy efficient transportation turn favorable and become reality (unless energy scarcity demands these changes nonetheless).

HANDICAPS

The transportation needs of some people are dictated at least in part by limitations on their physical and/or mental abilities. Physically handicapped individuals may find architectural barriers inhibit their ability to move in certain geographic areas, buildings, or transportation vehicles. People with less than normal mental capacity may be unable to safely operate a motor vehicle or travel unattended in public transportation.

The elderly or infirm as well as the very young may also be limited in the transportation they can use effectively. Poverty can handicap some people, especially in areas where public transportation is meager at best. Rural residents in particular usually feel the most frustrations in attaining a reasonable degree of mobility despite their handicaps.

TRANSPORTATION OPTIONS

The practicality of various modes of transportation is limited only by their ability to move people and things from one designated location to another within the restraints of time, energy, and dollar costs set by the person initiating this movement. Transportation can and does include movement across land, water, or air with human, animal, or mechanized power sources.

However, since the main purpose of transportation has been moving people between home and work, the discussion of options will focus on four basic modes of transportation for use over land. These include walking, cycling, driving a privately maintained motor vehicle, and using mass transit. The unique aspects of each and the potential for combining them to maximize resources will serve to exemplify the diversity of factors in transportation decision making and how to effectively cope with them.

TWO FEET

All physically healthy human beings have the capacity to walk from one place to the next. This is by far the oldest form of transportation and one of the most adaptable to differences in climatic conditions and terrain. Carrying things along on the trip will be limited by the strength of the walker, although this capacity can be greatly expanded by pushing or pulling items on a wheeled cart.

The primary costs of walking are personal since it takes time and human energy. Dollar costs are reflected primarily in the use of shoe leather and appropriate attire for the climate. Opportunity costs are reflected in the reduced hours and personal energy available for other activities when walking is the preferred mode of transportation.

The accepted transportation criterion used in estimating regular walking distances is a 1/4-mile maximum.[6] Therefore, persons choosing to walk as the primary mode of transportation must make appropriate lifestyle adjustments to accommodate this decision. In a self-contained environment like Doreen's college campus, the effort involved in this adaptation is minimal because the lifestyle is geared to walking. This is especially true since most of the basic needs of resident students, including food and shelter, are handled for them. Systems are even developed to improve environmental safety for walkers to reduce pedestrian-related crime and provide the necessary priority in motor vehicle zones.

In noninstitutional environments, it takes much more careful planning to walk to work. Urbanized areas have sometimes encouraged this mode of transportation when residential areas have been built to incorporate necessary related services from medical practitioners to grocery stores and shoe repair shops. Usually this is the result of planned communities or neighborhoods that must be carefully searched out. Sometimes these areas are geared to retirement living when proximity to a work place is no longer essential. At one time, central city residence provided a similar pedestrian-oriented environment all over the country. Now safety problems, suburban sprawl, and an eroding tax base have limited the probability that many cities can still meet this need. Attempts are being made through redevelopment to bring this lifestyle back to reality, but the process is slow. It is also hampered by the small but growing problem of the "reverse commute" or city residents who must travel to the suburbs to find work.

The addition of wheels to human leg power can greatly increase the distance to be covered in a set period of time. This mode of personal transportation is most economically achieved by using a bicycle. That increases the dollar commitment toward transportation. When the same distance to be traveled is calculated for walking and cycling, less time is generally needed for the cyclist. The total personal energy expended may remain constant or actually increase (when calculated in calories burned).

TWO WHEELS

The primary advantage of the bicycle is the potential to cover more distance than walking in less time. The opportunity cost involves trading money to purchase and maintain the bike for the time saved in moving from place to place. When safety factors require locking the bike at each destination, the time savings can be reduced on frequent short trips. The same is true if transporting things becomes cumbersome due to limited storage space on the bike or if the terrain and/or traffic pattern of the area deters easy cycling. Some college campuses prove the futility of efficient routine bicycle travel for these very reasons. In addition, dollar costs can skyrocket if frequent vehicle replacement is required because of damage or theft (although insurance protection is available under a homeowner's or tenant's policy).

Direct dollar costs involved in bicycle transportation include purchase of the vehicle, maintenance, and licensing (if required by local ordinance). Purchase costs vary with the design, comfort, durability, and pedaling ease of the bicycle, as well as its weight and portability. The purposes for bike travel as well as the household budget will determine dollars allocated to this purchase. Individual stature will also affect purchase decisions because a bicycle must fit the rider properly to be comfortable and safe.

Maintenance costs generally include tire and some parts repair and replacement, or a new coat of paint to protect exposed metal from weather deterioration. In addition, headlights, reflectors, horn, and brakes must always be in good working order. Local licensing programs are, in effect, safety inspections that also help to identify bikes in the event they are lost or stolen.

Indirect costs of bicycle transportation are essentially limited to depreciation and the energy costs inherent in producing the bicycle. Regular innovations in bicycle design have brought planned obsolescence into this area of transportation. Yet this urge to replace existing equipment because of style changes is not as advanced as it has been in the automobile field. Some communities also spend portions of their tax dollars to build special bike paths and recreation areas for cyclists or accommodate parking needs by supplying bike racks at frequently used destinations.

When a motor is added to this two-wheeled vehicle, the dollar costs rise as travel, time, and personal energy use decline. Mopeds and motorcycles rely on gasoline powered motors rather than human energy to move. Therefore, purchase costs mount, operating costs grow to include fuel and special insurance, licensing requirements may expand, and maintenance becomes more expensive because of the mechanical complexity of the motor. In addition, indirect costs rise due to air pollution and depletion of world fuel reserves. Operating risks also rise because of increased speeds of travel. Like bicycles, these motorized cousins are considered unsafe to use in snow and icy road conditions. More protective clothing is also needed on motorized bicycles for increased safety and comfort of the rider. The size and weight of the vehicles also increases storage costs since they no longer readily portable.

FOUR WHEELS

By far the most popular form of transportation in America today is the private automobile. Available in numerous sizes, shapes, and prices, this vehicle is prized for its comfort and capacity for transporting several people at once and many things along with them. It is the only vehicle cited so far that can effectively carry more than two people simultaneously plus a large assortment of possessions.

Like the other modes of transportation already discussed, the auto allows its driver to decide when and how it will deliver him or her to the predetermined destination. Numerous roads are accessible to the auto, connecting various routine and unique points of travel. In general, personal energy is conserved because of the limited physical exertion required for driving. When traffic flow permits, considerable travel time can be saved as well. Comfort is obviously increased over walking or bicycling, as is convenience in most cases.

However, the dollar cost tradeoffs for these transportation advantages are substantial. In fact, some financial analysts have proposed that the long-term costs of auto ownership exceed those of home ownership because cars depreciate in value while homes generally appreciate.[7]

A method of calculating specific automobile transportation expenses is effectively presented in *Rideshare and Save—A Cost Comparison,* available from the Federal Highway Administration, U.S. Dept. of Transportation, Washington, D.C. 20590. It includes the out-of-pocket costs of car ownership and operation, the savings possible from carpooling, and depreciation of the vehicle. Other indirect costs of auto ownership *not* included in this formula are environmental, especially related to air pollution and the inefficient use of natural fuels in the production and operation of autos plus their limited durability and planned obsolescence.

Opportunity costs of auto ownership are personal as well as environmental. With an increasing percentage of disposable personal income being spent on transportation, less actual dollars remain to meet other needs and wants. A Labor Department analysis of American household spending patterns indicate that in the last two decades transportation expenditures increased more than spending on food and housing, primarily because of the higher prices for cars, finance charges, maintenance, and gasoline.[8]

This perception of auto transportation as a priority item in financial planning is verified even during a recession. In an attitudinal study of American household spending practices during 1974-1975, respondents indicated a preference to trim other spending in order to meet the rising costs of their automobiles.[9] Despite the strain that a recession places on many households, the majority of respondents also concluded that having a second car was no longer a luxury nor was taking a Sunday drive.[10]

Auto transportation is far from trouble free, however. For several years problems with car repairs have led the nationwide list of consumer complaints. Traffic jams are common to virtually all urbanized areas, thereby greatly increasing the time it takes to commute by car to work and home again. This time commitment is further lengthened by parking problems due to insufficient storage space for the total number of vehicles in use. While physical energy expenditures remain low for driving, mental fatigue and tension can drain much vitality from a harried rush-hour commuter.

MANY WHEELS

Buses and trains of various sizes and shapes are another mode of transportation that can be used effectively in many circumstances. As motorized transport vehicles, they resemble cars in the ability to move people and things fairly rapidly between locations with limited personal energy expenditure. They also offer the potential for significant time saving over nonmechanized forms of travel.

Another attraction of mass transit is the possibility of lower dollar costs for the individual. The basic direct cost for transportation is the fee charged to rent space on the vehicle—plus an allocation for getting to and returning from transfer points of the transit system. Indirect costs include housing and work site selection to accommodate mass transit usage, as well as taxpayer subsidy for development and operation of some lines.

Of increasing importance are the reduced fuel consumption and the reduced air pollution by mass transit vehicles in comparison to autos. In addition, the potential exists for more efficient land use since mass transit vehicles spend more hours per day in use than autos and require less parking space per occupant. They also offer the hope of reducing travel time for commuters because they can carry more people in less space, thus reducing vehicle congestion on transportation corridors.

Opportunity costs reflect the inadequacies of the present systems. Accessibility to mass transit is generally limited to urban areas. Even when it does exist, the reliability of mass transit may be questionable, especially in maintaining time schedules. In some areas, overcrowding is common and equipment used is far from comfortable by anyone's definition. While the users of mass transit make no direct investment in the purchase of mass transit vehicles, nor assume responsibility for maintenance needs, they suffer the consequences of poor decision making in these areas. In addition, they remain frustrated by the inability of the transit owners to accurately accommodate demand for their services.

COPING STRATEGIES

Logical decision making among transportation alternatives often means finding the least objectionable choice to meet your needs. As needs change, choices must also vary when the goal is to maximize the use of total resources. For example, your housing selection may allow you to walk to work. But carrying groceries home, even 1/4 mile, may require wheeled transport if you're shopping to feed a household of five members for a week. Recreational travel for one person can be most economical on public transit, yet cheaper by car for the four-person household.

END USE

The conclusion therefore requires the wise consumer to match transportation choice to the purpose of the trip. A bicycle may be used to travel to the local recreation area, a bus to commute to work, and a car to visit relatives across the state—all by the same household. Each mode of transportation may be realistic in terms of time, dollar, and energy costs only for the trips just described. Attempting to interchange the systems could negate the benefits of each just like fixating on the use of auto transit alone can raise transportation costs beyond the means of many Americans, especially in urban centers.

Transportation costs in relation to end use should be made per traveler rather than per vehicle to account for economics of scale. This is especially important when values conflict with economics. For example, in a progressive urban center, government subsidies may allow residents to travel to work by bus at a lower cost than using other forms of transportation. But the commuter obliged to carry that thirty-pound sample case could find bus travel most inconvenient despite the economy. He or she could, however, make travel by private auto a more realistic alternative by arranging a four-party carpool with co-workers to compromise comfort and economy as well as environmental impact.

PURCHASING OPTIONS

Walking is almost free of direct costs. Using public transit also limits these costs because space is merely rented as needed. Use of bicycles and all forms of private motorized transport require more complex decision making because they can be rented or purchased in a variety of sizes and shapes to meet the intended end use and personal preferences. Wise selection is based on finding the best size, shape, and price range to meet household needs.

Since automobiles remain the overwhelming favorite among these private vehicles of transport, they will be the focus of this discussion. In many cases, the basic principles considered in selection of an appropriate auto apply almost equally to other private vehicles, with necessary modifications to accommodate design differences. An investigation into safety and performance characteristics of the vehicle, plus comparison shopping among reputable dealers, will always help in the selection.

Owning. The pride of ownership (plus clever salesmanship) encourage most Americans to purchase the cars they drive. When the car is well maintained and retained by the owner for its full useful life of ten years or 100,000 miles, car ownership can also be the most economical way to obtain this type of transportation. However, such things as individual driving habits, climate, garage facilities, type of road traveled, purpose for which the car is used, and sometimes luck can affect the service life and costs of operating that vehicle.

The largest single cost of ownership (after the purchase price) is *depreciation*. This is defined as the loss of values of the automobile during ownership due to (1) passage of time, and (2) the mechanical and physical condition plus the miles driven. Actual figures for depreciation are determined by national automobile dealer groups who canvass selling prices of cars by make and model for geographic areas. These tables of car resale values are published quarterly by the dealer associations and available at newsstands, car dealerships, and lenders' offices for review by interested parties. As a general rule, cars depreciate most rapidly during the first year of ownership (up to 30 percent of the purchase price). In subsequent years, the rate of depreciation slows to about 10 percent annually.

Since automobiles are continuously exposed to the possibility of damage, whether on the roads or parked, they need insurance protection of this investment plus personal liability coverage in the event of an accident. Insurance costs vary with the types and amount of coverage, purpose for which the car is used, and location where it is operated. Insurance costs also vary with the age and driving record of the car owner. The present high cost of automobiles and their replacement parts, and the growing price tag on personal liability and medical payments have made the costs of auto insurance a substantial factor in car ownership. (For more information, see Chapter 8.)

Financing costs also reach all car buyers either as interest paid to a lending institution to purchase the car on credit, or interest lost on savings to buy the car for cash.

In a study of cash versus credit auto financing, the application of interest lost on savings withdrawn would make buying on credit cheaper with (1) a 6 percent rate of inflation during the term of the loan, and (2) income tax deductions for taxpayers in the 35 percent tax bracket who itemize their federal income tax returns.[11] In addition, inflation would also significantly reduce the difference in effective cost between the thirty-six- and sixty-month loans.[12]

When income tax deductions are not itemized, short-term loans are indeed less costly than long-term loans and very close to the effective cash price of the purchase in a time of 6 percent inflation. Those calculations thus imply that people in higher income tax brackets may actually pay less for a car purchased on long-term credit contract than for cash. Lower income earners will do better paying cash or selecting short-term car loans. For those people who have enough cash on hand to buy for cash or credit, these results should encourage decision making in relation to current income versus savings lost rather than economics alone.

Registration, title, and sales taxes are all additional costs of ownership paid to the government of the state in which the car's ownership is registered. A registration fee is due annually, although title and sales tax are generally only levied when the car is purchased. However, some states charge a titling tax each time the car changes ownership. Other states and/or their municipalities charge an annual personal property tax on automobiles (see Chapter 3 for details). Many also require official safety inspection of each vehicle one or more times during the year.

Leasing. In order to avoid some costs of car ownership, it is possible to *lease* a car—or contract to rent the vehicle for a specified period of time, usually from several months to several years. In some cases, it can be cheaper to lease because there is no large down payment involved, long-term loan, or savings withdrawal. Leasing can prove economical for people who drive long distances of 20,000 miles per year or more, as well as for business and professional people who can deduct auto expenses on federal income tax returns. Because of first-year depreciation, leasing may also be cheaper for some people who want a new car each year. Leasing can stabilize the monthly cost of auto operations if insurance and maintenance remain the responsibility of the leasing company and you need only buy gas and oil and find a parking place. However, this type of convenience can also make the price of leasing beyond the reach of many Americans. After all, in order for the leasing company to make a profit, they must charge enough to cover all of the routine costs of car ownership plus a little extra.

In order to provide consumers with the true costs and terms of leasing, Congress passed the Consumer Leasing Act of 1976. This law mandates that enough information be provided to consumers to compare the costs of various leases as well as the difference between leasing and buying. The law applies to all leases at least four months in duration for a contractual obligation of $25,000 or less, and goods used for personal, family, or household purposes. It requires consumer leases to include a description of the property, installment payments, due dates, insurance coverage, warranties, maintenance responsibilities, purchasing options, etc.

Renting. If a car is only needed for short periods of time on an occasional basis, renting an appropriate vehicle can be a viable option. Although the daily cost may be high in comparison to owning or leasing, total annual car costs are modest if the vehicle is only rented a few times a year. Rental fees also vary with the size of the car, its age and the miles to be driven as well as if it will be returned to the original point of rental or another office of that company. Renting can be ideal for the household who needs a station wagon for that camping vacation once a year or the city dweller who wants to go to the country. It can also postpone the purchase of a new car for households who find their existing vehicle may be inappropriate for one special purpose but otherwise satisfactory during the year.

COMPARISON
SHOPPING

Whether a car is purchased or rented, it is important for the consumer to do some planning before making a selection. This involves four basic steps:

1. Research specific cars concerning safety, comfort, and economy, in relation to end use.
2. Test drive the vehicle(s).
3. Locate a reputable auto dealer for purchase, lease, or rental.
4. Study contract terms for cost comparisons and comprehension of responsibilities.

There is a wealth of information written annually about the performance and other aspects of new cars. The reliability of the information depends on the thoroughness and the objectivity of testing methods and sponsors. Sources of this information include car manufacturers, the federal government, and numerous automobile-related periodicals. One source known for its objectivity is *Consumer Reports* magazine, which devotes its annual April issue to automobiles and selected additional pages throughout the year. Cars are purchased for the test, and methods are carefully described for interested readers with cost, safety, and comfort factors considered. In addition, a "Frequency of Repair" record is included based on a reader survey to help future buyers to anticipate possible repair problems and/or locate a potentially good quality used car.

Reading about a car is not enough to decide if it is appropriate for your needs. It is imperative to test drive the car. A person five feet tall with a six-and-one-half-foot mate may not be able to safely or comfortably drive the same vehicle. A household of six large people may not be able to fit into a compact car despite its presumption to hold six adults with ease. The size or shape of trunk space may not accommodate commonly carried things. The list continues because of endless differences in human needs and wants.

It can also be helpful to talk with present or past owners of the car(s) you are considering. Long-term use can reveal many insights not obvious in a short test drive or not relevant to the car tests you've studied. This type of informal survey will also aid you in assessing servicing problems, costs, and dealer reputation. No matter how good a car model appears to be, it must be backed by an honest and reliable seller or leasor in order to make this particular selection worthwhile.

Some consumer protection agencies can also help consumers find a reputable car dealer. However, since few can endorse a particular dealership, the information they can provide is often limited to the number of complaints filed against a dealership and the nature of their resolution. Some government consumer protection agencies have opened their files of consumer complaints to the public. In these localities it is possible to actually read the histories of these complaints to make your own assessment of dealer's reputation. It is important to remember that the number of complaints filed does not accurately reflect dealer reputation. Some firms do a higher volume of business, so the percentage of complaints in relation to sales may actually be small. Nor are all complaints legitimate. Therefore, it is important to ascertain the nature of the complaint, how it was handled, and if customer satisfaction was achieved.

After researching cars and dealers, it is time to actually go shopping for the best vehicle at the best price. Bargaining is expected on new and used domestic cars most of the time, although some imported car dealers adhere rigidly to the sticker or list price for their new cars. It is the buyer's responsibility to negotiate the best possible price for the car selected—and to be sure that the contract accurately reflects the final offer.

There are many games played by car dealers to entice consumers into their showrooms and psychologically trap them into buying or leasing more car than they want. Sometimes this is done by adding more options than the consumer wants, or finding that the manager will not agree to the salesperson's price offer, etc. The best defense against these tactics is to shop with a clear head and an objective mind, focusing on the written agreements made, not hasty oral promises. The contract to buy or lease the car must specifically list all characteristics of the vehicle, costs to you, delivery dates, and terms under which the contract can be voided, if at all, by either party. A contract is a legal document. When in doubt about its validity, consult an attorney about how to protect your rights and your investment.

Since most cars are purchased on credit, it is equally important to shop carefully for the money you need to borrow to pay for the car. While many new and used car dealers can arrange financing for their customers, their costs can be higher than individually arranged loans from the same bank or finance company. Comparison shop first. Convenience usually costs extra. As explained in Chapter 6, the source of a loan, its length or purpose, as well as the borrower's credit worthiness will all affect the cost of borrowing.

SAVINGS

There are many ways to reduce the costs of car ownership for the purchaser who values economy over luxury and convenience. The first of these is to consider a used car rather than a new one in order to reduce depreciation losses. However, used cars require extra care in selection because each vehicle will have unique characteristics depending upon its use and abuse by previous owners. Therefore, an important additional step in comparison shopping is to have an independent mechanic assess the condition of the used car before you buy. The mechanic's fee for this service will be well worth the cost if it helps you locate a used car in good condition.

If you shop for a used car at a new car dealership it may also be possible to examine the service and repair records of the vehicle if the maintenance work was done there. This will be especially helpful if the car was purchased from the dealership and regularly serviced there since the records will show a thorough history of vehicle performance. In other cases, it may be possible to locate the previous owner with the help of the used car dealer to obtain some service-related information. Since this person no longer owns the car, he or she may be quite willing to provide this information. On the other hand, people selling used cars privately may be hesitant to reveal too many problems with the vehicle for fear of losing a customer.

The Federal Trade Commission has proposed a trade regulation rule that requires all used car dealers to disclose certain key information about the vehicles they sell. This will include facts related to the nature of prior use, and any major repairs performed during reconditioning. (Federal law already requires a written statement of accuracy on odometer readings.) In addition, dealers would be required to disclose if the vehicle is to be offered for sale with or without a warranty, and the terms of that warranty, if one is offered. All of these details are expected to be written on a sticker affixed to the car window. However, it will be of no value unless this rule, proposed in 1976, becomes enforceable.

The selection of a used car can be particularly economical for the person capable of doing his or her own repairs since maintenance costs generally increase with the age of the vehicle. It will also be less costly in terms of property tax assessments if this fee for car ownerhip is charged in your locality. There is also a reduced likelihood of theft for residents of high crime areas and a lower cost for used parts if they are accessible from local junkyards.

For those people who are not mechanically skilled and can afford the down payment, a new car may be a more realistic choice. Although this choice means extra costs for depreciation and style, the warranty accompanying this purchase can leave the buyer free of major repair costs for all or most of the first year of ownership. In addition, new parts should be less likely to malfunction than older ones so the vehicle's reliability may be greater than a used car. This would be particularly important for people who drive extensively on highways, away from home, or alone.

Many new car costs can be minimized through careful model selection. Choose a reputable dealer and bargain for the best possible price. Compare the price of this year's car with a new leftover from the previous model year. If a generous price reduction is allowed on the older model, it could be a wise choice. This is especially true for the driver who travels substantially more than 10,000 miles per year since used car values are lower on high mileage vehicles. If a car is perceived to be one year older because of its model year, the average annual mileage will be calculated at a lower rate when the vehicle is sold. People who keep a car for its full useful life may also benefit from buying an older model car because they will no longer be concerned about resale value.

Limiting the optional equipment purchased with the vehicle can also save money. That is why it is important to obtain an itemized list of all options included with a new car purchase. A few options, like automatic transmission and power steering, may increase resale value. Most do not; therefore, they should be scrutinized to avoid paying hundreds of dollars for useless luxuries. If you can drive the car safely without the options and meet the storage and transport needs of your lifestyle, eliminate options whenever possible.

Try to buy a car already in stock, if you can find one with the minimum options to meet your needs. The dealer has already invested in this vehicle and may be more anxious to sell it than a special order car. That also means you may be able to negotiate a lower price. This is especially true during slow seasons like the heavy winter months in cold climates.

Always bargain for the cash price of a new car, even if you will use it to replace an existing auto. This will make comparison shopping easier and prevent you from accepting a price because of a good trade-in offer alone. Very often you can get more money from your used car if you sell it privately instead of trading it. However, this takes time and can tie up some of your money if the old car is not sold by the time the new one is ready for delivery. For some buyers, that can pose financing problems that they prefer not to handle.

Repairs and maintenance costs can contribute substantially to the costs of automobile operations. Therefore, it will also be wise to comparison shop among the warranties available for the new or used car you choose. Read carefully to determine the length and content of warranties as well as buyer and seller responsibility to keep the warranty in force. While most autos carry only a limited warranty, the details can vary significantly by manufacturer and/or dealer. This is another reason for careful scrutiny of the dealer's reputation, since the warranty is worthless unless it can be enforced.

Accordingly, the routine service requirements of many cars are changing due to new technology. Some cars require fewer oil changes, etc., because of this. Others come with standard equipment like radial tires that have a longer than average service life. Any or all of these factors can save money for the careful auto buyer. Fuel economy factors are also growing in importance as the cost of gasoline rises. Anything that reduces operating costs of the auto can pay for itself many times over its original purchase price.

OPERATING COSTS   The most obvious cost of automobile operation is gasoline. The size and weight of the car, load carried, fuel efficiency, the operator's driving habits, and road conditions all affect fuel consumption. These costs can be minimized through careful vehicle selection and handling. Perhaps the greatest savings can be realized by reduced vehicle usage. That means carefully planning all auto trips to reduce miles traveled when less costly transportation is available. Sometimes just rearranging your schedule to run errands while en route to work or school can reduce fuel consumption. Carpooling will help as well.

A growing abundance of self-service gas stations can reduce the price per gallon of gasoline if you are willing to exchange time and energy for money. However, in doing so, it is important to take responsibility for the other routine maintenance checks performed by the full service gas station—like checking fluid levels in key parts of the car. Carelessness here can mean costly repairs later.

New cars generally burn little oil, so the cost of this maintenance factor is limited to the manufacturer's requirements for oil changes. Older cars may use substantial amounts of oil between recommended oil changes depending upon their condition. Since oil is essential to protect vital engine parts, this service need must be carefully followed.

Tires also require routine replacement due to regular wear. Of the three basic types of tires, bias ply tires are the least expensive although they ordinarily will not last as long as the other types. However, they are safe and their low cost makes them a wise choice for mainly suburban and urban driving. Radial tires are the most expensive but they can be expected to travel many more miles than bias ply tires. Their durability is greatest for highway travel where tests show that they roll more freely, thus saving up to 5 percent in fuel consumption. When most travel is in heavy traffic at slow speeds, the savings are substantially reduced. Bias belted tires fall between the other two types in performance and cost.

For maximum wear life, tires must be carefully maintained. This begins with proper inflation for the load carried, rotation as specified by the manufacturer, and accurate wheel alignment. Tires are directly related to operating safety so they should be a top priority in maintaining any vehicle.

Repairs and other maintenance costs are hard to predict. Some service needs like brake linings, fan belts, and battery replacement can be anticipated with age and miles driven. Mechanical failures are less consistent. They may or may not occur. While frequency of repair records for earlier models of the same vehicle may offer some clues to probable repair needs, the same problems do not always occur for all cars of the same model. In addition, good quality service under the warranty can sometimes prevent costly repairs later if malfunctioning parts can be repaired or replaced with new parts at the manufacturer's expense shortly after purchase.

According to both government and industry leaders, "inadequate, unnecessary or fraudulent car repairs" exceed all kinds of consumer complaints.[13] Most complaints deal with improperly done repairs, although 10 percent occur because of fraud.[14] Major reasons for these problems fall on both consumers and repairers. Few auto owners really understand the mechanics of their vehicles to know what repairs are needed and if they are done correctly. Accordingly, many auto mechanics have limited knowledge of the cars they attempt to repair although the mechanically ignorant consumer will not know this until after he or she pays for the repairs.

The best strategies for reducing auto repair costs are (1) learn their probable causes, (2) shop carefully for car repair services, and (3) learn where and how to complain effectively and follow through. Your bargaining position is far greater when you understand the repair needs you're buying and can knowledgeably check workmanship as well as the repair diagnosis. For persons unskilled in this area, enrollment in evening school courses in auto mechanics can help. Even if you never perform the repairs yourself, you will know what the mechanic you hire should be doing. The costs of equipment for auto repairs can sometimes wipe out any actual savings on the job for do-it-yourselfers. However, a growing number of firms are appearing on the market that rent tools and repair space by the hour to help reduce these costs and encourage do-it-yourself car repairs.

Finding a skilled mechanic who charges a reasonable rate takes time and thorough searching. Since licensing of mechanics is not generally required, word of mouth may be the only way to judge the reputation of various repairers. Consumer protection agencies may also be helpful in a manner similar to their assistance in locating the best car. Some states have now passed legislation requiring auto repairers to provide a written estimate of work needed plus its cost for all repair to customers upon request. That can greatly aid in comparison shopping for the best buy in car repairs, especially for persons moving into a new neighborhood or community.

One clue to locating a good mechanic is the repairer's participation in the National Institute for Automobile Service Excellence mechanic certification program. Through a series of tests that take up to six years to complete, this organization can help verify the abilities of trained mechanics who really know their trade.

Car manufacturers supply written warranties on their new cars in an attempt to prove that product quality is good. The promises made in that warranty can offer some clue to the performance you can expect from their vehicle. Some groups of auto dealerships belong to AUTOCAP, a national program started by the new car automotive retailing industry in 1973 to mediate disagreements between participating new car dealers and their customers. A few automobile clubs offer car diagnostic services or related programs to help protect their members from car repair problems as well.

Sometimes none of these preventive measures can protect you from car repair problems. So it also is important to learn appropriate complaint handling procedures in case service and repair problems do occur. Begin by keeping precise written records of the repairs made. Always get a receipt for all work performed and request the worn or malfunctioning parts that were replaced (unless the service is performed under a new car warranty and these parts must be returned to the manufacturer). Then if the repairs do not prove satisfactory, approach the owner or manager of the repair garage for help in resolving the problem. Let the manufacturer know of your plight if the car is under warranty. If that fails to receive satisfactory results, contact one or more consumer protection agencies *in writing* about the problem. Present the facts clearly and concisely, then be persistent about seeking a resolution to the problem. Although these efforts can be time consuming, your persistence, including court action when necessary, will only help to obtain satisfactory future performance for yourself and others.

DECIDING AMONG ALTERNATIVES

Sometimes selecting the most economical transportation alternative for a particular situation is unclear. It is often hard to predict performance or anticipate comfort and convenience factors far into the future. Changes in the age, size, and lifestyle needs of household members can necessitate reevaluation of transportation alternatives despite economics. Doreen Elliott must change her ideas about acceptable forms of personal transportation when college graduation throws her into the world of work and possible commuting. It may be impossible to find a job and residence that makes it realistic to walk to work forever. Then Doreen must decide which takes priority—the job or the preferred mode of transportation to it. Perhaps, more realistically, what compromises, if any, can Doreen and others make to reduce the personal and environmental costs of transportation?

Although it is impossible to accurately predict the future, trends suggest that transportation costs will continue to rise with few real innovations to compete with existing alternatives. Because that means a continued dependence on the automobile for most Americans, it also means primary responsibility for transportation decisions rests on the household. Decisions on ownership and operating costs are, therefore, highly individualized. The one common thread is that preventive maintenance will increase vehicle life. Beyond that, individual driving habits, attitudes, and mechanical skills determine total transportation costs along with the practicality of alternate forms of transportation.

Perhaps the best solution is to prepare for contingencies. Automobiles break down. Gasoline becomes scarce. Buses stop running. Bicycles get rained out. Whenever possible, select appropriate places to go that are accessible by more than one type of transportation, especially when they require a regular commute. Then your transportation choices are more flexible to combat travel boredom, rising costs, comfort, etc.

Transportation choices cannot remain static. Circumstances change constantly. So the wise consumer of transportation services will maintain an awareness of these changes and their effect upon existing choices. It is best to review transportation in light of all major lifestyle modifications. When the status quo appears to take precedence in other areas, evaluate the reliability and economy of transportation being used at least once a year. In that way, you are less likely to be taken by surprise that car repair costs are skyrocketing along with bus fares and gasoline.

PROFESSIONAL GUIDELINES

Matching people and transportation alternatives takes a clear understanding of household values in relation to spending and end use. Therefore, the first goal of the money management professional in helping a household cope with transportation decision making would be to ascertain their values and preferred methods of exhibiting them. Does strong peer group influence encourage the household to maintain a private auto despite the cost? Are public transportation facilities truly inadequate or just perceived as such because they are viewed as unacceptable?

Research has shown that mobility problems may cause disadvantaged households to obtain automobiles whenever possible, often trading convenience for safety because alternative forms of transportation cannot meet their needs.[15] This is an understandable reality in some parts of the country, especially where the location of welfare and social service offices are virtually inaccessible by mass transit.

In other cases, the barriers to the use of alternate modes of transportation are psychological. Therefore, the role of the money management professional is accepting the task of locating the barriers and attempting to eliminate them through education. The non-English speaking resident may need guidance in using city buses instead of taxis to go across town—so will others with literacy limitations. The handicapped may find it less costly to minimize travel by using more telephone shopping services and free delivery. The higher price of groceries delivered from the neighborhood store may be less expensive than a taxi ride to get to the supermarket and back.

For those of higher income, tradeoffs may need to be emphasized to keep the household budget in balance. If luxury and comfort take priority, perhaps carpooling is more realistic than scaling down the type of auto selected. Becoming a one-car family may also be considered, or buying a used luxury vehicle instead of a new one.

The major obstacle for most people is developing a willingness to assess or reassess the multitude of options open to them. That often means breaking stereotypes and encouraging clients to dare to be different. Once the results begin to speak for themselves, in resources saved for other uses, this task is done. In fact, the motivating force in modifying transportation choices may well be reaching a previously unattainable goal.

Transportation is but one of many basic human needs in our modern society. Despite rising costs, it does not have to dominate spending patterns when household priorities lie elsewhere. But it takes careful planning and follow through to avoid this contemporary dilemma.

ENDNOTES

1. Advisory Commission on Intergovernmental Relations, *Toward More Balanced Transportation: New Intergovernmental Proposals* (Washington, D.C.: U.S. Government Printing Office, 1975), p. 19.
2. Ibid., p. 42.
3. Janice M. Hogan, "Family Decisionmaking and the Energy Crisis." From a speech delivered to the American Home Economics Association on June 29, 1977, in Boston.
4. Advisory Commission, p. 13.
5. Caroline Donnelly, "What's Down the Line for Commuters?" *Money* (March 1976): 69.
6. William J. Murin, *Mass Transit Policy Planning* (Lexington, Mass.: Heath Lexington Books, 1971), p. 25.
7. "Which Costs More—Your Home or Your Car?" *The California Federal Story* (annual report), January, 1970.
8. "Family Spending," *The Money Tree* (Newark: University of Delaware Cooperative Extension Service, August, 1977), p. 2.
9. Yankelovich, Skelley, and White, Inc., *The General Mills American Family Report, 1974–75* (Minneapolis: General Mills, Inc., 1975), p. 22.
10. Ibid., p. 86.
11. Caroline Donnelly, "New Long Term Car Loans at Short Term Prices," *Money* (September 1976): 44.
12. Ibid.
13. "The Rising Tide of Auto Repair Complaints," *U.S. News and World Reports* (May 15, 1978): 73.
14. Ibid.
15. Advisory Committee, p. 25.

SIX

Credit: A Mortgage on the Future

Robert Walters, age 61, and his wife, Jeanette, were in an exceptionally happy mood when Jessica knocked on their door. They had just mailed the final installment on their home mortgage. At last, they were completely free of debt after thirty years! It was, indeed, a relief. Neither had ever fully been able to accept the new "buy now, pay later" philosophy so widely advertised lately. Except for the purchase of this house, their only major investment, the Walters seldom found anything else important enough to buy on credit. Maybe they were too conservative, but this was the only way they could have peace of mind. Sure, Jeanette had a thirty-day charge account at the local department store, but that was purely for convenience. The bill was always paid in full when it arrived so no interest charges were ever added. They also had a gasoline credit card which arrived unrequested about fifteen years ago. They used it on their annual vacation and kept it for emergencies, but neither spouse has yet become comfortable enough to say "charge it" every time they buy gas.

The most interesting thing to Jessie was the sharply contrasting attitude toward credit held by their thirty-year-old son, Robert, Jr. Here to share in his parents' mortgage burning, Bob had also come to announce the approval of his mortgage application to buy his first home in a neighboring community. Although a bachelor seldom looks forward to caring for a homestead, Bob is very conscious of how inflation is eating away at the little savings he has been able to accumulate in recent years. As a counterattack, he has chosen to buy now and pay later—when each dollar is worth less. At an annual salary of $18,000, Bob feels comfortable carrying $500 per month in installment obligations and a small balance of $1,000 in savings. His future looks good professionally, the lenders have never turned down his loan requests, and he is enjoying the lifestyle he always wanted, without any more waiting. In fact, Bob was so proud of his credit decisions that he volunteered much of this personal financial information, even though Jessica explained that his residence in another town prohibited him from being part of the survey population.

Jessica left the Walters' house a bit puzzled. Robert and his family seemed to communicate well and share a mutually respectful relationship. They even exhibited many of the same values—except for credit usage. She had always assumed that heavy credit users like Bob were more impulsive and less stable personalities. They could never be so down-to-earth or serious about the rationale behind this decision making—or could they?

TRENDS IN CREDIT USAGE

Since the end of World War II the use of personal installment credit has grown rapidly and continuously. Home mortgages were the first generally accepted purpose for borrowing, followed shortly by the durable goods related to home ownership. Cars were expensive but necessary in many areas to maintain a suburban home. Labor-saving appliances became essential to ease the housewife's burden, especially as more and more women returned to work. As the economy prospered and Americans gained confidence in their earning power, they borrowed more.

By the mid to late 1960s, it became more acceptable to borrow for nondurable goods, like vacations, provided these bills were repaid before it was time to borrow again for the same purpose. At about the same time, the use of credit cards became widespread, and Americans were charging everything from gasoline and cosmetics to the family vacation. The convenience of using credit rather than cash became important. It was considered to be safer protection against rising crime rates, and it became easier to keep records for maintaining the family budget.

Today, even dentists accept credit cards for bill payment, as do craftspeople at their exhibitions, and some colleges for tuition costs. In a few retail stores, it can take longer to change a $20 bill to pay for a $5 item than it does to approve the same purchase for credit.

While there is some adjustment necessary to accept this "buy now, pay later" lifestyle, it has become commonplace, particularly among the post-World War II generation who grew up with it. In fact, consumer credit is now considered to be an effective money management tool when used wisely.

The connotation of consumer credit has become generally positive and normal for Americans. The credit card takes its place next to apple pie in terms of acceptability. Like that same pie, credit must also be handled with care by those persons who truly want to maximize its utility and prevent possible problems.

Let's take a closer look at why credit has now become so popular among American consumers. To begin with, it adds another dimension of flexibility to financial planning. With the addition of credit buying, you can postpone payment for some purchases up to thirty days or more (when it takes that long for the credit card bill to arrive). This could make it easier to repay other obligations on time in order to maintain a good bill-paying record and avoid late charges. You can also use credit as a method of forced savings in order to have the use of certain essential products as you pay for them. In so doing, you can concentrate on building your regular savings program to meet other long-range goals and investment needs. The Walters' decision to buy a home on credit is a classic example.

ADVANTAGES

Credit can sometimes save you money as well. If certain items are on sale now but you don't have the cash to buy them for an additional two weeks, you could lose out. But with a charge account or credit card at that store, you can buy the sale items on credit today and set your cash aside in two weeks to pay the credit card bill when it comes due at the end of the month.

On major purchases you often have the same advantage, even without price reductions on the merchandise, because the rate of inflation during your saving period may be greater than the cost of borrowing to buy now. With inflation computed at 6 percent annually, the net cost of buying a car with a three- to five-year loan varies by only $6, even though the actual dollar cost of interest varies by $465 in a recent cost comparison.[1] If you applied the same 6 percent inflation to the car's cash price and waited three years to save the money to buy that car, your total cost would be $627 more than if you purchased it with credit three years earlier! That could help explain why young Bob Walters was so willing to use credit for his major purchases.

Moreover, credit and the ability to obtain it are a source of security today. Since credit cards replace the need for carrying large sums of cash, your losses are reduced in the event of theft or carelessness. This is especially true for the affluent American who would otherwise carry hundreds of dollars regularly. When a credit card is lost or stolen, your maximum legal liability per card is $50. When cash is lost or stolen, your losses are only limited by the amount you carry.

In addition, your credit worthiness can expand your ability to borrow to meet various emergencies. If unexpected medical bills occur and you have proven yourself to be a good credit risk, you can generally borrow to pay these off in full, repaying the loan in modest installments. However, the life-long cash customer would have greater difficulty in the same situation since she or he has never proven an ability to handle credit wisely. Therefore, most lenders would be reluctant to allow you to borrow, or would charge a higher rate to compensate for the greater risk involved.

DISADVANTAGES   All of this does not mean credit usage is free of problems. On the contrary, the many disadvantages of credit can easily and quickly outweigh the advantages, especially when the credit user acts in haste.

The biggest single problem with credit is that it leads to overspending and impulse buying for many people. Despite the fact that limits are generally imposed by lenders on the amount of credit any individual can use at one time, generous discretion is often the guide for credit grantors on this matter. For credit-worthy individuals, maximum limits may be raised rather than denying additional usage as long as regular payments are being made on the credit account. This leads to a false sense of security. "If my creditor has confidence I will repay the loan, how can I doubt his or her professional judgment?" So many people, including Bob, Jr., keep charging until someone else stops them—usually at a time when their indebtedness is so great it is no longer easily manageable.

The growing indebtedness not only causes repayment problems, but it can substantially raise the cost of goods and services purchased with borrowed money. In the thirty-six-month car loan example previously discussed, the total dollar cost of borrowing was $698 above the cash price. That figure is calculated on regular repayment of installments. Most credit contracts carry a surcharge for late payments in addition to this prearranged interest charge.

Accordingly, heavy credit users sometimes begin to raise their standard of living above realistic levels for their income. This is a trap that ensnares many people for whom credit is relatively easy to obtain but far more difficult to repay when the slightest calamity strikes in the pocketbook. One reason for this, which will be explored more fully later, is the minimum payment required on many credit card accounts. This figure can be as small as 1/36 of the balance due, or payment may be interest only, depending upon the company. So when a $394 bill requires a $10.95 minimum payment, a typical credit user may easily meet this minimum without substantially reducing the balance owed. Nor will he or she be aware of the rapid growth of this balance in future months when the minimum payment grows only one or two dollars at a time. So the borrower continues to spend freely on credit, honestly believing he or she can afford to do so until someone or something pulls in the reins.

Misconceptions like this can cause rude awakenings at unexpected times, too. This is particularly common when the radio you bought with your credit card breaks before the bill is paid. When you use credit to buy things that are used up or worn out before they are paid for, the extra cost of credit buying hardly seems worthwhile, and the incentive to repay that bill diminishes with each passing month. After all, the enjoyment you derived from using the product while you are paying for it is now over if only the bill remains intact.

TYPES OF CREDIT AVAILABLE

After more than a quarter century of rapidly expanding credit usage, it can be no surprise that the types of credit available have become a real smorgasbord of choices to meet a wide variety of consumer needs and wants.

The original type of credit, seldom used today, is the *single payment note*. This is a contractual agreement that specifies the borrower will repay *principal* (dollar amount borrowed) plus *interest* (cost of borrowing) in one lump sum on a specified date. There is no contact between these parties during the time between the date of borrowing and the date of repayment. But the full burden rests on the borrower to meet this lump sum payment as agreed. For business people and farmers, etc., or people with seasonal incomes, this type of credit meets their unique needs well. They generally anticipate earning the money needed for loan repayment within a very short time just prior to the due date.

SINGLE PAYMENT
VERSUS
INSTALLMENT

In contrast, the average wage earner, who already has some difficulty saving to meet her or his needs, could have problems scraping together this lump sum when it becomes due. There are certainly exceptions. Nonetheless, it takes a conscious effort from the borrower to set money aside to meet this obligation since there are no reminders from the creditor to prompt this action.

To better meet the needs of wage earners, our credit industry has developed the *installment* loan, a far more popular type of credit among consumer borrowers. Here, the contract between borrower and lender stipulates that the loan will be repaid in fractions at regular intervals over a specified period with each fractional payment representing the repayment of a portion of both principal and interest. This type of loan repayment is easier for the wage earner to meet since it allows him or her to set aside a small sum from each paycheck for repayment, delivering these sums regularly to the creditor. In so doing, the borrower relieves the temptation to use this money for something else. It also provides a way for the borrower to watch the balance owed shrink continuously as a further encouragement to meet this obligation regularly.

To better achieve this goal, many lenders even offer borrowers a choice of installment plans to best fit in with their spending plans. These choices often include both length of the loan (which determines the size of each installment) and time of the month each payment is due. Coupon books are even offered to serve as gentle reminders of this obligation that must be met by a series of prearranged deadlines.

OPEN VERSUS CLOSED-END

The next step in expanding the variety of credit types available came by modifying the types of installment credit. The basic installment credit contract is "*closed-end.*" That means all of the terms are fixed at the time it is signed. So, if a borrower signed a $1,000 closed-end note, he or she would repay that sum plus interest in regular installments by the due date. If that borrower wanted more credit from the same lender during the term of the first loan or after, he or she would generally have to sign a second contract. This new contract could be separate from the first one, or it could cancel the first one by including the remaining payments due from that loan in with the payments due on the new contract. When lending was only done by financial institutions, this system worked fairly well.

The same system became cumbersome and time consuming when retailers began to offer credit at a specified fee for that service. For many years, retailers offered credit only via thirty-day charge accounts. These accounts gave qualified customers the option to pay for their in-store purchases in full upon receipt of a monthly bill. There was no interest charged for doing so, although the cost of merchandise in the store may have been raised slightly to cover these costs.

As customers showed more interest in stretching these payments beyond thirty days, many retailers chose to enter the field of credit granting rather than refer these customers to financial institutions who would lend them cash that is just as easily spent in someone else's store. Since many retail purchases are for relatively small amounts, closed-end credit became awkward to use. That led to the introduction of revolving charge accounts or *open-end* credit agreements—the credit card as we know it today.

With open-end credit, the contract signed by lender and borrower sets a maximum dollar limit that can be borrowed at any one time. A percentage of the amount borrowed plus a predetermined amount of interest is due monthly. But the contract is never-ending as long as these terms are met. The borrower may use any portion of the available credit offered, paying only for what is actually used. The rest remains in reserve, at no cost, until it is used. A periodic (generally monthly) statement of the account is sent by the lender to itemize activity on the account for verification by the borrower who receives a duplicate copy of all credit transactions as the sales receipt for purchases. This periodic statement also lists the installment payment due at that time. The fee varies with the amount of credit used during that billing period.

This is different from closed-end loans in which all installment payments are equal and fixed at the time the contract is signed. As a bonus, perhaps in remembrance of the thirty-day charge, many revolving charge accounts offer a grace period of twenty-five days or so in which this periodic bill can be paid in full, free of interest charges. That does not hold true in closed-end contracts. Yet that bonus may be the reason why people like Mrs. Walters bother to use this credit card at all. While retailers make no profit on the credit usage of people like Mrs. Walters, the credit card offers convenience to encourage them to purchase more goods and services which do yield a profit from these customers.

BASIC SOURCES OF CREDIT

To further increase your options in borrowing, you may select among these various types of credit from a variety of lenders. For simplicity we will break them down into two groups: financial institutions and other sources. The primary differences among these sources are (1) cost of borrowing, and (2) qualifications to borrow. The qualifications for borrowing are set by each individual lender, but state usury law intervenes to set maximum limits on how much interest various types of lenders may charge. These laws vary substantially across the country.

FINANCIAL INSTITUTIONS

The lowest cost loans are available through financial institutions called credit unions. These are legal entities organized under state or federal charter, by and for their members who already have a common bond. This bond may be their place of employment, labor union, church, or club. These people agree to save their money in a facility they own and operate (the credit union) and to make their collective savings available for low-cost loans to all members. Because access to the credit union is limited to members, there are lower overhead costs, which in turn mean lending rates can be lower. After all, profits from the lending operation go directly to the members who own the institution. Often this takes the form of a refund of interest paid on credit union loans. In addition, for employer-based credit unions, payroll deduction plans are available for savings and/or loan repayment at the credit union.

Banks, both commerical and saving, are the lowest cost public lenders. They offer many types of credit, depending on your needs, and a wide range of interest rates that vary with the purpose of your loan, etc. Available credit services often include single payment notes, personal, automobile, and mortgage loans, as well as revolving charge accounts. Rates of interest vary frequently.

Savings and loan associations are similar to savings banks in their credit offerings. Both specialize in mortgage and home improvement loans, although the variety of loans available is expanding regularly. Rates of interest are comparable to those offered by banks, although they may be slightly lower in home-related lending.

Finance or small loan companies also offer credit to the general public. Their requirements for borrowing are often more relaxed than the previously listed institutions. In financial jargon, that means these small loan companies will assume a greater risk—or lend money to people less willing or able to repay the loans in full or on time. To compensate for making credit available to this higher risk group, the law allows small loan companies to charge higher interest rates—sometimes two or three times higher than banks. State law also limits the maximum dollar amount these companies can lend to one borrower at any given time. While the law does not regulate the purpose of these loans, these companies generally specialize in personal and automobile loans.

OTHER SOURCES

The most popular other sources of credit primarily offer credit card or revolving charge accounts for various purposes. Their motive is to increase the convenience of borrowing to pay for the items they promote.

Oil companies offer both open-end and installment credit for the purchase of gasoline and automotive needs from car repairs to new tires. Most offer a grace period on their revolving credit account so you can avoid interest charges by prompt payment in full.

Travel and entertainment clubs offer revolving credit accounts for use in restaurants, resorts, hotels, nightclubs, etc. As clubs, many of these organizations charge a small annual membership fee and provide other member services such as package tours and charters. Some also allow cash borrowing to a specified limit for qualified members who apply for this option.

Retail stores offer both installment and revolving credit plans for the purpose of buying merchandise in their stores. Interest rates may vary for the various types of credit available from each retailer. Store profits rise sharply for the retailer who can sell a customer both the product and the money to pay for it, so retail credit is a very heavily advertised item, even though many of these stores also offer an interest-free grace period for prompt bill repayment.

Life insurance companies also lend money to holders of cash value life insurance. The maximum to be borrowed is roughly equivalent to the cash surrender value of the policy—or the savings feature. Rates of interest are specified in the policy and are generally lower than those available from any other credit sources previously cited. There are no regular installment payments or due dates for the loan. Interest payments must be paid along with regular life insurance premiums, but repayment of the principal is at the discretion of the borrower. If the loan is not repaid at the time of the policy-holder's death, the amount due is subtracted from the face value of the policy to be paid to the beneficiary. But the longer that loan remains outstanding, the higher the total cost of borrowing gets.

Pawnbrokers are another source of credit to qualified borrowers. To qualify for a loan from this source, the sole criteria is that you have an item of value to leave with the pawnbroker in exchange for cash in the form of a single payment note. The length of the loan is generally six months or less, and interest rates exceed those offered by small loan companies. In addition, the amount of the loan is usually only equal to about 50 percent of the auction value of the item you leave as security. If you fail to redeem your property as agreed by repaying principal plus interest, the pawnbroker has the right to sell this item for his or her own profit.

The only source of credit more costly than the pawnbroker is the loan shark or illegal lender. This person charges usurious or illegally high rates of interest that run as high as 500 to 2,600 percent per year! His or her practices further violate all existing lending laws because of harsh and sometimes abusive methods of collection. That means stay far away from this credit source since it spells nothing but trouble.

UNIQUE CREDIT ARRANGEMENTS

Although the combination of credit types and sources is already quite diverse, there are several credit options that deserve closer scrutiny so their uses can be easily comprehended.

Passbook Loans. Available from most savings institutions, passbook loans, like life insurance loans, involve using your own money for two purposes. With a passbook loan, you use a sum already in your savings account as security for borrowing an equal amount from the same savings institution. The rate of interest on the loan runs a few percent above what you are earning on the savings account. Interest payments are due regularly although the repayment schedule on the principal is at the borrower's option. However, your savings account is frozen for a sum always equal to the amount of the loan outstanding. Then, if you fail to repay the loan, the savings institution can easily get its money back directly from your account. It is an advantageous arrangement for both borrower and lender and should lead the list of loan sources to consider when enough savings are available to make this a viable option. This is especially true for the person who finds savings difficult and is therefore hesitant to use these monies for cash buying because he or she lacks the discipline to replace them.

Consolidation loans.   This type of loan is available from most financial institutions at varying rates. It is generally used to pay off old bills in order to (1) reduce the monthly installment obligation to these creditors because it is too high in relation to basic living needs, (2) try to reduce total interest paid by paying off high cost lenders early with borrowing from a lower cost lender, or (3) stop collection practices on delinquent accounts by paying them off via a new loan to a new lender who can be repaid on time. Sometimes this reasoning works well. That only happens when the borrower is highly motivated to live within realistic credit limits and profit from previous mistakes. Consolidation loans spell trouble when borrowing is increased to earlier levels or beyond. They also add to the cost of credit buying because borrowers are paying finance charges on the original loan and the consolidation loan.

Second Mortgages.   These closed-end installment loans are available through many financial institutions as a means by which homeowners can raise relatively large sums to be repaid in about a three- to ten-year period. These loans can be used for any purpose if you are willing to pay the price, which is usually equal to maximum legal rates of interest if borrowed from a second mortgage company. When taking a second mortgage through the lender holding the original home mortgage, interest rates can be much lower, but the longer repayment period available can substantially increase the total dollar cost of the loan. When dealing with the original mortgage lender to negotiate this loan, you can sometimes just rewrite or refinance the original mortgage note (which is merely a twenty- to thirty-year installment loan). In so doing, the interest rate would be changed to reflect present market levels and your monthly payment adjusted accordingly. The major drawback, however, is the old problem that the items purchased with this loan may be used up or worn out long before the loan is repaid unless this method of borrowing is used to finance a college education, major home improvements, etc., with long-term benefits.

Check Credit.   This form of revolving credit is available to qualified borrowers from their banks. This is an automatic line of credit that offers borrowers an instant loan of $100 to $1,000 or more by either writing an overdraft check on their regular checking account or using checks drawn to a separate account for this purpose. This type of credit can be used with automatic teller machines in some cases. As long as the loan amount remains in reserve and unused by the borrower, there is no charge for this service. Finance charges begin when you borrow, generally at an annual rate of 12 percent per year, or higher depending upon state law. Loans from this source are generally granted in multiples of $100, although the borrower may write the check drawing on this account for any amount preferred. The best uses for this type of credit are to prevent overdraft charges on your checking account and the embarrassment of bouncing checks. Check credit can also be convenient in emergencies to pay for a special item when cash is short and your credit card is not an acceptable method of payment. Since the length of the check credit loan can be as short as thirty days, it is also to the borrower's advantage to repay this loan as quickly as possible. For long-term borrowing, lower rates are generally available in closed-end credit instruments. There is seldom, if ever, a grace period offered for prompt repayment on check credit. Finance charges begin to accumulate the day the loan is made.

COST COMPARISONS

On single payment loans, the borrower has use of the total sum borrowed until the due date of the loan when the principal plus interest must be repaid in full. Interest on that loan was computed at the time of borrowing by either an "add on" or "discount" method of applying simple interest. If you borrowed $1,000 at 6 percent interest and were asked to repay $1,060, the interest on the loan would be "add on"—or above and beyond the original loan request since you would have use of the full $1,000 during the term of the loan. If the loan had been discounted instead, you would repay a flat $1,000 but receive only $940 to use during the term of the loan.

However, if you paid the same $60 as a cost of borrowing on an installment loan of $1,000 to be repaid by the same due date, the true annual rate of interest would be 11.08 percent for the "add on" method and 11.58 percent for the discounted loan. The reason is simple. Since you are repaying the loan in pieces, you actually have use of the full $1,000 borrowed for far less time than the term of the loan. So the rule of thumb to use when estimating the effective rate of interest on an installment loan or true annual percentage rate (APR) is approximately equal to *twice* the rate charged on a single payment loan.

While a precise mathematical formula has been devised for making this calculation accurately, the borrower's need to do so has been reduced by the passage of the federal Truth in Lending Law of 1969, after similar legislation was already in use in several states. In all cases, the law required a uniform method of calculating credit costs for the potential borrower and presenting this information for consumer use prior to signing the contract.

The main requirements of Truth in Lending are the presentation, in bold face type, on all consumer credit contracts of two figures: (1) true *annual percentage rate* or rate of interest for one year, and (2) *finance charge* or total dollar cost of borrowing.

From this information, a potential borrower can easily comparison shop by simply searching out the lowest figures in both categories. No additional calculations are necessary since the law requires almost all related carrying charges to be included in this calculation as made by the lender (with guidelines from the federal government). These additional charges include any mandatory fees the lender requires all borrowers to pay. Some examples may be a credit investigation fee to determine your credit worthiness, or a credit life insurance policy to insure repayment of the loan if the borrower dies.

By comparing both APR and finance charge amounts on all credit contracts under consideration, you will be able to determine which lender offers lower rates depending upon the term of the loan. For example, Bank A may offer a car loan at 9 percent APR for thirty-six months. Bank B may offer the same rate on a forty-eight-month car loan. While their APR is the same, the total dollars to be paid in finance charges will be greater for Bank B because you are borrowing the money for a longer period of time. This fact would become obvious when you compare finance charges offered by both lenders even though APR information gave no clues to this difference. That cost difference may affect your choice of loans since it certainly shows a difference in the dollar cost of borrowing.

There are many more details of the Truth in Lending Law that can prove very helpful to consumer borrowers. Each will be introduced as it applies at various steps of the credit granting transaction. At this point of comparison shopping for rates, the APR and the finance charge remain the most important figures to note. However, several additional elements of this law should be included.

1. These two previously mentioned figures must be provided to the potential borrower *in writing* before credit is extended. Generally, that also means many lenders will also reveal this information in telephone inquiries as you begin comparison shopping.
2. They are also required to reveal the information in all advertising of credit for consumers. In fact, the ad must include:
   a. the amount of the loan or cash price
   b. the annual percentage rate
   c. the amount of down payment required (or if any is required)
   d. the amount of each installment payment
   e. the length of the loan or number of installments
   f. the amounts deducted as prepaid finance charges.
   This same information and more will also be required in the credit contract offered to confirm the loan. The requirements here differ for open- and closed-end transactions.
3. Truth in Lending generally covers all credit offered in four or more installments for personal, family, household, or agricultural purposes up to $25,000. All real estate transactions for these purposes are also covered even if they exceed this limit.

It is also essential to remember that Truth in Lending is a disclosure law only. It *does not* in any way regulate the rates to be charged legally by lenders. That is the responsibility of state governments under usury legislation exclusively at this time. Truth in Lending only requires that borrowers be told the true cost of credit usage before they agree to sign a legal contract for this transaction.

A recent amendment to the Truth in Lending Law may, however, affect the cash price of an item purchased in a store which accepts bank credit cards or other revolving credit plans not offered directly by that retailer. When a retailer accepts these cards for the purchase of goods and services, he or she gets paid immediately by the credit card company for these transactions. There are no bills or collection problems for the retailer to worry about. For that convenience, the retailer pays a service fee to the credit card company equal to a small percentage of credit card purchases made in that store. The agreement between credit card company and retailer generally expressly forbids charging this fee directly to credit card users. Instead retailers were required to add these costs to the cash price of store merchandise so the credit cardholder would not hesitate to charge purchases. Of course, that amounted to having cash customers subsidize credit users. So for the present, these retailers can legally offer discounts of up to 5 percent of the purchase price to cash customers, provided the discounts are equally available to all cash customers. In the future, surcharges *may* instead be imposed upon credit card users.

APPLYING FOR CREDIT

After you locate reasonable sources and costs of credit in your area, you must formalize this request to borrow by completing a credit application. All applicants can be evaluated on uniform criteria in determining their credit worthiness. Once the application is completed, signed, and returned to the lender, all the borrower can do is wait for the results. It is the creditor's turn now to make choices.

Lenders use many different ways of evaluating potential borrowers in order to obtain the information necessary for informed decision making. Their goal, of course, is to lend money only to those persons with both the ability and willingness to repay the loan. The basic guidelines for this determination are the borrower's character, capital or collateral, capacity, and the conditions of the economy.

Character is interpreted to reflect your willingness to repay the loan. Did you tell the truth on the credit application? Will you keep your promises as set forth on the credit contract? Capital refers to your financial resources or assets that can be used as security or collateral for this loan. In other words, if you fail to make payments as agreed, can the creditor attempt to get the loan repaid by forcing the sale of some of your property? (For more details, see Chapter 7.) Capacity is your ability to repay the loan from present income. Conditions of the economy affect the money supply or dollars the lender has available for new loans. When money is tight, costs of borrowing rise and lenders are more cautious about the qualifications of potential borrowers. The situation reverses somewhat when the money supply is plentiful.

CREDIT REPORTING SERVICES

In order to more quickly process credit applications, local lenders often use a clearinghouse of information established for this purpose. This clearinghouse or independent business that provides information about borrowers' character and capacity is called a *credit reporting agency* or *credit bureau*. Whether privately owned or operated cooperatively by the local lending community, this agency collects relevant financial information about local borrowers and sells it to properly identified member creditors and select others.

This information is maintained separately for each individual on a report form called a credit file or credit record. The information included in this record comes from public records, newspaper articles, and creditors who report to the bureau the status of their client accounts. The bureau abbreviates the data to conserve space and assure uniform terminology for reporting.

Every borrower makes his or her own credit record. The credit bureau does not rate them. It merely collects pertinent information including credit history. The credit history section of the record shows only the present status of each account (current balance plus amount and number of payments past due) and the historical status of the account. Under the historical status category, the creditor indicates how many times, if any, the account was thirty to fifty-nine days past due, sixty to eighty-nine days past due, and ninety days or more past due, during the length of time reviewed.

Your credit record remains with you for life. When you move across the state or the country, your credit file will follow as soon as you apply for credit in the new location. That means you cannot run away from a history of poor bill repayment. But you can take pride in noting that a good credit record will simplify the process of obtaining credit in your new location. In fact, it can prove helpful to notify the credit bureau in your new community of your recent move and ask them to request a copy of your credit record. This will save time when you first apply for credit in the new location. There may, however, be a nominal fee for the service.

In an attempt to reduce the number of errors inherent in this mass of paper handling, the federal government passed the Fair Credit Reporting Act of 1971. Basically, this law allows all borrowers the opportunity to review the information contained in their credit files, obtain corrections for all errors, and present both sides of disputed issues. This becomes the borrower's way to check that all information provided to creditors about them is truthful. But this is exclusively the borrower's responsibility. All the creditor is legally required to do is (1) indicate to the borrower that the reason for rejection of the credit application was adverse information listed in his or her credit file, and (2) provide the credit reporting agency's name and address that supplied this information so the borrower can pursue the matter.

To find out what information is in your credit file, you should call or visit the appropriate credit bureau office to review your record. You must properly identify yourself to have this information released. If you phone for the information your request will be delayed long enough for you to complete and return a request application. When that has been received by the credit bureau, an employee will telephone you, verify your identity, and release the requested information. This bureau is required by law to release all information in your file and the sources of that information.

In addition, the bureau must tell you the names of those who have received employment reports based on this information within the last two years and all others who have received credit reports in the last six months. Only you and reputable business or professional firms under contract with the credit bureau have access to your credit file. Call numbers are used to identify each firm so that the information is kept confidential. One of the following conditions must be met before any information from your credit file can be released:

1. Response to a court order.
2. If the consumer/borrower asks for a report to be made.
3. If the person requesting information will use it for:
    a. credit granting, collection, or review of an account
    b. insurance involving the consumer/borrower
    c. employment purposes
    d. a legitimate business need involving the consumer/borrower
    e. determining the consumer/borrower's eligibility for a license or other benefit granted by an agency of the government which is required to inspect the applicant's financial status.

There is no charge to review your credit file if the request is the result of a credit rejection within the last thirty days. If the reason for your request stems from pure curiosity, then the bureau may charge a small fee for this service.

If the results of this review indicate to you that there is an error in the file, explain the problem to the credit bureau and request that they reinvestigate the matter on your behalf. This is a required service under the Fair Credit Reporting Act at no cost to the consumer. If the reinvestigation confirms that an error has been made, the credit bureau must delete this information from your file. Upon request, the bureau must also contact, at no charge to you, those persons who received erroneous reports from your file.

Sometimes a reinvestigation of this nature indicates that some information in your file remains in dispute between you and a creditor, etc. In that case, both sides of this story may be included in your credit file and provided to all persons making future inquiries. To include your side of the dispute, write a brief letter of one hundred words or less to the bureau explaining the dispute. This will become a permanent part of your credit file.

Adverse information in your file is often undisputably yours but reflects mistakes made years earlier. To provide a second chance for people who have mended their ways, the Fair Credit Reporting Act also limits the length of time some of this information can remain in your credit record. Bankruptcies may be reported for ten years. Tax liens, collection accounts, bad debts, and records of arrest, indictment, or conviction, etc., may only be reported for seven years. After that, this information must be removed from your record.

What this all boils down to is that your credit record can often make the difference between acceptance or rejection of a credit application. That record, therefore, must be handled very carefully. To preserve its accuracy, it is to your advantage to review the record personally every year or so. Preventive maintenance can save time and embarrassment when you need or want a ready reference for credit or some related purpose. Since the law allows another person of your choice to review this record with you, it is also wise to take advantage of this opportunity to have a witness to the transaction.

CREDIT SCORING   Credit bureau reports are not foolproof, though. The information may not be completely up to date unless regular reports are made by creditors to the bureau and unless bureau employees have time to compile data from local public records. In addition, creditors wishing to obtain information from the bureau must pay for this service. The fee is generally the same no matter how useful the information obtained may be.

Because of these factors, many creditors prefer to use alternate methods of evaluating the data provided on the credit application. One method growing rapidly in recent years is credit scoring. This is a method of assigning various point values to selected characteristics of the potential borrower as provided on the credit application. The points received are totaled and then compared to a minimum company standard for good credit risks. Persons scoring above this minimum are granted the loans requested. Those scoring below the minimum are rejected. Borderline cases are more fully evaluated through credit bureau reports, references, etc., to make a more verifiable decision.

A potential borrower may never see the actual credit scorecard used by the lender, but she or he can easily be alert to the types of information used because it is all reported on the application. Your length of residence in the community, on the job, and even in your present residence are clues to the creditor about your stability and willingness to repay the loan. Income, occupation, even the age of your car can be criteria for some lenders' credit scoring systems. These systems are based on a statistical history of each company's good credit risks. Because of this, the system varies regionally and by type of creditor as well as the type of customer generally borrowing from this source.

Credit scoring is handled by computer as much as possible to reduce human subjectivity. It is also kept confidential from customers to reduce risks of cheating on the application. For example, while it is assumed that higher income earners are always better credit risks, this has not proven accurate in some segments of the credit industry. That conclusion is therefore reflected in the point values assigned to various income levels by some firms. Since this fact is not obvious to most people, revealing it on the credit scorecard could be confusing and tempt applicants to stretch the truth in order to get a higher score.

EQUAL CREDIT OPPORTUNITY

Despite the introduction of credit scoring systems to make credit granting more objective, many complaints have arisen about criteria used in credit granting. Women and minorities in particular felt discriminated against by the attitudes of credit grantors and the questions asked on application forms as well as point values in credit scoring.

In 1975, the federal government acted to prohibit discrimination in credit on the basis of sex or marital status through the passage of the Equal Credit Opportunity Act. Amendments were made in 1977 to further prohibit discrimination because of race, national origin, religion, age, and receipt of public assistance. To uphold this law, creditors are limited in the questions they can ask an applicant and the criteria they can use in evaluating creditworthiness.

To comply with the law, creditors may no longer ask questions about your:

1. Sex, race, national origin, or religion.
2. Marital status if you apply for a separate, unsecured account—unless you live in the community property states of Arizona, California, Idaho, Louisiana, Nevada, New Mexico, Texas, or Washington.
3. Previous marriages (in relation to divorce or widowhood)
4. Spouse *unless*:
   a. your spouse is applying with you
   b. your spouse will be allowed to use your account
   c. you are relying on your spouse's income or on alimony or child support income from a former spouse
   d. you reside in a community property state.
5. Plans for having or raising children.
6. Receipt of alimony, child support, or separate maintenance payments unless the creditor first tells you that you do not have to reveal this information unless you want to rely on it to obtain credit.

Although a creditor cannot consider an applicant's sex, marital status, race, national origin, or religion in determining creditworthiness, he or she may ask and consider age of the applicant under the following circumstances:

1. The applicant is a minor (under eighteen) and therefore not legally forced to uphold any contract signed.
2. The applicant is over sixty-two and the creditor will favor him or her because statistically persons in this age prove to be good credit risks.
3. The creditor uses age to determine the meaning of other factors related to creditworthiness. For example, a creditor could consider your age to see if your income might be reduced during the term of the loan because you are about to retire.

Also, since some telephone companies will not list telephone numbers in the name of both spouses without additional charge, a creditor cannot use a telephone listing in the applicant's name as a criteria. The creditor may, however, ask if there is a phone in your residence since this is a common indicator of stability.

In evaluating the applicant's income, the creditor must be careful to treat all regular sources of income equally. The creditor always reserves the right to ask for proof that the income has been consistently received and to attempt to verify the probability of its regular continuation throughout the term of the loan. But in so doing, the creditor considers all sources of income equally (from public assistance, part-time employment, pension, annuity, alimony, child support, etc.) if the applicant is relying on this source of income to meet the payments on this loan. This means only the amount of income in relation to living expenses and its regularity can be used in evaluating creditworthiness.

While this is generally a boon to most credit applicants, it reinforces the need for applicants to realistically appraise their own financial situation, including plans for the future. For example, under ECOA it is illegal for a creditor to assume that a woman of child-bearing age will stop work to have or raise children. Therefore, when a couple applies for credit and both spouses are working, the creditor must calculate the amount they can afford to borrow on the basis of their combined income provided both are holding permanent jobs. If the couple's plans differ from that assumption, the applicants must communicate this pending change to the creditor during the application interview in order for the calculations to be realistically adjusted.

Revolving charge card limits and short-term loans do not indicate real problems in this regard for most couples. However, in long-term lending for mortgages, etc., it is imperative to communicate with the creditor about pending changes in income if the applicants are to regularly meet this obligation. In time, one spouse's income may grow to equal or exceed their combined income at the time of the loan application, thereby reducing this problem. Yet, that can take years with related living costs rising too. Moreover, either spouse can lose a job due to a variety of reasons. That can apply further strains on the loan repayment abilities of the applicants unless they have an adequate emergency fund set aside to deal with these problems.

Many lenders are hesitant to discuss these possibilities with loan applicants for fear they will be accused of discrimination. Because of that, the burden of determining ability to pay falls jointly on borrower and lender alike now more than ever. By the same token, it forces lenders to rely more heavily than ever on their ability to collect a loan because they are somewhat more limited in assessing creditworthiness.

In addition to the regulations ECOA requires of creditors, the same law offers new rights to credit applicants. These include the right to:

1. Obtain credit in any legal name of your choice. For many women this allows an option of using your maiden name, your first name and your husband's surname, or your first name and a combined surname.
2. Get credit without a cosigner, if you are creditworthy.
3. Have a cosigner other than your spouse, if a cosigner is necessary.

4. Keep your own accounts even after you change your name or marital status, reach a certain age, or retire (unless the creditor has evidence that you are unable or unwilling to repay).
5. Know whether your application was accepted or rejected within thirty days of filing it.
6. Know why your application was rejected if that is the case.

To assure fair treatment in all aspects of credit granting, ECOA has also established regulations regarding the reporting of credit histories by credit bureaus. Traditionally, credit histories for married persons were reported only in the husband's name, even for joint accounts. So when the wives wanted to establish credit in their own names as the law now allows, this task was difficult in terms of evaluating their credit histories.

To solve this problem, creditors who report credit histories to credit bureaus must report information on joint accounts in both names. In deciding how to report on past credit transactions (prior to 1977), the creditor may not use any unfavorable information about an account shared with a spouse or former spouse, if the applicant can show that the spouse's bad credit record does not accurately reflect his or her own willingness or ability to pay and vice versa.

The intent here was originally to protect women who were married, separated, divorced, or widowed. But the protection applies equally to married men whose wives or former wives have abused their credit privileges on joint accounts.

THE CREDIT CONTRACT

Once the application has been completed and signed, creditworthiness established, and the requested monies found to be available for lending, this agreement must be formalized by the acceptance of a legally binding contract. This contract may be known as an installment loan (or sales) contract, chattel mortgage, conditional sales agreement, bailment lease, or credit card customer agreement. While there are some slight differences by legal definition, once you have signed this document, you and the lender become obligated to live up to its terms.

To clarify the terms of a typical credit contract, we will review one such agreement in the form of a closed-end installment loan contract. It is presented in the new plain language format that is gaining popularity in common consumer law transactions. Similarities and differences will then be presented in relation to other popular types of consumer credit contracts.

As you will recall, borrowing is cheaper when the applicant is willing to guarantee repayment of a debt by giving the lender legal access to select items of personal property which that lender may claim if the borrower fails to make payments as agreed. These terms are, therefore, explained and signed in the relevant credit contract along with any required supplemental materials which become public record. An analysis of Figure 6–1 will explain these terms more precisely.

FIRST NATIONAL CITY BANK

Figure 6–1
Sample Secured
Credit Agreement

Consumer Loan Note   Date_____, 19_____

(In this note, the words I, me, mine and my mean each and all of those who signed it. The words you, your and yours mean First National City Bank.)

Terms of Repayment To repay my loan, I promise to pay you_____dollars ($_____). I'll pay this sum at one of your branches in _____uninterrupted_____installments of $_____each. Payments will be due_____, starting from the date the loan is made.

Here's the breakdown of my payments:

1. Amount of
   the Loan $_____

2. Property
   Insurance
   Premium $_____

3. Filing Fee
   for Security
   Interest $_____

4. Amount
   Financed
   (1 + 2 + 3) $_____

5. Finance
   Charge $_____

6. Total of
   Payments
   (4 + 5) $_____

   Annual
   Percentage
   Rate_____%

Figure 6–1 Continued	Prepayment of Whole Note	Even though I needn't pay more than the fixed installments, I have the right to prepay the whole outstanding amount of this note at any time. If I do, or if this loan is refinanced—that is, replaced by a new note—you will refund the unearned finance charge, figured by the Rule of 78—a commonly used formula for figuring rebates on installment loans. However, you can charge a minimum finance charge of $10.
	Late Charge	If I fall more than 10 days behind in paying an installment, I promise to pay a late charge of 5% of the overdue installment, but no more than $5. However, the sum total of late charges on all installments can't be more than 2% of the total of payments or $25, whichever is less.
	Security	To protect you if I default on this or any other debt to you, I give you what is known as a security interest in my 0 Motor Vehicle and/or_____ (see the Security Agreement I have given you for a full description of this property), 0 Stocks, 0 Bonds, 0 Savings Account (more fully described in the receipt you gave me today) and any account or other property of mine coming into your possession.
	Insurance	I understanding I must maintain property insurance on the property covered by the Security Agreement for its full insurable value, but I can buy this insurance through a person of my own choosing.
	Default	I'll be in default: 1. If I don't pay an installment on time; or 2. If any other creditor tries by legal process to take any money of mine in your possession. You can then demand immediate payment of the balance of this note, minus the part of the finance charge which hasn't been earned figured by the Rule of 78. You will also have other legal rights, for instance, the right to repossess, sell and apply security to the payments under this note and any other debts I may then owe you.
	Irregular Pay	You can accept late payments or partial payments, even though marked "payment in full," without losing any of your rights under this note.
	Delay in Enforcement	You can delay enforcing any of your rights under this note without losing them.
	Collection	If I'm in default under this note and you demand full payment, I agree to pay you interest on the unpaid balance at the rate of 1% per month, after an allowance for the

Figure 6-1
Continued

unearned finance charge. If you have to sue me, I also agree to pay your attorney's fees equal to 15% of the amount due, and court costs. But if I defend and the court decides I am right, I understand that you will pay my reasonable attorney's fees and the court costs.

Co-makers If I'm signing this note as a co-maker, I agree to be equally responsible with the borrower. You don't have to notify me that this note hasn't been paid. You can change the terms of payment and release any security without notifying or releasing me from responsibility on this note.

Copy
Received The borrower acknowledges receipt of a completely filled-in copy of this note.

	Signatures	Addresses
Borrower:	_____	_____
Co-maker:	_____	_____
Co-maker:	_____	_____
Co-maker:	_____	_____

Hot Line If something should happen and you can't pay on time, please call us immediately.

Personal Finance Department
First National City Bank

Reprinted with permission of Citibank, N.A.

The *terms of repayment* itemized at the top of the agreement provide the basic required information under Truth in Lending Law for the true costs of the loan, plus when and how it will be repaid. These provisions are the primary contract terms that apply to all borrowers. If you follow these rules exactly, none of the supplemental terms of the contract are likely to be enforced. To protect yourself, it is, however, essential to read and comprehend these additional terms for they are the guidelines for you and the lender to follow if either of you attempts to alter the terms of the original agreement.

Prepayment of whole note affects the conscientious borrower who pays the loan in full prior to the date agreed to in the terms of repayment. First, this clause grants the borrower permission to prepay. Then it explains how a refund of some finance charges will be computed since the borrower no longer requires use of the principal as agreed in the original contract.

If this loan is prepaid or replaced by a new one, the refund of finance charges will be figured by the "Rule of 78" or "Sum of the Digits" method. Obviously, this is *not* a simple fractional share of the finance charges based on the length of time the loan was outstanding. Many lenders claim refunding interest on that basis would cause them to lose money on the bookkeeping involved. Instead, the "Rule of 78" was devised as a more equitable formula from the lender's perspective.

Here's how the formula works. Based on a fraction, the numerator is found by determining the number of payments agreed to and then counting backwards from that figure a number of places equal to the payments actually made. These numbers are then added together. The denominator becomes the sum of the numbers from one to the number of payments contracted. For example, if you prepaid a twelve-month loan in six months, the Rule of 78 would allow the lender to keep 49/78 of finance charges and repay the remainder to you. The math involved would look like this:

$$\frac{12 + 11 + 10 + 9 + 8 + 7}{1 + 2 + 3 + 4 + 5 + 6 + 7 + 8 + 9 + 10 + 11 + 12} \times \text{finance charge} = \text{amount retained by lender}$$

Obviously, this is an amount far greater than one-half, the simple fraction equal to the time period in which you actually repaid the loan. If that fact discourages you from considering prepayment, you are following the lender's intent. The creditor prefers that you follow the original agreement. So, if you do plan to prepay a loan, be sure you do it early enough to make the refund worthwhile. If prepayment is only a month or two before the deadline, you might be ahead financially by leaving the money for these extra payments in a savings account to earn interest until they are due. Accordingly, you are also wise not to try prepaying a loan by making double or triple installments then skipping one or two, etc. This technique offers no financial advantage. It would be wiser to save the money for extra payments until that sum will repay the remainder of the loan in full. The combination of interest earned on the savings plus the small prepayment refund could lower your cost of borrowing a little.

Late charges are added to the cost of a regular installment payment only if that payment is not received within ten days after the due date passes. That means each installment has a ten-day grace period to compensate for common errors of forgetfulness or post office delays, etc. Payments received more than ten days late are penalized by a surcharge of 5 percent of the overdue installment, up to $5. For the chronically late payer, the total of late charges made on this total contract is also limited. From the borrower's perspective, late charges should be viewed as an incentive to make prompt installment payments. That is part of the reason the lender included this clause in the contract anyhow. In fact, some lenders who use coupon books write monthly payments to include the late charge and direct the prompt paying borrower to deduct them when the payment is made on time!

Security is the property you already own that you allow the lender to take away from you if you fail to keep your promise to repay this loan as agreed. In signing the loan contract you, the borrower, can generally choose which property will be used as security on this loan. The choice may include the property you will be purchasing with the money received from this loan. In fact, this option will generally be the lender's preference.

To be sure both parties to this contract clearly understand which property will be used as security, this property should be listed in the credit contract as shown in Figure 6-1. Then, a financing statement describing the property and the agreement which it secures should be filed for public record at the municipal clerk's office where the borrower resides. (The exception here is for motor vehicles registered in title states, a legal document on which ownership and lien information is already provided.) This is a provision of the Uniform Commercial Code (UCC). It protects the secured lender from having this same property seized by another creditor or sold without her or his knowledge. The financing statement, when properly filed, places a lien on the stated property that is public information to all prospective buyers. It prohibits the transfer of title to that property without payment of the lien to the creditor filing this agreement.

As you will note, under terms of repayment, a fee can be charged for filing this agreement. In addition, the law provides that the financing statement must be promptly removed from the borrower's record when the loan is repaid in full.

Insurance is required on the property used as security so that loss or damage to that property will not prohibit the lender from receiving full market value if he or she accepts this property in repayment for the loan. The lender may sell the borrower this insurance at a cost disclosed under terms of repayment, or the borrower may obtain a completely separate insurance policy. The creditor may, however, reserve the right to see proof of insurance coverage before the loan is granted.

Default occurs when the borrower fails to live up to his or her part of the credit contract. Generally that means when the borrower fails to make installment payments as previously agreed. In this particular contract, the lender also uses a second definition of default unique to this type of financial institution. It declares the loan to be in default if another creditor tries to take money from the borrower's checking or savings account, etc., held at that bank. This is legal under certain circumstances (explained in Chapter 7). This is another protection for the lender who anticipates a borrower is having money problems and may not repay as agreed.

The contract goes on to explain that if the borrower defaults, the remainder of the loan becomes due and payable in full now—minus unearned finance charges computed under the Rule of 78. It goes on to explain that if the note is not repaid in full as requested, the lender can *repossess* or take away the property you purchased with this loan or other security used. The lender can then sell the security and apply the proceeds of the sale to the balance outstanding on the loan. Legally, this can all happen if the borrower is eleven days late in making an installment payment!

The *irregular payments* clause is additional protection for the creditor. It allows the lender to accept late or partial payments without cancelling any of the other provisions of this contract. That goes one step farther by voiding the possibility that a partial payment will be accepted as payment in full if the check is so marked. In some cases, the cashing of a check marked in this manner could constitute a legally binding contract. Under the terms of this contract, that is not a possibility since it is negated here and agreed to by both parties.

Delay in enforcement allows the creditor to wait more than eleven days before using any of the rights granted under this contract without losing them. While this is intended to protect the creditor, it also tells the borrower that the terms of this agreement might be renegotiated if mutually agreeable revisions can be found. That means a borrower should always keep channels of communication open with the lender as a means by which she or he might delay enforcement of some of the negative provisions of this contract.

When a borrower fails to pay the loan in full immediately after default as required, the lender incurs certain costs in attempting to collect this money. These *collection costs* are charged to the borrower as explained here. To begin with, interest is charged on the total unpaid balance at the rate of 12 percent APR. Depending on the original terms of repayment, this may be a rate of interest higher or lower than the original contract. Either way, the finance charge is computed as 1 percent per month on the total unpaid balance.

This clause goes on to explain that any legal fees involved in collecting on this loan will also be charged to the borrower up to certain limits. However, if the borrower wins the suit, the lender will pay the legal costs involved for both parties.

Co-makers are all persons who sign this note along with the original applicant. In so doing they accept equal responsibility for repaying the loan as agreed or accepting the consequences as described in the contract. Moreover, the co-makers waive the right to notification of any changes made in the terms of repayment, etc., without cancelling their own responsibility for repayment. That means the co-makers agree to allow the borrower to change the terms of this agreement for them. So anyone signing as co-maker should have complete trust in the borrower to represent them in this manner. The co-makers should also have the ability to repay the loan just in case the borrower defaults.

Finally, the borrower must acknowledge receipt of a completed copy of this contract with all blanks filled. Provision of this copy is required under the Truth in Lending Law so duplicates are often kept as a reference for the lender to prove compliance with the law. A customer copy also becomes an important reference for the borrower to recall the terms of the agreement as needed.

UNSECURED CREDIT AGREEMENT

The terms of an unsecured loan are quite similar to those of a secured note. Some of the numbers are different, but so are the institutions offering the loan and the states in which they do business. The only significant difference in contract terms is the lack of a UCC financing statement or other evidence of saleable security to back up the borrower's promise to repay the loan.

Credit life and/or disability insurance is also a popular requirement on many consumer credit contracts. Both can be required by any lender, although the borrower has the right to purchase this insurance from someone other than the lender except in cases where the premium for the insurance is included in the basic finance charge.

CREDIT CARD AGREEMENTS

The numerous operational differences between open- and closed-end credit necessitate substantial differences in contract provisions between them as well. First, an explanation is usually given of how the credit card is to be used. This includes making a contract to pay for charged merchandise each time a sales slip is signed ordering that purchase to be paid from the cardholder's account. It also covers authorized sales orders made by mail and telephone, even though they do not include signed sales slips. The agreement may allow persons other than the cardholder to make purchases on this account if they have the cardholder's permission to do so. Hence, the salesclerk accepting the credit card for a purchase can request proof that the person carrying the credit card is either the cardholder or otherwise authorized to use it. The cardholder is required to match her or his signature on the back of the credit card with the signature on the sales slip. Authorized other users could be required to carry a note from the cardholder granting this permission, or otherwise indicate how this authorization can be verified.

Some retailers offer extra credit cards on the same account for the cardholder's dependents to carry to simplify this authorization procedure.

Open-end credit applications generally include a credit limit that indicates the maximum amount of credit available to the cardholder at any one time. The terms of the contract put some flexibility into that limit by allowing the cardholder to exceed it upon occasion. However, if that occurs, the creditor requires all charges that exceed the limit to be paid immediately upon receipt of the bill. In addition, the creditor accepts no obligation to raise the credit limit just because he or she has allowed it to be extended once in a while. In other words, to have the credit limit raised, you must make a formal request to the creditor for this purpose. It doesn't happen automatically.

The size of the installment payments made on the account can vary monthly, largely at the cardholder's discretion. Three repayment choices (from payment in full to a sum as small as 5 percent of the new balance) are given. A twenty-five-day grace period is usually also offered, during which payments can be made without the addition of a finance charge.

When finance charges are applicable, the method used for their computation is also explained, so potential cardholders may use this fact in comparison shopping. In addition, the provisions of Truth in Lending must be met in regard to the statement of finance charges and annual percentage rate.

An explanation is also included on how payments received will be applied to the cardholder's account. Since finance charges are repaid first, it should be clear that meeting minimum payments only each month will do little to reduce the balance on the credit card account. For some cardholders, that can mean following the creditor's own rules can put them more deeply in debt than they planned. Minimum payments on most credit card accounts provide a false sense of affluence for many cardholders if the account is used regularly. While the minimum payment grows in direct proportion to the balance owed, this is seldom obvious in terms of fixed dollars owed because the minimum payment is equal to a mere 5 percent of the new balance. Therefore, if bill repayment on this account is regularly fixed by the cardholder at the minimum payment level, it will be very costly and result in a long-term commitment to pay the bill in full. Yet this will not be readily apparent to the cardholder if the only figure he or she examines on the monthly statement is that minimum payment.

The conditions under which this contract can be terminated are explained, including a definition of default. All monies owed become immediately due and payable in one lump sum—even if the cardholder is not notified that he or she is in default! Acceptance of this contract can mean the cardholder waives the right to such a notice, if so specified in the contract.

The Truth in Lending Law limits any credit cardholder's liability for unauthorized use to a $50 maximum per credit card. This must be spelled out in the contract. However, that liability limit can be reduced to only those unauthorized charges made prior to notifying the creditor that the credit card was lost or stolen. This second provision can be extremely important if you consider that the cardholder's maximum liability would be $300 if six cards were lost—and even higher for the person who carries more cards! Prompt notification of loss or theft is so important that the law requires all creditors to supply a self-addressed, prestamped "notification of credit card loss" form to each cardholder to facilitate this reporting. A telephone call, telegram, etc., is also acceptable notification to alert the credit card company of the problem and should certainly be used to speed the oral notification processing. However, it is always important to confirm in writing.

Obviously, it is to your advantage to keep an up-to-date list of credit card numbers and addresses in a safe place separate from your credit cards. Then you are prepared to act quickly and accurately to stop unauthorized use of your card.

Use of a credit card is a privilege granted to the cardholder that is revocable at the creditor's discretion since the card actually remains as property of the creditor. The cardholder also has the right to cancel this agreement at will by returning the credit card and paying any remaining balance owed.

Since the creditor owns the card, she or he may also change the terms and conditions of this contract at any time as long as these changes are not made retroactive. This agreement can also be changed in accordance with new or revised state laws without cancelling the total contract.

The details of billing procedures on this account are also included as required by federal law under the Fair Credit Billing (FCB) Act of 1975, an amendment to Truth in Lending. (This statement may supplement the contract rather than being contained in it.) Because the issuer of a credit card agreement may allow a twenty-five-day grace period in which to pay the bill without a finance charge, the law requires that creditor to mail or deliver the bill to all customers at least fourteen days before the end of the grace period. Obviously, this timing is essential for the cardholder to review the accuracy of the bill and return the proper payment before the grace period elapses.

That same law requires credit card issuers to mail regular statements to all cardholders who have a credit or debit balance in their account of $1 or more. This assures that credit balances cannot be forgotten. For double protection, the law also allows cardholders to request a cash reimbursement of credit balances if they prefer.

In addition, FCB provides a nationally uniform policy for handling billing errors on open-end credit accounts. A major provision of this law requires that the cardholder notify the creditor of any suspected billing errors *in writing* within sixty days after the bill is received. The details of this procedure are required to be given to all credit cardholders upon opening their account and semi-annually thereafter. Alternatively, the card issuer may summarize the procedure on each monthly statement.

POST-TRANSACTION ACTIVITIES

After the credit contract is signed, there are a few additional transactions that can affect the relationship between the borrower and the lender, even though they may not be specifically written into the credit contract.

ASSIGNMENT OF CONTRACT

A common practice in closed-end credit is for the original lender of sales credit to assign this contract to another creditor, usually a financial institution. In effect, the original lender sells the contract at a discount to another lender in order to get prompt repayment of the contract. For example, a retail store may offer a $1,000 installment loan contract to a customer for the purchase of household goods. With finance charges added, a three-year note may require the customer to repay $1,300 by the end of the contract. But the lender may be able to sell that contract for $1,050 and get that money back now in one lump sum to reinvest as she or he chooses. That also means that the new creditor or *holder-in-due course* of the contract has to accept full responsibility for collecting on the loan.

Obviously, this assignment of a contract is advantageous to the original lender. Until recently it was also a very good deal for the second creditor since the holder-in-due-course was not legally responsible for any problems with the merchandise purchased under this contract. All complaints had to be handled under the original purchase contract. The newly assigned credit contract was viewed as a separate transaction involving only the lending of "X" dollars with a promise to repay. There was no merchandise agreement included.

Of course, that also posed complications to the credit buyer. If a problem occurred with the merchandise and the retailer refused to fix it, many credit buyers would withhold payment of their installment loan, hoping to get action on the complaint. Instead they would often find themselves in default on the loan!

Fortunately for consumers, this practice is no longer legal under federal and some state laws. New consumer rights under FCB protect borrowers using open-end credit. Similarly, a Federal Trade Commission trade regulation rule protects consumers' rights in holder-in-due-course transactions on closed-end credit accounts. This FTC rule requires all sellers to include a clause in any installment sales contracts which notifies consumer borrowers that they have a right to make any legitimate claims and defenses resulting from defective merchandise, etc., against the original lender and/or any creditor who subsequently purchases the contract. These claims are, however, limited to the amount already paid on the installment loan.

The result of these legal changes from the mid-1970s means that all credit buyers retain their rights to the correction of merchandise faults whether the contract is assigned or not. In addition, commercial banks, sales finance companies, etc., who regularly purchase the assignment of credit contracts, must be more selective. If they continue to buy "paper" from lenders with questionable reputations, these financial institutions may suddenly find themselves in the business of repair and replacement for faulty merchandise!

Occasionally a merchant will offer a credit customer a perfectly legal credit contract for the purchase of certain merchandise. This will be accepted and signed by the customer. Then the merchant will break the contractual promise by delivering different merchandise to the customer and requesting a signed receipt acknowledging delivery and acceptance of the merchandise.

DELIVERY OF GOODS AND/OR CREDIT CARDS

To avoid this problem and the need for possible future legal action to correct it (see Chapter 7), a wise consumer will take some additional precautions upon delivery of the merchandise.

1. Be present to verify that the merchandise delivered is the same condition and quality as that ordered.
2. Check model and serial numbers on contract and merchandise to be sure they match.
3. Refuse to accept the merchandise in fulfillment of the contract unless the first two conditions are met.

Accordingly, when a credit card is received, the contract terms and credit limit should be reviewed for accuracy, as should the name and address of the applicant(s). Then the accompanying information on notification of loss and handling billing errors should be filed in a safe and convenient place for easy access when needed.

Keep a copy of this record with other important household records. Make another copy to keep in your office and a third to carry with you when you travel (separate from your credit cards). Then you will always have this information readily available if your cards are lost or stolen. Any delays in notifying the credit card company can cost you money (up to the $50 maximum liability per card).

BILLING ERRORS

Check the accuracy of credit card statements promptly upon receipt to be certain all charges are correct. The first responsibility for correcting a billing error belongs to the cardholder. If he or she fails to notify the creditor *in writing* of a possible error within sixty days after that first incorrect bill was received, the creditor is no longer obligated to make the correction.

To assure adequacy of information in verifying credit card charges, the cardholder should keep purchase copies of all credit card transactions in one convenient location. These receipts can then be compared to the itemized account on the monthly statement to see if they were correctly billed. For additional protection, it is wise to attach the appropriate receipts to the customer's portion of the monthly statement and save these records for at least one year. They can help to provide proof that a charge was already paid in case of double billing. This could facilitate processing a correction.

The cardholder should also keep a carbon copy of all billing error inquiries to verify the date the notice was sent, etc. This is important since the credit card issuer must correct your bill within thirty days or acknowledge receipt of the complaint within that time and respond to its validity in ninety days after receipt.

Recordkeeping accuracy and proof of proper notification become essential to verify your adherence to these provisions of the FCB law. Otherwise, it becomes difficult if not impossible to enforce this important consumer protection legislation.

SECURITY AGREEMENTS

Creditors offering a secured loan must generally file a document for public record to make their interest in this security legally binding. While this can be done for any secured loan, the filing is only required by the Uniform Commercial Code on consumer goods with a purchase price of $2,500 or more in most states. In addition, this holds true only when the purpose of the loan is to purchase the product used as security. For example, it is quite common for a UCC financing statement to be filed by a lender for the borrower who purchases a car (except in states requiring a title to show proof of ownership for vehicle registration). It is less likely to be filed for the purchase of a color TV because of the price difference.

In addition, notification that this financing statement has been terminated by payment in full of the loan is also required. This must be done by the secured lender within ten days after the loan is repaid or that creditor can be fined $100 to be paid to the borrower. That means ten days after a secured loan is repaid you should check the public records at your municipal clerk's office to determine if you have received clear title to your security. If not, take the appropriate actions to rectify this situation and collect your $100.

A multitude of credit laws have been presented in this chapter. Each is enforced by its supervising federal agency. State counterparts of these laws are similarly enforced by a variety of state agencies. All carry penalties for noncompliance. Selecting the appropriate agency for help when a problem arises can, therefore, be a time-consuming process.

VIOLATIONS OF
THE LAW

The simplest thing to do when government action is necessary is to contact your local information and referral center of the state government for assistance. If the problem is a federal matter, the state counterpart will refer you accordingly. Talking with a person about where to go for help will often be faster than writing a letter which must be forwarded through several agencies for action. Therefore, it will probably be easier to locate the correct agency and their address before your complaint is written and mailed. However, if this tactic becomes costly or impossible to deal with, the logical place to write is to your Congressional representative or:

Director, Office of Consumer Affairs
Department of Health, Education, and Welfare
Washington, D.C.

Both of these agencies make referrals regularly on matters of this nature. They will generally be able to offer the help you need, although a reply may take several weeks because of their regular backlog of correspondence.

PROFESSIONAL GUIDELINES

It is no secret that complexity and some confusion are inherent in many credit transactions for consumers. While recent legislation has attempted to reduce these problems, the success of this project remains questionable. Yet all indicators point to an ever-expanding rate of consumer credit usage in our nation.

That places a heavy burden on helping agency professionals and creditors alike to assist consumer borrowers to understand their rights and responsibilities in credit usage. Plain language credit contracts are a big step in the right direction. More importantly, consumers must learn to read and question contract terms before they sign these contracts. And lenders should be capable of clearly explaining these provisions without consulting the corporate attorneys.

Stronger channels of communication between creditors and their borrowers must be built either directly or through a liaison with helping agency representatives. For this to be accomplished, more attention must be given to helping all clients to accept credit as a privilege to be earned, with equal access by all parties. Creditworthiness and the enforcement of credit legislation are valid educational concepts. They are two sides of the same coin to be treated with equal respect by ethical professionals.

Credit education is a prerequisite for consumers and their professional representatives in the field of personal money management. It takes time and effort to do so, but consumer borrowers will only give greater attention to their own credit education if this is perceived to be important in obtaining and using credit. For this perception to become reality, lenders and helping agency staff must make this task perfectly clear through their own handling of credit and its related problems.

ENDNOTE

1. Caroline Donnelly, "New Long Term Car Loans at Short Term Prices," *Money* (September 1976): 44.

SEVEN

A New Definition of Debt and Its Implications

Jessica breathed a heavy sigh as she left the interview at 49 Congress Street. The residents there certainly had their hands full of problems. Joe Carter, the family head and sole breadwinner, was a construction worker who earned $20,000 a year or more. The work was seasonal but he and his wife, Donna, had been able to manage. They tried to keep their fixed costs to a modest level in order to manage through the leaner winter months. They even made double installment payments on all of their credit contracts to be sure they stayed current all year. Then Joe got injured on the job! The doctor feels it will result in a permanent disability.

While the medical bills are all being taken care of by insurance, they are about the only thing being paid regularly right now. Worker's Compensation hasn't yet settled Joe's claim. Social Security hasn't decided if he is eligible for disability benefits. Joe's not eligible for unemployment benefits because he's not able to work. With two new cars, a house, and a recreational vehicle, the Carters own too much to qualify for welfare. Their modest savings account is almost depleted, and the bill collectors call weekly. Neither Joe nor Donna know what to tell them. They really want to pay their bills, but they don't know how—or when they'll have the money.

Right now they're living on credit cards to buy gas for one car and using their savings to buy food. They're trying to sell the recreational vehicle, but they've been unable to find a buyer. No one's going hungry yet, but there is no immediate resolution to their plight either. Even if one of the government aid programs accepts their application, the benefits make no provision toward debt repayment other than the mortgage. Their only hope is that the Worker's Compensation settlement will be generous and soon.

The Carter family has really tried to live within their means, and they ran into problems. What would happen to people like Bob Walters, Jr., if he ran into the same type of emergency? He used credit to try to beat the inflationary spiral so he gambled heavily on his freedom from disaster to pull him through. "But disasters can't always be prevented," Jessica reminded herself. Yet living on a cash only basis, or close to it, like Bob's parents had done can sure restrict your enjoyment of the world. There must be a logical compromise . . .

EXPLORING ATTITUDES TOWARD DEBT

There is ample evidence that American attitudes and practices in relation to consumer debt has grown considerably more accepting since World War II. The percentage of disposable personal income used for debt repayment has grown from 6 2/3 percent in 1950[1] to 23 percent in 1978.[2] That certainly makes it sound like credit usage and its resultant levels of indebtedness are now facts of life.

In a recent study of this topic, the conclusions generally supported this assumption. Two-thirds of the families surveyed used credit for everyday expenses, from the purchase of gasoline to toiletries and even food.[3] They also use credit, along with insurance and savings, as a way to cope with financial emergencies.[4] The whole behavioral change is rationalized by a new definition of debt. For the families interviewed in the pilot project for this study, debt was said to mean "falling behind in payments,"[5] not just owing money.

Therefore, while Americans are readily using more credit than ever before, they are not fully in command of this lifestyle adaptation. As discussed in Chapter 1, they perceive that anyone who develops the necessary skills to earn money will automatically also acquire the skills to spend it wisely, without any specific preparatory training at home or school. Yet the records show that as personal income and credit usage rise, more and more Americans are floundering with this management task. Late payments and the failure to pay bills altogether rise with each recessionary trend as more and more borrowers choose not to accept responsibility for their contractual obligations. According to one analyst, Americans who don't pay their bills are increasing at a rate of about thirty-two times faster than those that do.[6]

Even so, the problems of personal debt management are far from insurmountable. Oftentimes they need only to be dealt with honestly and openly to be resolved. Money management education and counseling can and do help resolve these dilemmas. This is especially true when debtors and their creditors accept joint responsibility for these problems and work together to eliminate them.[7] Therefore, the remainder of this chapter will be devoted to fostering a clearer understanding of creditor and debtor rights and responsibilities in relation to these management tasks. This will be in addition to a discussion of realistic coping skills for prevention of and rehabilitation from a financial crisis.

EXAMINING DANGER SIGNALS

Between the flood of persuasive advertising encouraging credit usage and the insatiable nature of most human wants, it is sometimes difficult to know when you've taken on more debt than you can realistically handle. While the level of affordable indebtedness will vary with other lifestyle choices, the following guidelines are a composite of expert opinions on the subject of possible debt overload:

1. Spending more than 20 percent of your after-tax income on debt repayment (not including the home mortgage).
2. Charging day-to-day expenses like gasoline or personal grooming needs because you can't afford to buy them otherwise.
3. Borrowing money to pay fixed annual expenses like insurance premiums and taxes.
4. Making only the minimum payment on revolving charge accounts each month.
5. Borrowing money to pay existing credit obligations.
6. Skipping payments to one or more creditors each month in order to make ends meet.
7. Making some or all installment payments late despite the additional cost.
8. Receiving regular letters from your creditors reminding you to pay your bills.
9. Maintaining liquid assets in a savings account or other emergency fund of less than $400.

Living with two or more of these danger signals could spell trouble, especially if disaster strikes your already strained finances. To handle the situation wisely, the debtor who senses pending difficulties should act immediately to try to reduce or eliminate the problem. Contingency plans can be very helpful. It is especially important to know where to go for help and when, as well as the type of assistance you can expect from each resource. It is equally important to realistically appraise your own management abilities as well as those with whom you share a household in order to determine the usefulness of a self-help program versus third-party intervention between you and your creditors.

ASSESSING THE SITUATION

When the warning signals first begin to appear, it is time to take a comprehensive and careful look at your spending and saving patterns. The primary goal here is to see if you are living within your income. The most objective way to do this is to follow the guidelines in Chapter 2—collect receipts for all of your expenditures in one month and compare this total to your monthly take-home pay. Be sure to include a monthly amount set aside for all annual expenses.

If the total of basic monthly living costs, plus installment obligations, and the amount set aside toward annual expenses exceeds your income, it is time to make some changes *now*. You must either reduce spending or increase income to avoid pending financial problems.

SURVIVAL NEEDS

Begin by determining your basic survival needs budget that is adequate for good health and human safety. This will include both fixed and flexible expenses. For most people it will focus on food, shelter, medical care, transportation, and utilities. Various lifestyle needs may add to that list. However, it should be a "no frills" package that tells you what your *minimum* needs are if you are ever faced with a crisis like Joe Carter's. The basic budget can easily be expanded when more money is available.

To determine if your pending financial problems will allow for additional living costs, subtract the survival needs budget from your net monthly income. Then subtract the total of your monthly installment obligations from the remainder. If any money is left, you can use it to modify your monthly expense plan or increase debt repayment schedules, depending on your values and goals.

COMMUNITY RESOURCES

Many Americans growing up in our more affluent times may have difficulty finding and using money substitutes to reduce their spending and still meet household needs. These people can begin at the local library by reading about how others cope with hard times. Knowing you are not alone in this struggle can build confidence in your ability to overcome the problem. In addition it can provide numerous suggestions for implementing the required behavioral changes.

In many cases, the answer to some of these cost reduction needs can be found around the community. Resources here offer a wide variety of goods and services just waiting to be used—most of which you have already paid for through tax dollars or charitable contributions. Some of these many resources include recreational facilities, well-baby clinics, free lunches (and/or breakfasts) for school children, free clothing stores, fuel banks, emergency food shelves, tax relief programs, garden plots, etc. These are all in addition to the basic government programs of Medicare, Medicaid, food stamps, Social Security, and welfare, all of which were developed to help people meet minimal needs for living.

To find out more about the existence of these services locally, contact the information and referral agency serving your community. Their primary task is to put people in touch with the services they need. If no such agency exists in your area, contact the municipal clerk's office, county extension agent, or other helping organizations to get this information.

Earning more money can also offset some problems of overspending, provided the benefits outweigh the costs of doing so. When overtime work at the same job site is available, your costs are often minimal if you can: (1) maintain the same commuting arrangements (carpool, etc.), (2) wear the same uniforms, and/or (3) continue responsibility for the same at-home tasks despite the reduced time available for them.

INCREASED INCOME

When these conditions cannot be met, extra hours of work can mean extra costs as well. Moonlighting or sending additional household members to work can also have a limited positive effect on increasing your income when costs rise in conjunction with earnings. Taxes on your income rise with virtually any increase in earnings. In addition, child care, meals away from home, extra transportation, clothing, household help, etc., can make the extra earnings disappear very quickly.

Before choosing this alternative as the means by which you would resolve your financial problems, calculate the true net benefits of the job. Do they meet your income needs or add to your problems?

If increased earnings can really add to your net spendable income without jeopardizing the health and safety of individual household members or the group, this can be a wise choice. However, it cannot logically be the selected alternative unless the extra work is presently available to you. With today's tight job market, it is unrealistic to assume anyone can easily find a means by which to quickly increase earnings. On the other hand, long-range planning for financial security can include the development of hobbies and other skills to a level at which some earnings could be achieved if necessary.

ADJUSTED PAYMENTS

Once you begin to fall behind on installment obligations it is often difficult if not impossible to catch up, especially when there is no extra cash available for this purpose. If changes in spending and income cannot help you to reach this goal, it is appropriate to talk to your creditors about modifying your contractual agreements.

Creditor/debtor communication is essential for a positive working relationship. It is only logical that, during the many years a loan is outstanding, you may have occasion to miss a payment. Many creditors have come to accept this as reality. In fact, some creditors now advertise their loans with a built in "miss a payment" feature that allows one monthly payment each year to be skipped and paid at the end of the loan term.

However, when late or skipped payments become a common occurrence, then creditors begin to worry about your willingness and ability to repay the remainder of the loan. This is only natural since these lenders generally stand to lose substantial sums if you completely default on the loan. As explained in Chapter 6, missing just one payment can place you in default according to some contracts.

When you become aware that you will be unable to meet a regularly scheduled installment payment, contact your creditor to explain the reason. Then work together to determine a mutually agreeable method of compensating for this breach of contract. This is the only way your creditors will know that you still accept full responsibility for your obligations. It is important to maintain a mutually respectful relationship.

You usually have three choices when requesting an adjusted payment schedule. Depending on your needs, you can ask a creditor to let you:

1. Skip one or more payments now and have them added to the end of the loan term.
2. Make partial payments (often interest only) until you can see your way clear to reassume the original payment schedule and gradually make up the missing amounts.
3. Reduce the payment schedule permanently by stretching the length of the loan.

Any of these modifications can increase the total cost of finance charges on the loan because you will have use of the creditor's money for a longer period of time. In addition, any of these changes may require you to accept a new contract based on the adjusted terms, since no provision is generally made in the original contract for making these revisions legally binding.

DEEPENING INDEBTEDNESS

If your indebtedness continues to grow despite an honest attempt to assess this situation and modify your spending, your financial troubles may be deeper than first anticipated. This is especially true if continued mismanagement or lack of motivation to change are the reasons for the growing indebtedness. Accordingly, when multiple catastrophes strike, your coping skills may be diminished from excess stress or exhaustion.

Any of these circumstances can mean you need professional help in dealing with your debt management problems. This help is often available from clergy, lawyers, mental health counselors, a variety of financial advisors, as well as friends and relatives.

However, inappropriate assistance, no matter how well meaning, can often compound the problem. To choose wisely among these many advisors you must learn the background and abilities of each in relation to your needs. In addition to an awareness of the reasons behind your default, this requires a basic understanding of the collection process and creditors' rights against default debtors as well as your rights in this process. Only then can you make an informed decision.

COLLECTING PAST-DUE ACCOUNTS

The contract that you signed for credit buying will be your first reference in determining the consequences of default. As discussed in Chapter 6, the contract spells out what can happen if or when you fail to make a payment on time. While most creditors are not immediately required to implement these collection procedures, these are all terms you agreed to when signing the contract. Therefore, you should be aware of these actions before you contact the creditor to renegotiate your contract.

CREDITORS' RIGHTS UNDER THE CONTRACT

In the contracts presented to date, the following consequences of default were included: (1) late charges, (2) title retention (right of ownership under the security interest), (3) acceleration of payments (right to demand immediate payment of the balance due if one installment is skipped), and (4) repossession.

Other common contract terms affecting delinquent accounts include:

1. *Balloon payments*—a final payment under the contract that is more than twice as large as regular installment payments.
2. *Confession of judgment*—a clause in which the buyer agrees to let the creditor take legal action to collect this account without first notifying the buyer of this action.
3. *Cross collateral*—a clause allowing the seller to retain ownership (title) to all goods purchased under a single installment contract until the last item is paid for in full.
4. *Deficiency judgment*—a clause allowing the creditor to collect from the buyer the balance owed on the contract after sale of the repossessed goods.

5. *Wage assignment*—a contract condition which allows the creditor to collect payments on this delinquent account directly from the buyer's wages by demanding a payroll deduction by his or her employer—without first notifying the buyer.

When any or all of these terms are to be used, they are written into the terms and conditions of the credit contract, which in turn must be accepted by buyer and seller. If the contract is signed with these terms included, the agreement is considered to be legally binding and enforceable.

However, most consumers have little or no legal training. They may read the words of the contract but seldom understand the legal jargon, nor do they have many alternative sources of borrowing if the majority of local lenders use the same contract terms. Therefore, the judicial process in our country has sometimes banned enforcement of some of these clauses because they can be unfair. Few borrowers anticipate falling behind on their payments when they sign the loan contract. So they may willingly accept these legal terms without any realization of their ramifications.

In fact, the incidence of lawsuits on this issue has been so great that many states have passed laws limiting or prohibiting the use of some of these collection remedies in consumer loan contracts. The laws regulating this aspect of consumer credit transactions are the Retail Installment Sales Act and the Small Loan Act.

The most common prohibitions are against the confession of judgment and wage assignment clauses. Installment payments must also be substantially equal. Or balloon payment contracts, when preferred by the customer, must allow for refinancing of this large payment in order to avoid default. Cross collateral clauses are generally only allowed if the creditor's security interest on each item purchased under the installment contract is released as that item is paid for in full. Late charges and acceleration of payments can be regulated under these laws. In addition, creditors may have to choose between repossession and collection of a deficiency judgment.

The federal courts have also taken one very important step in helping default debtors nationwide. Since 1970, it has been mandatory that a court hearing be held to determine the legality of a creditor's claim to a debtor's property before any goods can be repossessed or otherwise taken away from the debtor in payment for the loan. At least in this manner, the debtor is well aware of the creditor's actions and can defend himself or herself accordingly.

NONCONTRACTUAL COLLECTION EFFORTS

Implementing most of the contractual terms just presented can be quite costly to creditors. This is especially true when legal fees are involved. Court actions impose a high degree of impersonality to this procedure, which can result in poor public relations between borrower and creditor. Since the default may be caused by a simple oversight, misunderstanding, or temporary financial setback, most creditors prefer to begin the collection process with a more friendly approach. In no way do they want to alienate the good customer who has fallen upon hard times. Creditors want to keep your business. Their profits depend on it. So their reputation in the initial stages of collection must be humane and client-centered—at least until they discover an unwillingness to pay, or turn the collections over to an independent agency that has no need to preserve goodwill.

The collection process generally begins with gentle persuasion and/or clever reminders of the status of your past-due account. It will be sent when the payment is about one month past due. If that yields no response from the debtor, an appeal letter will soon follow, asking if a problem exists with the merchandise purchased on credit or the terms of repayment. This contact may also take the form of a telephone call to see if there is a way to avoid further delinquency on the account. The dialogue will be polite but persuasive, encouraging the debtor to pay all or part of the past-due installment immediately, or come in to the creditor's office to discuss rewriting the loan.

If these actions do not generate a positive debtor response, subsequent collection efforts will be more direct and firm. This is especially true if the debtor has ignored all correspondence on this matter to date or has made promises to pay which have not been kept. Both actions indicate an unwillingness to pay which runs contrary to the original contract. Communication at this phase of the collection process informs the debtor of the legal consequences of his or her failure to pay as agreed, or more nebulous types of "drastic action" that can only be avoided by paying this bill now. The rationale behind this approach is that most debtors know little about their legal rights or the internal operations of the credit industry. So in an attempt to preserve their future borrowing ability, many debtors will find a way to pay this bill—even if it means going into default on another credit contract to do so.

When even this firm persuasion is not enough to collect on the account, creditors may begin legal action or turn the account over to an independent collection agency, whose sole purpose is to persuade people to pay their past-due accounts. Legal action may start in the form of polite collection letters sent directly by an attorney. Even the first few contacts by the collection agency will follow the same stages of collection just completed by the creditor.

However, both collection attorneys and independent collection agencies generally work on a commission basis. Their fees are based on a percentage of past-due accounts that they can collect. If they can't get any money from the delinquent debtors, their efforts are wasted for they receive no other form of compensation from the creditors that hire them. That provides a strong incentive to persuade the debtor to pay. Moreover, these collectors are not concerned with preserving customers since they have nothing to sell. This results in the use of a more forceful approach, tempered only by legal limits on debt collection practices.

For many years, debt collection practices were substantially unregulated by law at the state or federal level. When debtors tried to get a legal reprieve from harsh and abusive collection tactics, their recourse was limited. Collection efforts across state lines were regulated only by a Federal Communications Commission Act that made it a criminal offense to use the telephone to annoy or harass anyone for any reason. Civil remedies applied under state laws if the creditor could be proven to be at fault for: (1) intentional infliction of emotional stress, (2) defamation of character, (3) abuse of process, or (4) invasion of privacy.

Generally, the result of successful court cases in this area means it is, or can be proven to be, illegal for creditors to contact the debtor in any way that might harass or embarrass the debtor. For example, that means the creditor or collector *may not:* (1) telephone the debtor at unreasonable hours, (2) telephone the debtor frequently and repeatedly, (3) threaten to use violence if the debtor does not pay, (4) use offensive language in talking to the debtor, or (5) contact the debtor's employer or others to gain assistance in collecting the debt.

However, where there is an absence of laws dealing specifically with these and other aspects of debt collection, each court case must be decided on individual merit and proof of harassment in relation to one of the four violations listed above. To simplify this process, many states have passed debt collection laws that range from licensing debt collectors to regulating the manner in which they do business to assure no harassment of debtors will take place. Essentially, they prohibit any unfair and deceptive trade practices used to collect a debt. Of course, because these are state laws, they affect only debt collection practices within their boundaries—not across state lines.

The federal protection against collection abuses began in 1968 under the Federal Trade Commission's authority to prevent unfair and deceptive trade practices. Under this administration procedure, the FTC could ultimately take legal action against fraudulent debt collectors who:

1. Use any deceptive ways to collect or try to collect debts or to obtain information about debtors.
2. Attempt to hide the purpose of their business by using forms, letters, or questionnaires that conceal the real reason for the correspondence.

3. Attempt to be represented as a government agency when this is not true.
4. Try to represent themselves as a credit bureau or collection agency, etc., when this is not true.
5. Threaten to take any action (such as credit bureau notification, lawsuit, etc.) that can adversely affect the debtor unless that action is actually taken.

While these restrictions affect interstate debt collection practices, FTC enforcement powers are limited to cases that this government agency can or will pursue on their own behalf. The process is long and slow, beginning only with "cease and desist orders," which ask violators to stop using objectionable practices. Moreover, an individual debtor who claims harassment by a creditor has no protection under this regulation other than to report the violation to the FTC for investigation and possible government action.

To strengthen these consumer protection efforts, Congress passed the Federal Fair Debt Collection Practices Act which took effect on March 20, 1978. The new law makes it a federal offense for independent debt collection agencies to threaten consumers with violence, use obscene language, or contact consumers by telephone at inconvenient times or places. It further prohibits debt collectors from publishing the names of debtors in default, impersonating government officials or attorneys, obtaining information under false pretenses, and collecting more than is legally owed.

The new federal law takes priority over weaker state laws and provides civil penalties in both individual and class actions. A debt collector who violates this federal law is liable for the debtor's legal fees as well as any additional damages determined by the court up to $1,000. The debtor may also claim additional compensation for any losses suffered due to harassment (loss of job, etc.). In the case of a class action, total penalties can be as high as $500,000 or 1 percent of the collector's net worth.

The Fair Debt Collection Practices Act also sets guidelines for how a reputable debt collection agency should operate within the law. After an initial contact with the debtor, the collection agency has five days to send a written notice to the debtor indicating the amount owed and to whom. This letter must also indicate to the debtor that the collector will assume this debt is correct unless otherwise notified within thirty days of receipt of this letter. If the amount owed is in dispute, the collector must ask the creditor for written certification that it is, in fact, correct, and then mail this directly to the debtor.

In addition, if a debtor prefers not to discuss this debt with the collector, the debtor may write a letter asking for all contacts to stop. That forces the collector to go to court to pursue the matter further. When a suit is begun, it must be filed in the county where the debtor lives or where the original credit contract was signed.

While a debt collector may still contact the debtor's friends or employer to locate the debtor, no mention can be made that a debt is owed, nor can a collector call the debtor at work if such phone calls are prohibited by the employer. In fact, the collector can no longer ask a debtor's employer to help in collecting the debt without permission from either the debtor or the court.

The one caution to debtors seeking defenses under this law is that it does not apply to retail stores, hospitals, or other creditors that handle their own collections. It affects *only* the collection activities of independent collection agencies across the country. But some state laws do cover the activities of creditors seeking to collect their own debts, so protection may be available locally in this regard.

WAGE AND PROPERTY ATTACHMENTS

Since not all delinquent debts are the result of installment credit contracts, the law provides two additional legal means for collecting past-due accounts. Both require court action and notification to the debtor that these legal remedies are being implemented.

The more common of the two is *wage garnishment*. This involves a court order asking your employer to pay your past-due bill for you by deducting this sum owed directly from your wages before you receive them. The amount of your pay that can be garnished is limited under the federal Truth in Lending Law to 25 percent of your weekly take-home pay or that amount in excess of thirty times the minimum wage, whichever is less. Stronger state laws take priority over this federal law, so it is possible your creditor may be limited to attaching a smaller portion of your paycheck.

Stronger state laws also take priority if they allow more than one garnishment (the federal requirement) before an employee can be fired for excessive garnishments. In addition, state laws outline whether or not garnishment proceedings can be initiated prior to a court hearing on this matter.

Attending the hearing can be most beneficial to a delinquent debtor even though it is not required. The debtor can explain the reasons for the delinquency and attempt to negotiate a voluntary repayment schedule with the creditor and the court, thereby possibly avoiding the garnishment and related court costs that must be paid. This could save the debtor's job as well, if her or his employer resented the additional expense of processing numerous wage garnishments. Also, if the debtor's only source of income is public assistance or unemployment compensation, the debtor is considered "judgment proof" and no garnishment can be processed.

If you defaulted on an unsecured loan, the law allows your creditor to sell some of your property in payment for the debt. To do so, the creditor must sue in court for the amount owed, win the case, and hire a sheriff to process a *writ of attachment* against specific items of your personal property which will then be sold to pay off the debt. The property taken must be owned outright by the debtor and described to the sheriff before the writ can be processed. That means the creditor must locate your attachable property (exemptions vary by state law) before this legal remedy can be fully implemented. Obviously, the process is more costly to the creditor than wage garnishment, unless the property to be attached is a bank account with a sufficient balance to pay off the debt plus court costs. Then the creditor must locate the bank account prior to processing the writ of attachment.

Even though the default debtor violated a contractual agreement by failing to completely repay money owed, the law provides some protections for him or her as well. After all, this problem is not the fault of the debtor alone. In the late eighteenth century, historical records indicate that one in three household heads were taken to court as defaulting debtors.[8] Yet debtor's prison was legally abolished in 1838 and methods by which an impoverished debtor could find release from his or her debts were tried as far back as colonial days in the hope that debtors could be rehabilitated rather than a growing burden on society.[9]

DEBTORS' RIGHTS

As we have seen in reviewing the collection process, debtors are now protected against abuse and harassment from creditors. All collection activities initiated under the original contract or otherwise must be handled in a fair and reasonable manner. Even in regard to repossession, attachment, or garnishment, creditors must follow the rules of judicial due process. Any sale of property to discharge a debt must also be accomplished in a commercially reasonable manner whether public or private. Also, a debtor must be allowed to redeem repossessed property prior to its sale by paying the bill owed in full plus repossession and legal expenses incurred by the creditor.

In addition, the law provides debtor protection against inequities of the bargaining process when a contract is first made. It is *unconscionable* and thus illegal for a creditor to use fraudulent or unfair sales techniques, charge an excessive price, conceal important aspects of the product, or use misleading wording to encourage a consumer to sign an unfair contract. Therefore, if any of these actions can be proven to have taken place in negotiating the contract now in default, the consumer can take legal action to have the original contract cancelled or revised to eliminate the unconscionable provisions. Of course, legal action costs money and decisions on this matter vary with individual circumstances, so alleged unconscionability of a contract does not guarantee dissolution of that contract and the debtor's responsibility to pay.

This and other consumer protection measures should not be overlooked as potentially effective debtor remedies. In a study of 1,320 default debtors living in four major cities, 36 percent felt misinformed or deceived in the credit transaction,[10] thereby limiting their motivation to pay as agreed. The largest proportion of these problems dealt with defective merchandise, while other consumer problems included delivery of the wrong merchandise, price and insurance misrepresentations, or claims of persuasion to sign contracts under false pretenses.[11] Therefore, it is important for all borrowers to know and use their legal rights as consumers, irrespective of cash or credit payments for the goods and services in question. These same rights can sometimes save delinquent debtors from the consequences of default.

In all truthfulness, most default debtors are the primary cause of their own problems in this regard. Their own mishaps and shortcomings have led them into default, as Caplovitz confirms,[12] and the debtor remedies just described only serve to bring reason and order to the collection process. The real problem of finding ways to pay off this indebtedness remains.

Since debtor's prison and indentured servitude has long since proven ineffective in resolving this dilemma, other options had to be devised to reach this goal. *Bankruptcy,* the court-ordered sale of assets to discharge total liabilities, was introduced as one alternative back as far as colonial times. The idea was that if poverty prohibited a debtor from full bill repayment, his or her possessions (with certain exemptions) would be sold to provide some compensation equally to all creditors. Then the default debtor could make a fresh start, free of overburdening indebtedness, but once again able to meet the survival needs for herself or himself and dependents, thus relieving the community of this burden.

In effect, what has happened is that default debtors, unwilling or unable to pay their debts, may use the threat or promise of bankruptcy as an instrument of negotiation with their creditors. The result can be a compromise since few debtors today have unencumbered assets, the sale of which would be sufficient to pay off any substantial portion of their liabilities. Oftentimes the creditor is better off accepting partial payments after limited collection attempts rather than forcing costly judicial proceedings and/or bankruptcy. Many creditors and debtors are well aware of this cost consideration. They are equally cognizant of the growing acceptance of bankruptcy as a remedy for overburdening debt and its occasional planned use as a means by which the debtor can temporarily feel successful in counterbalancing the power of creditors in our money world.

For example, Joe Carter and his family could choose bankruptcy as a remedy for their indebtedness if creditors failed to help them seek realistic alternatives that would alter their existing credit contracts. In so doing, they would readily relinquish assets to cancel debts since little income is available for this purpose. Based on the family values presented, they would probably scale down their standard of living to avoid a repeat of this dilemma in the future.

Bob Walters, Jr., on the other hand, has probably always considered bankruptcy as an easy option if his debt load becomes overburdening. He realizes his right to bankruptcy and its lack of effect on his job or his income. Therefore, he figures it would probably always be relatively easy to make a fresh start, as long as he can find work. With his rate of pay and only himself to care for, even cash buying could provide many of the luxuries of life. Credit purchasing just presents the possibility of satisfying more wants sooner, and if he fails again to meet these obligations, he can always choose bankruptcy again . . . and again . . . if he times it properly.

CHOOSING AMONG DEBT MANAGEMENT ALTERNATIVES

When you are aware of creditor and debtor rights and responsibilities after default, you can make a more informed decision about the course of action to follow to resolve the problem and try to prevent its recurrence. The debtor has four basic alternatives in this regard:

1. Develop a self-help program to negotiate personally with all creditors to find an acceptable compromise.
2. Seek professional representation to intervene and negotiate creditor agreements for you.
3. Obtain legal relief from indebtedness under provisions of the Bankruptcy Act.
4. Avoid the creditor in the hope that he or she will ultimately write off the loans as a bad debt and stop trying to collect on them.

The first two alternatives require voluntary agreement between creditor and debtor. The third is court supervised and administered under the law. The fourth is illogical and often self-defeating because of the added stresses it can place on daily living until the goal is achieved. It is, unfortunately, also the first choice of many debtors who are unaware of the other alternatives or who are unskilled in implementing them. Let's analyze these options, then, to determine when and how to use each one advantageously.

If a debtor has been following recommendations presented earlier in this chapter, she or he would have already begun a realistic self-help program. The first step is to assess the depth of the problem. This is initiated by reviewing all spending in relation to income to determine the size of the gap between them and how it can be closed. Cutting basic living costs, increasing income, and renegotiating contractual obligations are the logical possibilities, generally in that order.

Few, if any, creditors will consider renegotiating a credit contract unless there is a valid reason. This request is a signal to them that you may

SELF-HELP PROGRAMS

have been unrealistic in assessing your ability to repay the loan. Because of that, it is important to prove that you now have a better understanding of your financial condition and can really meet the new arrangements under consideration. You should be prepared to explain your living costs and level of total indebtedness with the creditor who requests this information. In addition, this type of candid financial reassessment will help you, the debtor, to better understand the sacrifices required to meet your obligations. For these reasons, plus related cost factors, it is wise to use contract renegotiations as the third step in a self-help program.

When this step is needed, the negotiations can be done by mail, telephone, or in person with each creditor. A sample letter reviewing the suggested content of this negotiation is presented in Figure 7–1. As you will note, income and basic living costs are an integral part of this presentation to be sure the creditor has sufficient information on which to make an equitable decision about your request.

Naming your other creditors and the amount owed to each shows the creditor your honesty in dealing with this dilemma and your willingness to provide full information about the problem. It provides the creditor with an opportunity to verify your commitments with other creditors listed to be assured of fair treatment for all. In addition, much of this information was already provided to the creditor on the original loan application. So it is not new unless all of the other credit obligations are more recent.

However, if you are hesitant to provide creditor names, etc., that is your choice. It is only important to include a statement about: (1) the total number of creditors owed, (2) the total indebtedness to this group, and (3) the total monthly installment obligation you are now trying to reduce. These figures tell the creditor something about the depth of your indebtedness and the likelihood of meeting your goal with the proposed adjusted payment schedule.

Reducing monthly payments on a "pro rata" basis means lowering the payments to all creditors by the same proportion. For example, if you owed $100 per month in installment obligations and could only afford to pay $75, you would request a prorate at 75 percent of the regular payments, treating all creditors equally in this adjustment. While this request sounds reasonable, it is not always acceptable to all creditors. Secured creditors, in particular, often feel that they deserve priority in debt repayment because they have the option of implementing contract terms regarding repossession and sale of your collateral to clear the debt. Since few debtors are willing to forfeit these possessions, they are frequently persuaded to favor secured creditors and others who can convince the debtor to do so.

The debtor approached by one or more creditors with this request for priority repayment has a delicate compromise to negotiate. Without the cooperation of all creditors, this proposed debt adjustment program will

Figure 7–1
Sample Letter to
Creditors
Requesting
Reduced
Payments

Street address
City, State, Zip
Date

To: All of my creditors:

At this point in time, my financial circumstances are such that I simply cannot pay all of my bills. Therefore, I am writing to you to request your cooperation in accepting a proposed schedule of reduced payments until my debt is repaid or I can afford to increase the payments to the original figure once again.

I'm sure you realize the importance of your cooperation with this request, since this adjusted payment schedule is my only alternative to filing for bankruptcy. I accept the full responsibility for my debts and would sincerely like to repay them. I simply need more time to do so under my present circumstances.

My net income from all sources (including my spouse's income and/or the children's part-time jobs) is $_____ per month. My minimum monthly expenditures for necessities are as follows:

Housing (rent or mortgage plus taxes)	$_____
Utilities (fuel, telephone, water, garbage collection)	_____
Food and household supplies	_____
Replacement clothing	_____
Laundry and dry cleaning	_____
Medical	_____
Transportation	_____
Insurance	_____
Other	_____
Total	$_____

This leaves me approximately $_____ for debt repayment. My total of unpaid bills is as follows:

	Name of Creditor	Approximate Balance	Due Per Month
1.			
2.			
3.			
4.			
		Total: $_____	Total: $_____

**Figure 7-1
Continued**

Obviously, I cannot pay all of my bills on my present income. I have no savings. Therefore, my only alternative is to divide the $_____ I have available for debt repayment proportionately among all of my creditors. This would result in my paying each of you _____ % of your regular monthly payment, until the bills are paid off or I am able to increase the payments.

If all of my creditors will accept this plan, the proposed payment schedule will be:

Name of Creditor	*Amount Per Month*
1.	
2.	
3.	
4.	
	Total: $_____

If you will accept the proposed reduction in payments, please let me know immediately by signing the enclosed copy of this letter and returning it to me with an up-to-date statement of the balance I owe you. If you prefer, I will rewrite my contract according to the new terms.

I hope you will also freeze the interest as its present dollar level so that I can work toward reducing the principal amount that I owe. This would serve to reduce the interest I must pay monthly by extending the total interest owed over the new longer term of the note. In effect, this means I will pay the balance on my account in full; I just need more time than I expected when I signed the original contract.

Unless all of my creditors approve this plan, it cannot work and I will be compelled to file for bankruptcy. I hope you will help me avoid this court action by accepting the proposed plan.

Please reply to this request as soon as possible. I must have your answer no later than <u>(a date ten days away).</u>

Thank you in advance for your patience and understanding.

Sincerely yours,

We agree to the foregoing:

Name of creditor: _____

By: _____

Balance: _____

Interest will be
adjusted as
follows: _____

not work since it is based on voluntary compliance. The program can there-fore be renegotiated irrespective of the prorate formula until it is ultimately acceptable to all concerned. The debtor *can* stand firm with her or his orig-inal proposal in the hope that the mention of bankruptcy will encourage creditor compliance. However, the success of either alternative varies with the persons involved in the negotiation and their individual communication skills as well as corporate policy among creditor firms.

The same dilemma can develop with the request for reduced or frozen interest charges. Again, this is the ideal method for expediently reducing total indebtedness. If interest continues to accrue at its original rate, even though payments are now reduced, total indebtedness will decline slowly, if at all, despite the resumption of regular monthly payments toward this goal.

Many creditors, however, will only accept a reduced payment schedule if the debtor agrees to sign a revised credit contract for the new terms. While this can mean a higher total finance charge because of the longer repayment period, it is a compromise worth considering. In so doing, the debtor is no longer in default, so his or her reputation with the lender is improved by this renewed display of an ability and willingness to repay the loan. The credi-tor, in turn, feels more secure about recourse if payments once again cease, because the terms and conditions of the adjusted payment schedule are made legally binding through the new contract. In addition, total finance charges may ultimately be less than anticipated if the reduced payment schedule works as planned. As small loans are repaid in full on this sched-ule, payments can be increased on the larger installment obligations to re-pay these loans ahead of time and thereby receive some rebate on the fi-nance charges.

While the adjusted payment schedule is the most popular self-help pro-gram requested, it is only useful to debtors who have sufficient income to repay at least a portion of their indebtedness regularly. Families like the Carters could not even consider this program until their income is somehow reestablished. The same would hold true for other households suffering from illness, unemployment, etc., and therefore temporarily unable to pay their bills on time.

These people would be better advised to request a *moratorium* or tem-porary suspension of debt repayment until their financial circumstances stabilize. To be effective, the moratorium should be requested as soon as possible after it becomes necessary so creditors are always up to date on negative changes in a debtor's financial condition that affect his or her ability to repay obligations as originally contracted.

Obviously, development and implementation of a self-help plan takes time, patience, communication skills, and perseverance. Debtors attempt-ing to try this alternative must have a good working knowledge of their rights and responsibilities, confidence in their abilities to negotiate, and a firm commitment to follow through on their promises. This will be easier to accomplish for well organized people who can be objective in their financial decision making and who are self-disciplined enough to handle this whole process independently.

The benefits of accomplishing this task center around economy and confidentiality. While both are qualified benefits, the dollar costs of a self-help program are limited to postage for correspondence and/or phone calls or visits to creditors plus the possible addition of extended finance charges if those cases where interest is not frozen as requested. Only the debtor and her or his creditors are involved in this self-help process. Except where the debtor voluntarily offers a list of all creditors as part of the negotiation, this self-help approach assures the greatest privacy of information since it involves no outsiders in the process.

Of course, these benefits can also negate themselves if the debtor succumbs to creditor persuasion and agrees to unfavorable terms and conditions. One sure possibility is a creditor's offer of a *consolidation loan*—or one new loan large enough to provide for repayment of all or most existing bills. Then all past-due payments, defaults, etc., can be paid off in full with only one new bill to be met each month, probably at a payment level well within your income limitations.

While the idea has some merit, it has two major drawbacks. First, the debtor may wind up paying more total finance charges by following this procedure. Interest is first paid to the original creditors, then to the consolidator for use of the same money. Unless the consolidation loan is obtained at a rate of interest lower than the original loans, the debtor's total costs can skyrocket. As you will recall from Chapter 6, prepayment of a loan refunds interest charges by the Rule of 78, a formula favoring creditors and only adding to debtor costs when the loan is being refinanced through consolidation or otherwise. Second, consolidation can deceive some debtors into believing they can afford more credit since all the small bills are now repaid. If a credit grantor agrees, their total indebtedness can quickly return to an unmanageable level.

Accordingly, it should be clarified now that self-help programs in personal debt management should not include playing tricks on your creditors to pretend you are paying your bills as agreed. Also, they should not center on avoiding creditor contact in an attempt to deny the existence of a problem and the need for resolving it. While numerous books have been written on various strategies to avoid bill repayment, they have limited, if any, usefulness. Ultimately, they suggest utilizing one of the four options under discussion, with a special emphasis on bankruptcy as the preferred alternative since it hurts the creditors the most.

It is far wiser to seek professional help to rationally resolve the dilemma of your indebtedness and its underlying causes. Running from your creditors only hampers your future ability to borrow and that of others who are innocently forced to follow more stringent creditor regulations developed to limit the probability of "deadbeats" and "skips" who run away from their financial obligations.

Sometimes the maze of collection efforts and household problems, etc., surrounding indebtedness reduces coping skills to the point that it is unrealistic to attempt a self-help debt management program. In other cases, third party intervention between creditor and debtor is essential to convince both parties a proposed plan is workable and will be followed. For whatever the reason, professional help in debt management should be sought out as needed—before the problems seem insurmountable and emotions begin to overrule logic.

PROFESSIONAL GUIDANCE FROM TRADITIONAL AGENCIES

The type of professional help available is extremely diverse, varying from one community to the next and one agency to the next. Few formal training programs exist to produce competent professionals in this field with the necessary background to cope effectively with all money problems and their causes as well as their resolutions. Therefore, it takes time to find just the right help for a particular debtor's problems. If that appropriate help is not located, use of an alternate but inappropriate source can compound the problem and hinder its resolution. Therefore, it is important to learn the various types of help available and how to evaluate them in relation to your needs.

In some communities, familiar helping agency personnel, from clergy to social workers, marriage counselors, and/or Extension Home Economists can provide needed assistance in coping with debt problems. Yet their counterparts in another town may have little or no expertise in this area. To find out if debt counseling is available from these professionals, contact their offices directly, or use the services of the local information and referral clearinghouse.

The nature of debt counseling services will also vary among these agencies. The chart in Figure 7–2 will help you compare agency services and choose among them. If this decision making is difficult, sometimes explaining your specific problems to the information and referral service will result in suggestions for appropriate help. In reality, the answer may lie in a team approach with assistance needed from two or more of these sources to piece together a comprehensive helping program for the troubled debtor. Often this is done through referrals from one agency to another, with joint follow-up from both to assure consistency and coordination of helping efforts.

Figure 7–2
Comparing Local
Debt Management
and Counseling
Services

Agency Name			
Address			
Phone			
Hours			

Services available:
Budget planning
Psychological
   counseling on
   money in
   relation to
   emotional
   problems
Debt adjustment
   programs
   suggestions only or
   administration on
   your behalf
Legal assistance
Consumer protection			

Cost			
Eligibility: Income level Geographic area Membership			
Regular follow-up			
Teamwork with related agencies			
Credentials and/or licensing/certification			

Comments:

One often vital member of this helping team that has not yet been mentioned is the lawyer. Sometimes debt adjustment negotiations conducted via an attorney are more readily accepted by creditors than the same negotiations presented by a layperson. The use of legal stationery is often interpreted as a more serious commitment to the proposed plan. It is also recognized that an attorney is knowledgeable about the debtor/client's rights under the law in terms of collection practices and relief through bankruptcy. That generally implies that if creditors fail to agree to the proposed debt adjustment plan, the debtor's next alternative will be court action.

However, few lawyers are equally well trained in budget planning since this is not their business. Yet for a debt adjustment plan to be followed by the debtor, it must be realistically established. That may require the assistance of an agency professional (like a home economist) who is knowledgeable in household budgeting. A home economist may need to help the debtor draft a realistic budget and recordkeeping system for basic living expenses including a sum set aside for debt repayment. This "formula" must then be presented to the attorney for proration of debt payments and creditor negotiations. Once the plan is accepted by the creditors, subsequent follow-up with the debtor could be maintained by the home economist unless a problem arose in relation to debt repayment when the lawyer may again be called upon for assistance.

Either half of this team might willingly attempt to do the whole job and succeed, especially after considerable experience in the field. But professionals with such diverse skills are few and far between. Therefore, it is wise to be aware of ways to piece together required expertise in problem solving when no one individual or agency can provide the full scope of services needed.

Of course, when various community services appear to be in demand, but limited in availability, someone often decides to enter this field for a profit. That was the rationale behind the development of "debt poolers" or commercial prorate firms who made a business of establishing and administering debt adjustment programs for financially distressed clients.

SPECIALISTS IN DEBT MANAGEMENT AND COUNSELING

While the basic idea was sound, the implementation was expensive and sometimes fraudulent. Profits were made on this business by charging debtors a service fee based on a percentage of funds disbursed to creditors. But even that was not the worst problem. Many debtors were so relieved to have someone else take charge of their bill repayment, it was worth the price. However, some greedy debt poolers weren't satisfied with this level of profit, so they expanded their earnings by failing to make the agreed disbursements to creditors. Of course that resulted in renewed collection efforts by the original creditors and court action against the debtors who really believed they were meeting their payments!

Legislative action was then initiated and passed in more than half of the United States to prohibit or regulate the proration of debts for a fee by individuals or firms other than attorneys. However, because comparable nonprofit agencies had begun to emerge to offer legitimate help to troubled debtors, many states provided an exemption for nonprofit debt management and counseling programs.

First publicized in 1957, these nonprofit "Consumer Credit Counseling Services," as they were called, grew rapidly across this country and parts of Canada to meet a growing demand for their services. (A list of all CCCSs across the United States and Canada is available from the National Foundation for Consumer Credit, 1819 H. Street, Washington, D.C. 20006.) Comprehensive in nature, the services provided include budget planning, establishment and administration of a debt adjustment program, and counseling to find the underlying cause of the money problems and realistic means of preventing their continuation or recurrence. Team efforts may be initiated when referrals are needed to work with related personal, family, or legal problems. In fact, in some communities, sufficient rapport has been established for CCCS counselors to have garnishments suspended, mortgage foreclosures stopped, and divorces reconsidered.

Fees charged by the CCCS are generally modest. To share the burden, many of these agencies charge a token client fee up to about $10 per month for administration of a debt adjustment program, with the bulk of the cost charged to creditors at a rate up to 15 percent of disbursements. Budget planning and counseling are often free. Supplemental funds are, however, solicited from the business and professional community to help make these services available to everyone interested and to support the educational efforts of these agencies to prevent future debt management problems.

Unfortunately, though, the services provided by the CCCSs vary locally. Some are far more helpful than others in meeting client needs, particularly in regard to counseling, realistic budget planning, and coordination with other helping agencies. While the CCCS could be the perfect alternative for many debtor households, reality does not always meet this ideal. Hence, cautions must also be observed in evaluating this debtor help agency. Remember, commercial and nonprofit debt adjustment agencies are often registered or licensed with the State Department of Banking where their reputations can be checked by potential clients.

LEGAL REMEDIES   **Chapter 13.**   Sometimes any of the previously discussed plans for voluntary compliance with a debt adjustment program will fail because one or more creditors refuse to cooperate. When that happens, the debtor can seek legal help to resolve the dilemma.

When a debtor sincerely wants to pay off his or her indebtedness and has some income with which to do so, creditor compliance with the debt adjustment program can often be obtained via a "Chapter 13" or "Plan for Adjustment of Debts of An Individual With Regular Income" (formerly the "Wage Earner Plan"). All creditors can be required to accept the proposed court approved debt adjustment schedule, provided the benefits paid are at least equal to what they would receive in straight bankruptcy.

To qualify for the program, a debtor must have regular income from virtually any source with which to repay bills as ordered by the court. Maximum allowable indebtedness is $100,000 in unsecured debts and $350,000 in secured debts. The length of the program is about three years, although special cases may receive court approved extensions to five years.

All interest and late charges are frozen upon inception of the plan for the duration of it. All creditor attempts at collection must cease at this time as well. In addition, collection actions against co-makers are prohibited as long as the Chapter 13 Plan is in effect.

Chapter 13 plans offer some flexibility to the debtor in making needed adjustments to reflect changing circumstances in emergencies or fluctuations of income. The court may even temporarily suspend a Chapter 13 plan if illness, unemployment, etc., reduces the debtor's ability to pay as agreed. However, it is also expected that a Chapter 13 debtor will refrain from any new borrowing without first obtaining the court's permission.

In addition, a court appointed Chapter 13 Trustee will work with the debtor to determine if an *extension* or *composition* plan should be selected. When sufficient funds are available to fully repay the indebtedness and court costs in about three years, the plan used is an extension of debts or lengthened period of repayment under court supervision. If available funds over the same time period would allow only a partial repayment of the total indebtedness, the plan is called a composition of debts. If a composition plan is used, it is implemented on a pro rata basis for both secured and unsecured creditors, although there are sometimes exceptions made at the discretion of the Chapter 13 Trustee. Plans for Chapter 13 can be implemented as often as necessary to help a debtor meet her or his obligations as long as at least 70 percent of the indebtedness is repaid each time. Otherwise, there is a six-year waiting period between filings. Administrative fees paid to the court or trustee are about 10 percent of the funds disbursed. There is also a filing fee of $60 per person or married couple.

Like the other debtor alternatives presented so far, Chapter 13 projects debt repayment out of future earnings. It does not require the sale of any assets to reduce total indebtedness. However, the sale of assets for this reason or a release for voluntary repossession may be part of the negotiation with creditors to help gain acceptance of the proposed debt adjustment program.

Another feature used to promote the Chapter 13 program and some CCCS programs (when allowed by state law) is a voluntary wage assignment. This involves the signing of a written statement by the debtor that his or her employer may deduct a sum of money each month for direct deposit with the court, etc., for disbursement to creditors. Of course, this usually assures a greater likelihood of compliance with the program. Since the debtor never handles the money taken from her or his paycheck via the wage assignment, there is less temptation to spend it for other things. Hence, the creditors are more likely to be paid as agreed. The only drawback with this is freeing the debtor of the self-discipline required to prioritize spending. After the Chapter 13 program is complete, the debtor generally no longer has the crutch of payroll deduction to prompt bill repayment.

The common drawback to Chapter 13 is its focus on debt adjustment with limited efforts toward budget planning and debtor rehabilitation in particular, although some states have begun to focus greater attention on these behavior modification needs of the Chapter 13 debtors. Ironically, even ordinary Chapter 13 services are only made available to debtors at the discretion of the U.S. District Court bankruptcy judge or referee in that state. That sometimes means the Chapter 13 program is essentially unavailable in that jurisdiction.

Straight Bankruptcy.   When Chapter 13 programs are not available, there is little or no income to be used for debt repayment, or the debtor is unwilling to pay existing bills, the logical alternative is straight bankruptcy. In this older and more traditional form of bankruptcy amended in 1979 along with Chapter 13, the debtor agrees to turn over all nonexempt assets to the court for sale in exchange for a discharge from all allowable debts. The proceeds of the sale of assets are divided among all creditors in proportion to the debts held, although some priority claims take precedence. A debtor's future income or lack thereof has no bearing on these proceedings, although the debtor must pay a $60 filing fee for the bankruptcy. This fee can be paid in installments or waived in hardship cases, at the discretion of the bankruptcy court referee.

Federal law now allows the following list of exempt property to be claimed by each bankruptcy unless otherwise limited or liberalized by state law:

1. Your interest up to:
   a. $7500 of equity in a home or burial plot
   b. $1200 in value of one motor vehicle
   c. $200 for any single item of household goods and personal effects
   d. $500 in jewelry
   e. $750 in professional tools and/or books
   f. $4000 in cash surrender value of any unmatured life insurance contract.

2. Any professionally prescribed health aids.
3. Any other property worth $400 plus any unused portion of the $7500 homestead exemption (to avoid discrimination against renters).
4. Social Security, veteran's or disability benefits, alimony, child support, pension, or stock or profit sharing plans necessary to support the debtor and dependents.

In addition, the law allows the debtor the opportunity to reject certain secured debts and provide for the return of the merchandise in full satisfaction of the indebtedness—as though it had been repossesed, but at the debtor's option. Repossession initiated by the creditor can actually be invalidated for certain kinds of exempt property, especially when that property has been used as security for a personal loan. Perhaps most importantly, it is now almost impossible to revive (or reaffirm) an old debt after bankruptcy discharge unless the court rules that reaffirmation is in the debtor's best interest.

On the other side of the coin, not all debts are dischargeable in bankruptcy. Debts *owed* for taxes of any kind, alimony and child support, fines, fraudulent debts, and debts owed because of intentional injury to persons or property must be paid despite the bankruptcy. Of these, fraudulent debts provide the most confusion since they are often unintentional. For example, if a borrower listed only four outstanding debts on the loan application because there were only four spaces provided for this information, he or she could be accused of giving a false financial statement if it was later proven that the borrower had six outstanding debts at the time of the application. This loan could then be considered a fraudulent debt and denied discharge in the bankruptcy since most loan lenders would claim that the missing information could have caused them to deny the loan.

Personal debts can only be discharged in bankruptcy once every six years. If an overburden of debts develops in less than six years after the discharge, the debtor must seek help from another alternative because straight bankruptcy is not an available option under these circumstances. The debtor can, however, seek help from the bankruptcy court via an extension plan under Chapter 13 if desired.

A lawyer can be most helpful in evaluating the pros and cons of bankruptcy and in handling the necessary paperwork and creditor meetings required in straight bankruptcy and Chapter 13. Costs for these services range from many hundreds of dollars to no charge when the debtor is eligible for legal aid (where bankruptcy help by this program is offered). Often, all or part of these legal fees must be paid in advance of the filing. The remainder, if any, are due after bankruptcy and cannot be discharged in the proceedings. However, a lawyer is not necessary to handle a bankruptcy. The debtor/applicant may handle all required transactions personally with assistance from the clerk of the bankruptcy court.

While bankruptcy is the only alternative listed that offers direct relief from indebtedness, it also has the most long-term ramifications. Bankruptcy is even the only entry that can remain on your credit record for ten years.

AVOIDANCE
MECHANISMS

The added stress of overindebtedness on the demands of daily living sometimes prompts irrational behavior, especially when the awareness of debt management alternatives is limited. Unfortunately, the results often compound the stress and do nothing to resolve the debt burden.

Perhaps the most common example of this behavior is total creditor avoidance when delinquencies occur. The troubled debtor refuses to speak with creditors by phone, answer letters, or meet in person. He or she is embarrassed to admit an inability to pay now or in the foreseeable future, so the debtor avoids confrontation on the matter. Sometimes he or she rationalizes the situation to the point that monthly bills and collection letters are destroyed when they arrive in the hope that the problem will disappear, at least for a while.

Some debtors will carry this to an extreme by disconnecting their telephone (or obtaining an unlisted number), changing place of residence, leaving town altogether, or changing their name and identity. But creditors are wise to these and other tricks used to avoid bill repayment. Well trained collectors quickly learn the necessary detective work of "skip-tracing" to find runaway debtors and apply due process of law to have the past-due bills paid.

What many debtors fail to realize is that most creditors can be flexible when an emergency arises that reduces a debtor's ability to pay. They are not likely to immediately invoke contractual provisions for default because they want to preserve goodwill and keep collection costs down. Therefore, when a delinquency occurs, the creditor's primary concern is to determine if the cause is due to a change in the debtor's willingness or ability to repay. If ability to repay is the only reason, the creditor will generally help the debtor work out a more viable repayment schedule. But if there is evidence of unwillingness to pay through the implementation of avoidance mechanisms, the creditor will use the full power of her or his legal rights to aid in collection because of the fear of losing the money loaned.

The more logical approach, therefore, is to communicate with creditors immediately about repayment difficulties and work with them to select a mutually agreeable compromise. If defective merchandise or other consumer problems affect your willingness to repay, follow the Fair Credit Billing guidelines described in Chapter 6 and enlist the aid of appropriate consumer protection authorities.

However, it should be noted that some debtors may legally postpone or avoid paying bills. These include:

1. *Servicemen and women,* who under the Soldiers' and Sailors' Civil Relief Act, are protected against the repossession of property purchased under an installment contract signed and partially paid prior to entering the service as well as default judgments. Both may be postponed at the discretion of the court until he or she leaves the service.

2. *Minors* (under eighteen years old in most states) who may cancel contracts since they are not legally responsible for contracts signed except for the purchase of necessities not supplied by parent or guardian.

3. *Anyone holding an invalidated debt* whereby three to eight years (depending on state law) have elapsed without the debtor making any payments on the debt, promises to pay, or being sued to pay. Accordingly, state law also limits the time during which a judgment can remain effective under the statute of limitations.

PROFESSIONAL GUIDELINES

As this chapter has explored, there is a lot to learn about appropriate techniques for debt management. Existing choices have multiple intervening variables that can complicate decision making, especially since the availability and quality of community services in this area lacks national uniformity.

Therefore, professional responsibilities for persons working in money management are twofold. First, they must keep informed of existing debt management services, their strengths and weaknesses, plus relevant legislation on creditors' and debtors' rights and responsibilities. Second, they must be able to help debtor clients to assess existing alternatives and choose among them realistically.

Charts similar to that used in Figure 7–2 can help organize information about existing alternatives if they are updated regularly and based on personal contacts rather than hearsay. Client follow-up, including debtor perceptions of the quality of services rendered, can be most enlightening in this regard—so can conversations on the topic with other money management professionals. In addition, development of a cost-benefit chart based on local figures can prove invaluable in clarifying the differences among alternatives to your clients.

While it is often easier for you to make decisions for clients, this service can become a permanent crutch limiting the client's ability to function independently. Therefore, caution should be observed in how much you do for a client versus how much you guide the client to do. In addition, employer policies in regard to handling client funds, etc., may limit your personal assistance in this area. That should be clearly explained to all clients with appropriate referrals (and follow-up) to fill in the gaps.

With this type of comprehensive assistance, households like the Carters' can improve their coping skills to resolve financial crises and strive to prevent future ones because you have supplied the building blocks for informed decision making. Even well informed debtors like Bob Walters, Jr., may reconsider his perception of debtor rights and responsibilities if exposed to meaningful cost-benefit considerations.

ENDNOTES

1. U.S. Board of Governors' Federal Reserve System, *Federal Reserve Bulletin*, numbers 41–62 (Washington, D.C.: Federal Reserve System, Division of Administrative Services), 1955–1976.
2. "Are We Overloaded with Debt?" *Changing Times* (July 1979): 24.
3. Yankelovich, Skelley, and White, Inc., *The General Mills American Family Report, 1974–75* (Minneapolis: General Mills, Inc., 1975), p. 88.
4. Ibid., p. 91.
5. Ibid., p. 91.
6. Glen H. Mitchell and Martha G. Christie, *Summary: Consumer Education and Financial Management Conference January 13–14, 1977* (Blacksburg, Va.: Virginia Polytechnic Institute), p. 52.
7. Margery K. Schiller, *The Development of Selected Consumer Credit Counseling Services and Their Impact on Family Units from 1967 to the Present.* University of Connecticut, unpublished Master's thesis, 1974, p. 19.
8. Peter J. Coleman, *Debtors and Creditors in America: Insolvency, Imprisonment for Debt and Bankruptcy 1607–1900* (Madison: State Historical Society of Wisconsin, 1974), p. 187.
9. Ibid., p. 9.
10. David Caplovitz, *Consumers in Trouble: A Study of Debtors in Default* (New York: The Free Press, 1974), p. 37.
11. Ibid., p. 91.
12. Ibid., p. 55.

EIGHT

Options for Protection
Against Financial Disasters

Just three years ago today, Nancy Shroder, age thirty-three, died in a car crash leaving behind her husband, Donald, and two school-age children. Although the tragedy was awesome to these residents of 203 Congress Street, adjusting to a new lifestyle was easier because of the financial compensation provided from their insurance. The auto insurance company paid for the few medical bills incurred from the fatality as well as the cost of replacing the family car. Social Security helped out with a stipend toward funeral costs and a regular income for the children until they reach age eighteen. Nancy's employer-paid life insurance policy even provided $5000 to cover remaining costs related to burial and readjustment.

As he recovered from the shock of this tragedy, Donald began to realize many of these insurance benefits were reaped despite careful planning, not because of it. Therefore, he spent many long hours reviewing his present insurance protection and supplementing it in an attempt to cushion the blow of any possible future losses. Although that meant insurance costs now took a good sized bite out of every paycheck, the peace of mind was worthwhile. That feeling was further reinforced when he met and hired Minnie Simpson, a fifty-five-year-old housekeeper who came to care for the family after Nancy's death.

Minnie actually completed most of Jessica's survey before Donald Shroder came home. After three years with the family, she knew quite a bit about their purchases and style of decision making—and she openly envied their luck with insurance. The premiums were so costly, Minnie was pleased someone had reaped benefits. Her own circumstances were not very favorable.

Minnie was widowed seven years ago. Her husband, a self-employed carpenter, died of cancer after a lengthy battle against the disease. Their private medical insurance policy paid most of the hospital bills, but only part of the doctors' fees and none of those last few months in a nursing home. It took all of their savings, including the life insurance proceeds, just to break even. By selling their big house and moving to smaller quarters, Minnie was able to raise her teenage sons and even provide some help with college costs in addition to their Social Security benefits. But when her youngest son turned twenty-two and finished school, Minnie no longer had an income. Her Social Security checks stopped until she reached age sixty-two. Essentially untrained, she had no choice but to go to work in the only field she knew. After the thousands of dollars her family had spent on insurance and taxes, Minnie never expected to be in this position—but here she was.

Jessica was quite familiar with the inadequacies of many insurance programs through her career in social work. Her daily activities focused on helping those hardship cases resulting from catastrophe for which many individuals and families were unprepared to cope. These same experiences also made her painfully aware of the inadequacies of the social welfare system to fully help those in distress. Therefore, she has always felt that the only comprehensive protection against disaster was a combination of liquid assets, private insurance protection, and government benefits. Without careful planning, the Minnie Simpsons of the world would multiply and add to their struggle instead of relieving themselves from some of their financial distresses.

GENERAL PRINCIPLES

The primary purpose of insurance is protection against disaster—death of a family breadwinner, fire damage, theft, etc. The principle is simple. Many people contribute modest sums of money each year to a common fund used for the protection of those group members who suffer a disaster covered by the insurance they carry. The member stricken by disaster then claims a pre-arranged sum from the group's accumulated reserves. The rest of the money remains in the common fund until needed by other group members. Those contributors who escape disaster have paid for peace of mind. They generally receive no other return on their investment.

Therefore, the key to wise insurance purchasing is to protect yourself and your dependents from *major* financial losses resulting from the *unexpected,* including legal responsibility for someone else's disaster. This is the only way insurance costs can be minimized without shortcutting protection. However, the task is not always an easy one since insurance is often sold through persuasion and psychological appeals rather than purchased to meet basic needs.

Like Donald Schroder, many people pay little attention to their insurance needs because they refuse to believe they will ever be faced with a real catastrophe, or they feel cheated unless there is some predictable return of their investment. Then they choose policies that cover recurring small expenses better than infrequent big ones.

Small crises like scratching an auto fender or pulling wisdom teeth can and should be taken care of through routine financial planning for these foreseeable occurrences. Then insurance protection can focus on the really big losses that could use up all of your assets and more. Although this philosophy will mean less direct financial return on insurance dollars for those who escape disaster, it reduces the total cost of insurance. It also allows for a greater return on the investment when catastrophe does strike, as it also provides more comprehensive protection for the dollars spent.

REDUCING FINANCIAL LOSSES

When analyzing insurance needs, it is important to consider all of the possible ways in which an unexpected turn of events can cause a financial loss and the effects of that loss on caring for yourself and dependents. Obviously, if property that you own is stolen or destroyed, you will suffer a financial loss. The same holds true if accident or sickness prohibits you from temporarily or permanently working for a living. These are very obvious financial losses and relatively easy to calculate because you are dealing in known quantities.

Larger potential losses can be suffered from your liability or legal responsibility for property damage or injury to others. Legally, all adults are expected to act as reasonable and prudent people to protect the health and safety of others. Therefore, insurance can easily be the most important protection you have against potentially staggering financial losses. (Because liability insurance is commonly associated with auto and homeowner's insurance, it will be discussed in more detail with these package plans rather than as a separate form of protection.)

SELECTING TYPES OF INSURANCE

Almost anyone or anything can be protected with insurance—for a price. A large number of private, nonprofit, and government insurance programs exist to help qualified applicants to protect themselves against financial losses. There are limits on the type of coverage available from these various sources and the qualifications for obtaining coverage. In addition, the costs of the insurance will vary with the risk involved in providing the protection as well as the efficiency of administering the program and marketing it.

The most common types of insurance include: (1) property and casualty, (2) health and disability, and (3) life.

Almost everyone needs to carry some form of insurance protection. The types and amounts will vary with lifestyle choices and can change in each stage of the life cycle. Age, income, place of residence, community characteristics, condition of health, and occupational choices may affect the types and amounts of insurance available and the sources of it.

Insurance rates are determined by statistical analysis of the probability of certain catastrophes occurring to policyholders. As the frequency of catastrophe increases, so do insurance costs. In some cases, when the costs of providing certain types of insurance becomes prohibitive to private companies, the federal government intercedes to offer this protection at a more affordable rate to qualified citizens. Medicare, Medicaid, flood insurance, and property insurance in high crime areas are some examples of government sponsored insurance programs.

In addition, the government also provides a unique type of insurance protection in the form of unemployment compensation. Loss of wages, even for nonhealth-related reasons, can be catastrophic for the household that has only one breadwinner and little or no savings. Therefore, various levels of government have agreed to intervene on the part of qualified applicants to provide some source of income during the transition between jobs. Eligibility for the program is based on hours of work performed, salary earned in a given time period, and employer contribution to the system. Assets have no effect on eligibility nor does household income. However, qualifications to collect benefits vary by state law as do the amount of benefits paid.

Comparison shopping for this type of insurance is very limited. Only a change in the state of employment can effect benefit dollars received or eligibility. While some states allow unemployed persons to collect benefits despite the cause of job termination, others restrict benefits to people laid off due to lack of work.

CALCULATING BASIC NEEDS

To determine the kind and amount of insurance you need, begin by analyzing your lifestyle in relation to net worth (see Chapter 2). What amount of financial losses could you frequently absorb in the event of catastrophe? For example, if you broke your leg, could you support yourself and pay the related medical bills from present income and/or the sale of assets? Could you do so if an auto accident left you paralyzed from the waist down?

It is a very rare person who lives a full life without some cause for hospitalization or some form of comprehensive medical care. With good financial planning and a thorough program of health maintenance, insurance needs in this area can concentrate on catastrophic illnesses or accidents only. In other words, insurance protection can begin only after the insured is already paid a predetermined sum (deductible) in out-of-pocket medical expenses annually. This theory applies equally to disability needs.

Insurance on both home and auto can also be purchased with deductibles to reduce policy costs. The theory remains priority protection against disaster with self-insurance against predictable mishaps. However, in this circumstance, insurance must focus first on liability protection because of the potential losses inherent if you are at fault for someone's accident or injury.

Life insurance coverage is best calculated by determining the financial needs of your dependents in the event of your immediate death. The key here is *dependency*. A self-supporting single person may not need life insurance although his or her counterpart with three school-age children may need a sizable sum. After the amount of need is established, calculations must continue to reduce this figure by assets available to aid dependents and government programs which will also help. The Shroder children, for example, receive regular stipends from Social Security because their deceased mother contributed sufficient sums to this government program to meet eligibility requirements for survivors' benefits.

Since most forms of insurance protection are available from a variety of sources, it is important to take enough time to read and understand policy terms in order to choose wisely among available options. It is equally important to determine gaps in coverage and decide how to handle those circumstances when insurance protection is weak or nonexistent.

SELECTING COVERAGES

A skilled insurance agent or salesperson can be very helpful in this regard. However, selecting an appropriate agent means developing sufficient knowledge of insurance principles to locate and work effectively with that agent. Since many agents represent only one insurer, it would be wise to begin with some library research on the financial stability and reputation of potential insurers. The former can be found in *Best's Insurance Reports,* and the latter in various publications including some issues of *Consumer Reports* and *Changing Times*. You then will be more informed to select among the multitude of companies and agents selling insurance. Even independent agents that sell policies of several companies are not authorized to carry the policies of all companies, nor do they choose to do so. When in doubt about a company's reputation and license to do business in your state, contact the State Department of Insurance which regulates this industry.

An insurance policy is a legal contract that says the policyholder will pay a specific sum each year in exchange for a prearranged dollar limit of financial reimbursement if overcome by a catastrophe listed in the policy. If the policyholder does not make payments as agreed, the policy is void. If a catastrophe occurs not specified in the policy, the policy is not applicable to the situation and no payment is required by the insurer. Moreover, oral agreements between the insurer or agent and the policyholder cannot legally alter policy terms. Any changes must be made in writing.

Unfortunately, the complicated legal language used in most insurance policies makes it very difficult to understand contract terms. The company's representative or sales agent is trained in this field and should be able to explain contract provisions to the potential buyer. But if the agent misrepresents certain provisions, the buyer has no recourse to force compliance with the oral terms.

Some companies have begun to realize the frustrations of policyholders faced with these dilemmas, as have several state departments who regulate insurance sold within their borders. Their goal is the introduction of readable, or plain language, policies. In most cases, these are still in developmental stages, but several have already enacted legislation to provide all insurance customers with summaries clearly explaining policy provisions and costs in order to aid customers in comparison shopping.

An easily understood insurance policy alone is not enough for wise selection among the maze of policies on the market. It is equally important to realistically calculate insurance needs to acquire the appropriate amount of protection.

Avoid High Pressure Sales.   It is often said that most people are sold insurance; they do not shop for it. Since this product is a fairly complicated one to buy wisely, these people defer to the salesperson's greater knowledge of insurance to help in selecting appropriate protection. Yet, the salesperson may be faced with conflicting interests. Often her or his commission on the sale will be greater for policies less able to meet the customer's needs or budgets. Then the uninformed customer can fall victim to a salesperson's desire to achieve personal financial rewards. The result can become an inappropriate purchase camouflaged as adequate protection through rationalization by buyer and seller.

While this procedure is illogical, it is quite common, especially in purchasing life insurance which is commonly sold in the home, often by unsolicited door-to-door salespeople. (Yet, despite the potential for misunderstanding, insurance is not included in the Federal Trade Commission rule providing a seventy-two-hour "cooling off period" on door-to-door sales!) One reason for the problem is that many people readily postpone dealing with the grim facts of life and may only face the realities of their needs when someone else initiates the action. Others falsely assume all insurance companies are alike, hence, comparison shopping can reap no benefits. Research has, however, shown that the true cost of a life insurance policy may vary as much as 170 percent for the same coverage with different firms.[1]

While price is not the only criteria on which to select an insurance policy, this vast cost range does exemplify the need for comparison shopping. Even if an insurance salesperson initiates your analysis of certain insurance needs, the wise shopper will confer with several firms to compare benefits and price before making a purchase.

Because the healthy, accident- and disaster-free household receives no return on years of pure insurance payments, some of these people feel cheated instead of thankful. In order to encourage these fortunate individuals to maintain comprehensive protection, some agents encourage the purchase of higher cost health or property policies that return some of the dollars invested for minor claims like routine medical examinations or dented fenders. Ironically, the high annual insurance premiums for these predictable occurrences can exceed the return. More importantly, they divert attention from the main reason for insurance—to protect against the big losses. This sometimes results in inadequate total coverage, although the dollars spent would be sufficient to provide for household needs if priorities were maintained.

The same principle applies in life insurance. To provide a return on investment to long-life policyholders, many companies promote the sale of cash value life insurance, or a combination policy that incorporates savings and protection. Because savings for retirement is more pleasant a thought than providing for dependent survivors, the focus of the protection may once again be skewed in favor of the insurer rather than the policyholder.

Insurance buyers who prefer to avoid this emotional approach to protection need to carefully analyze their household needs before approaching an insurance agent for information about available products. Fortified with the facts in writing, it is easier to adhere to the primary purpose of your shopping. It is also easier to find an insurance agent and company interested in realistically meeting your needs because their analysis will replicate your own findings, so the results are far more likely to be satisfactory.

Seek Economy in Groups. Because so many people need some relatively similar types of insurance protection, it is often possible to save money by purchasing insurance through a group. It takes less agent time and less agent cost to sell one group policy than the corresponding individual policies to all group members. Therefore, some of the economy reaped by the insurer with this mass merchandising method can be passed on to the policyholder via lower insurance rates or premiums.

Accordingly, some high risk individuals who might not otherwise be accepted for a particular type of insurance will be included in many group policies because their increased probability of filing a claim is offset by a greater number of persons who will never need the insurance protection they are buying through this group.

Therefore, a wise shopping guide is to seek out all eligible group insurance programs before buying individual policies to meet insurance needs. While it may take more effort to locate and evaluate the benefits of several policies, as well as maintain them, the dollar savings should be well worth the extra time and energy involved.

Although there are many principles of insurance applicable to all types of coverage, the nature of protection provided often dictates specific characteristics of the policy. Therefore, the remainder of the chapter will focus on the specific types of insurance used to meet most household needs.

PROPERTY INSURANCE

Owning property can result in financial losses if that property is damaged or destroyed, or if someone sustains injury because of your negligence in caring for the property. Since the potential losses from a lawsuit can be particularly staggering, insurance protection can be a wise investment, especially for your home, personal property, and auto.

RESIDENTIAL
INSURANCE

Homeowners and tenants should carry insurance to protect against the loss of real estate and/or personal property, as well as protection against lawsuits initiated due to liability for accident or injury occurring on this insured property and away from it. Most of these policies are sold in packages which include insurance against: (1) fire; (2) theft; (3) natural, man-made, or mechanical damages; (4) judgments due to negligence resulting in accident or injury to others; and (5) additional temporary living expenses incurred in the event of covered disasters (above normal expenses in this regard).

As the cost of the residential policy rises, the protection increases against a larger number of perils. For example, in the basic form package policy (HO-1), protection is generally offered against damage by fire, hail, lightning, windstorm, explosion, riots, aircraft, glass breakage, vandalism, and theft. HO-2 is required if protection is sought against the additional risks of building collapse, freezing, damage by electrical equipment, etc. HO-3 covers all risks to insured buildings except damage due to war, nuclear disaster, flood, termites, depreciation, or normal wear and tear.

However, liability protection, medical payments, and damages to the property of others remain constant for all of these policies unless you purchase amendments to the policy or endorsements to raise coverage in one or more of these three areas where you feel the policy is inadequate to meet your lifestyle needs. It may be particularly important to upgrade liability coverage.

Tenants and condominium owners need less property insurance than homeowners. The landlord or condominium association is responsible for the building and grounds. Therefore, their residential insurance is less costly than the homeowner's and generally as comprehensive in damage protection as an HO-2 policy without protection on the building. Liability, medical payment, and other coverage is comparable to that available to homeowners.

When property damage occurs and a claim is filed, most residential insurance policies will pay only the actual cash value of the property lost. Actual cash value is defined as "the replacement cost of the property minus depreciation for years of use." In most cases, this is not enough to actually replace the damaged property. However, if the residence is insured for at least 80 percent of rebuilding, the insurer will pay full replacement cost on losses up to the face value of your policy. That means if a home with a replacement cost value of $50,000 was insured for $45,000 and it burned to the ground, the insurer would pay up to $45,000 toward the cost of rebuilding it on the same site. (When calculating homeowner insurance needs, it is essential to remember that the insured property includes the dwellings and related buildings, not the cost of the lot.)

Some companies now also sell replacement value insurance on personal property or the contents of the home as well. This pays fully for lost items, even if they cost substantially more now than at the time of purchase. This type of coverage raises the homeowner's premiums about 15 percent, so it can be costly in relation to other policy benefits, but it may be worthwhile when the majority of possessions are old enough to carry limited actual cash value but important to the household lifestyle.

It is also important to note other limits of coverage on the residence. Only certain dollar amounts are reimbursable for cash losses, securities, deeds, manuscripts, etc., as well as valuables like jewelry and silverware. However, most companies will allow policyholders to protect these items for additional value by purchasing "personal property floaters," or amendments to the residential policy that compensate for the true value of these articles.

In addition, personal property lost, stolen, or damaged away from the insured residence may not be fully covered by the policy. This is true when policies limit the amount of protection on property away from home to a predetermined percentage of the insurance carried. Most commonly this is as low as 10 percent of the face value of the property per location away from home. Those people who travel with possessions of a value beyond this sum must carry a rider or addition to their existing residential policy to obtain greater protection.

As a protection for homeowners whose property values are rising rapidly, many insurers offer an inflation guard endorsement that may be purchased as an amendment to the residential policy. This endorsement automatically increases the policy coverage by a predetermined rate each year. When this rate is equal to or greater than the rise in local property values, the endorsement offers good protection. In those select areas of the country with rampant housing booms, even the inflation guard endorsement may be insufficient protection. In those cases, it would become imperative to review your insurance coverage at least annually to adjust for realistic replacement values.

Some people assume they can get around the low reimbursement on actual cash value claims by stretching their losses or overstating the value of the original property or its location when lost. While this has certainly worked successfully many times, it is important to note that this type of action constitutes fraud. If detected by the insurer, it can result in criminal charges, a cancelled policy, and/or a denied claim.

Therefore, in order to substantiate your losses it is important to maintain an up-to-date inventory of your possessions, complete with descriptive information (for possible recovery in the event of theft) and date of purchase (to calculate actual cash value). A copy of this list belongs in your safe deposit box. Once possessions begin to accumulate, this recordkeeping is no easy task. One way to provide interim records and verification of ownership is to photograph the rooms of your dwelling with cupboards and closets open to display as many possessions as possible for a camera record. Another temporary aid worth saving is the household movers' inventory sheets which are required to be completed for all interstate moves. Of course, the pictures and the inventory lists belong in the safe deposit box if only one copy of each is available.

Not all personal property is covered under a residential insurance policy. All motor vehicles and some boats require separate policies against loss. Whatever your preferred mode of transportation, you will generally need to carry a separate insurance policy on it for both property damage and liability protection. The only exceptions are bicycles (*not* mopeds) which are covered under the residential policy, and legs protected under medical insurance and some aspects of the residential policy.

MOTOR VEHICLE INSURANCE

If you own and/or drive an automobile, truck, or motorcycle, you need motor vehicle insurance protection against suits for property damage and bodily injury claims. In some states, a minimum amount of insurance coverage is required to register your vehicle and drive within the state. All states require proof of financial responsibility or verification that drivers have assets at least equal to the minimum liability limits required by that state. These liability limits are usually at least $10,000. Most drivers meet these legal requirements through insurance, although it is sometimes possible to find alternate ways to do so. In some states, you must show proof of insurance protection in order to register a car.

The only people that can realistically avoid purchasing motor vehicle insurance are those who never drive a motorized vehicle on our roads. Bicyclists are protected under their residential insurance for property damage and theft, and under their health insurance for accident or injury. Mass transit users and people who walk need comparable coverage for protection when traveling. If liability protection is desired beyond the limits of the residential (or motor vehicle policies), most insurers will sell their clients an umbrella policy which can provide up to $1 million dollars or more in liability coverage. This protection is against most liability claims, not just those arising from motor vehicle accidents.

Since so many Americans own and operate a motor vehicle, it is important to understand automobile insurance[2] in order to select appropriate coverage at economical rates. Auto insurance is available for protection against financial losses due to: (1) bodily injury liability, (2) property damage liability, (3) collision, and (4) natural disasters.

In addition, depending on state law, your auto insurance claims may be handled by your own insurer (under no fault legislation) or by the insurer representing the driver responsible for the accident or injury that prompted the claim. While the latter is the more traditional approach, the time lags and legal costs inherent in this program make it slow and often ineffective. The following analysis of these components of auto insurance will serve to clarify their contributions to this form of protection against disaster.

Liability Coverage.   This type of insurance protects the policyholder (vehicle owner) against the bodily injury or property damage claims of another person (third party) that resulted from an accident caused by the policyholder's car. The "other person" may be a pedestrian involved in the accident or the driver (or passenger) of another vehicle. The insurance company that carries your liability coverage will also provide an attorney to defend you if you are sued for alleged bodily injury or property damage to others, even though the suit may be groundless or false.

Reasonable limits of liability insurance would currently be about $300,000 per accident, although the legal minimum required can be as low as $10,000–20,000. In some types of policies, this limit would read "100/300/10." That means bodily injury liability claims would be paid up to $100,000 for one person, $300,000 per accident (the sum of all bodily injury claims to be paid), and $10,000 for property damage. Since a liability suit is not limited to the amount of insurance carried by the person responsible for the accident, someone carrying this liability policy could be sued for $500,000 by the three people who were injured in this one accident. If the court awards these damages to be paid, the person being sued would have to pay the additional $200,000 not covered by insurance. While collecting this uninsured sum could be difficult, it can be done via wage and property attachments, etc. (See Chapter 7 on collection methods.)

Uninsured motorist protection also safeguards the policyholder and her or his family or passengers in the event they are injured while riding in the insured vehicle while it is struck by an uninsured motorist or a hit and run driver. The policyholder and family are also protected by this policy when walking if hit by an uninsured motorist or hit and run driver. Like other types of liability protection, this type of insurance is required for all drivers in some states.

Damage to the Insured Vehicle.   If your car is damaged by overturning or collision with another object (like a telephone pole) or vehicle, the costs of repairing your car can be covered under the "collision" insurance portion of your auto policy. Although this coverage is optional, it can help significantly to defray repair and/or replacement costs of the insured vehicle. However, since the benefits paid are limited to the present market value of the insured vehicle, it may not be a worthwhile investment for cars worth less than $1,000. After a car reaches ten years old, some insurance companies refuse to offer this coverage even if you want to buy it.

Collision coverage is usually only sold with a "deductible" or small sum the policyholder must pay out-of-pocket before the insurer pays the remaining costs. In recent years, a $200 deductible per claim has been common, although higher and lower limits are available. The higher the deductible, the lower the cost of the collision insurance and vice versa. The appropriate deductible for each policyholder is determined by the amount of emergency funds available in the event of auto damage, and the time involved to replace those funds in case multiple emergencies strike at about the same time.

A version of fire and theft insurance is also available for your car. Called "comprehensive," it pays for loss of or damage to the insured car for any cause other than collision or upset (such as fire, theft, vandalism, windstorm, hail, flood, smoke, falling objects, etc.) This is generally also purchased with a deductible to reduce the costs of coverage.

Medical Payments. A portion of your auto insurance protection also covers necessary medical, hospital, professional nursing, or funeral expenses resulting from an accident in which the insured car was involved. It covers the policyholder and family as well as passengers in the car. For many drivers, this coverage duplicates health insurance protection carried under a separate policy. Therefore, it may be possible to reduce auto insurance costs by limiting medical payment coverage carried under this policy.

Fault versus "No-Fault."   Traditionally, auto insurance companies required a court case to determine who is at fault for the accident before any claims would be paid. In those cases where two or more people shared liability for causing the accident, the court would even have to decide how much liability each person had in order to calculate damages to be paid. Of course, such a procedure could take years and considerable legal expense.

In an effort to reduce time lag and legal expenses, some states have initiated a no-fault liability insurance system. Under no-fault, *your* insurance company pays your claims (up to the policy limits) without regard for who is responsible for the accident. (Existing no-fault plans apply to bodily injury liability claims only.) Although the details of these no-fault plans differ by state law, this coverage is mandatory in states where it has been enacted into law.

No-fault coverage replaces medical payment coverage, up to certain dollar limits, beyond which the old fault system takes over. It also adds wage loss or disability income protection and substitute service coverage to pay for household help or assistance with other routine services that cannot be handled while recuperating from injury. In other words, if you lived in a no-fault state and were injured in a car accident that prohibited you from working at your profession for two months and required household help to care for dependent children, etc. (a job that is usually your responsibility), your insurance company may pay for all or part of this financial burden.

Other advantages of the no-fault system include more prompt payment of auto insurance claims for cases where no lawsuit is allowed. This reduction in legal fees and claims for pain and suffering has also meant slightly lower insurance premiums in some no-fault states. Unfortunately, the projected economics of the system have not reached their potential, largely because of the relatively low limits set before a liability claim can be filed in court under the old fault system. In some states, bodily injury claims for medical bills, rehabilitation, lost wages, etc., need only total a few hundred dollars per person before the traditional liability system takes over.

Cost Factors.   At present, the costs of auto insurance are still derived by a statistical analysis of claims paid, as determined by the following criteria used to classify policyholder:

1. Age and market value of the car.
2. Policyholder's accident and driving record.

3. The accident record and insurance statistics for the area in which the car is "garaged" or kept (in the event that this differs from the state in which the car is registered, etc.).
4. The amount of regular driving done by the policyholder and family drivers (especially commuting and/or business use of the vehicle).
5. Age, sex, and marital status of the policyholder and family drivers.
6. The company from which insurance is purchased.
7. The number and characteristics of all regular drivers for family vehicles.

High risk drivers with lengthy accident records are required to carry auto insurance in most states. Since no insurer really wants these drivers as clients, state law requires all insurers licensed to do business in that state to share the burden of insuring these drivers through participation in an "assigned risk pool." Customers are assigned to these companies in proportion to the amount of business conducted by the insurer in that state. A lottery system is also used to determine which insurer is required to provide coverage for each high risk driver. The only compensation the insurance companies have for carrying these policies is the option to charge significantly higher than normal premiums to drivers covered by the assigned risk pool.

It should also be noted that insurance companies often raise their rates after each claim filed against the policy. In some states this is illegal if the claim falls below a certain dollar limit.

The best ways to cut costs in auto insurance are comparison shopping and a good driving record. Additional savings may be reaped by carrying a $250–$500 deductible on collision and comprehensive coverage,[3] minimizing duplicate medical payments coverage, and taking advantage of all available discounts. Some companies discount policies when more than one family auto is covered under the same policy, or if student drivers have good grades, successfully complete driver's education classes, or drive the car infrequently because they attend school more than one hundred miles away. In addition, paying premiums annually, when allowed by the insurer, can save finance charges and prevent a raise in premiums during that full year.

MEDICAL INSURANCE

Automobile accidents are far from the only reason that people require medical attention. Mild and catastrophic sicknesses can and do strike when they are least expected, as does that inevitable accident that occurs when you are in a hurry, unskilled, careless, or a victim of natural disaster. While good health planning and a strong safety consciousness can help to reduce medical care needs, it cannot promise to eliminate them. Today's costs of hospitalization and medical care can quickly and relentlessly devour anyone's emergency fund, often forcing the sale of significant assets or producing overpowering indebtedness. That is why careful financial planning includes the purchase of adequate medical insurance to protect household members from possible substantial financial losses due to catastrophic sickness or an accident. While the government does provide some medical insurance coverage for large groups of people, the qualifications for these protection programs eliminate millions of people who must first use up all available assets and/or meet age and income guidelines.

The primary types of accident and sickness insurance fall into three categories: (1) basic medical coverage, (2) major medical coverage, and (3) dental coverage.

PRIMARY POLICIES

Basic Medical Coverage. This is the first layer of insurance protection called upon to pay all or part of the policyholder's bills for hospital room and board (usually semi-private), as well as doctor and surgeon fees incurred during the hospitalization. Some policies also pay for doctor visits outside the hospital. Related services such as blood transfusions, drugs, etc., *may* be included in this policy. In addition, there will probably be limits to the length of the hospital stay covered by the policy or the amount of doctor fees, etc., that are paid per sickness or as a lifetime maximum. Some insurers pay almost the full costs of hospital care; others provide far less protection even when the price of the policies is similar.

Major Medical Coverage. Designed to protect the policyholder from financial losses due to long-term sickness and/or serious accidents, major medical insurance provides coverage that begins after the basic medical policy has produced its maximum benefits. Most major medical policies provide all of the basic medical coverages and more for extended periods of hospital confinement and treatment. Sometimes coverage is broader than that provided in the basic medical plan. Hospital ancillary services like blood, drugs, physical therapy, etc., may be covered, as well as treatment for mental illness and convalescent needs including some skilled nursing facility care or private duty nursing.

As in the basic medical policy, there are usually dollar limits to the major medical coverage offered per policy. However, these limits may be for larger lifetime claims by the policyholder or five or more years of benefits, etc. Since fewer policyholders make claims against their major medical coverage, the insurers can provide more comprehensive coverage at fairly reasonable rates.

Dental Coverage. Traditional medical insurance only pays benefits for dental work resulting from an accident, if at all. The increasingly popular dental expense insurance offers protection against the costs of routine dental care as well as accident damages. Normally, coverage is comprehensive, including everything from oral examinations to dentures and orthodontics. However, this type of insurance is generally only available through group insurance plans.

Exclusions and Limitations. In order to discourage people from purchasing medical insurance just prior to surgery or other anticipated medical expenses, most insurance companies restrict coverage to reduce this probability. A common policy provision is a required waiting period of thirty, sixty, ninety, or more days before coverage takes effect. In the case of maternity benefits, payments may only be made if conception occurs eight to nine months after the policy becomes effective.

To compensate for some of these limitations, it is important to retain your existing insurance protection during the waiting period for a new policy so to prevent a void in total coverage. Because health insurance is so often tied to employment fringe benefits, many people routinely suffer from a gap in coverage due to job changes or waiting period delays. Since few people choose to be in that predicament, several insurance companies have begun to offer "stop gap" health insurance. This is a nonrenewable basic medical policy with coverage effective immediately but limited to 60 to 180 days and modest dollar benefits. In addition, many states now require employers to allow departing employees to buy up to thirty-nine weeks of additional group coverage in order to make continuous medical coverage possible during the transition between jobs.

A second common policy limitation is the exclusion of benefit payments for *preexisting conditions*—sicknesses and physical defects which were known prior to taking out the policy. Usually this exclusion is for a specified period of time, such as one or two years, rather than for the term of the policy.

As a compromise, reputable companies will require the prospective policyholder to take a *medical exam* or complete a medical history questionnaire, the results of which will determine acceptance or rejection of the policy and the rates charged. One company might exclude any claims related to heart problems if this health condition was preexisting. Another company could include coverage for heart problems but charge a higher rate to this policyholder because of the preexisting heart condition.

When the insurance application requires medical history information, you should disclose full information about your past and present injuries, illnesses, hospitalizations, etc. If you fail to include information about a previous condition and later incur medical expenses resulting from the same condition, the insurance company may deny your claim on the basis of misrepresentation or failure to disclose full information. It is not unusual for a policy to contain a provision under which the company may deny a claim or withdraw medical coverage if a misrepresentation occurs within a specified period after the policy takes effect. This period is generally two years. After that time, the policy essentially becomes incontestable and the company must pay the claim.

Other exclusions and/or limitations are sometimes found in medical insurance policies. These vary by company and policy type and may include:

1. Losses resulting from war or military services.
2. Suicide, attempted suicide, or intentionally self-inflicted injuries.
3. Losses that are payable under Worker's Compensation (as discussed later in this chapter).
4. Services or treatment provided by any hospital owned or operated by a government agency.
5. Alcoholism and drug addiction.
6. Extended care facilities and nursing homes.
7. Psychiatric treatment.

A recent survey of major insurance companies indicated that the majority of *group* insurance policies offered now include provisions for alcoholism treatment, nervous and mental disorders, skilled nursing care facilities, and voluntary sterilization and abortions. However, individual policies often still fail to provide this type of comprehensive coverage at affordable prices.

PURCHASING OPTIONS

Obviously, there are numerous pieces to put together in building an effective health insurance protection package. In some cases, the policyholder can select the desired benefits from one policy. In other cases, the medical insurance is offered in one package plan. If that is not acceptable, additional protection may need to be purchased in a second policy, possibly from a second insurer. In order to help you gain a greater understanding of the purchasing options available, let's analyze the more common alternatives.

Service Benefits versus Indemnity.   Insurance companies can either pay for covered medical services on a flat fee (indemnity) basis or at full cost (service benefit). Someone hospitalized for three days for a minor operation could receive bills totaling $200 a day for hospital room and board plus a $500 surgeon fee. An indemnity policy may only pay $60 a day to the hospital and $350 to a surgeon for that type of operation. So the indemnity policyholder would still owe $270 out-of-pocket to cover these medical expenses. In contrast, if the policy provided service benefits, the full $1,100 would be paid by the insurer.

Group versus Individual Policies.   Health insurance is one of the most common employee benefits in America today. Employers may simply provide access to lower cost group insurance rates for their employees or they may absorb some or all of the costs of insuring their employees and qualified dependents. In either case, the benefits of a group insurance program warrant careful scrutiny for economy and comprehensive coverage.

The advantages of group health insurance go far beyond lower costs. Many group plans reduce or eliminate waiting periods and exclusions, and charge regular rates even for preexisting conditions. They often offer broader types of coverage. For example, many basic medical policies pay all or part of doctor office visits, whether or not they are related to a recent hospitalization. Some also pay for prescription drugs, routine lab tests, etc. However, most still require an eight- to nine-month wait for maternity coverage.

The primary disadvantage to a group medical insurance policy is that you lose your coverage when you leave the group. If you lose your job, you may simultaneously lose your insurance protection (at least after thirty-nine additional weeks). The only possible way to continue coverage with the same insurer is to convert your group coverage to an individual policy when you leave the firm. The individual policy will cost more and provide less comprehensive protection, but it will be immediately enforceable.

Accordingly, there is very little anyone can do to comparison shop for group insurance, since you must qualify to join a group before you can be considered as a policyholder. Other things being equal, you may select one job over another because of better insurance benefits. You may even join a particular fraternal or professional association in order to qualify for their group insurance. You can also work to improve health insurance benefits for the group or groups to which you presently belong.

If you are not eligible for group medical insurance, you will need to purchase an individual policy to protect yourself and dependents. Comparison shopping in this case will be very helpful since you have a wide range of policies from which to choose. The variables to consider during this selection are also numerous.

The first line of insurance protection purchased should be the broadest, most comprehensive catastrophic sickness and accident policy you can afford. From this perspective, major medical insurance is a greater priority than basic medical because it offers more total protection in the event of serious long-term health problems. The potential costs that would be incurred before a major medical policy takes effect are sufficiently large that it is *also* important to carry basic medical coverage whenever possible.

Minnie Simpson and her husband are a good example of the ramifications felt when catastrophic losses are not adequately covered. Minnie and her husband carried only basic medical coverage purchased through an individual family policy. It sounded like good protection when they bought the policy fifteen years earlier. But they never dreamed their insurance needs would be so long term or expensive! Major medical insurance was not affordable on their tight budget, and at the time it seemed enough to carry coverage for routine expenses. Did they have a lot to learn! Mr. Simpson even had enough employees to obtain group coverage for them all. Ironically, he was the loser from failing to take advantage of this opportunity.

Group insurance never cancels a member's policy as long as the policyholder maintains membership status in the group, nor will they fail to renew an individual's policy for reasons other than nonpayment of premiums. That is not the case for individual medical insurance policies though. Unless otherwise stated in the policy terms, individual policies can be cancelled or denied renewal at the discretion of the insurer. Therefore, it is important to select a policy that is *noncancellable* (whereby premiums and coverage remain constant during the life of the policyholder) or *guaranteed renewable* (whereby rates can rise but no individual policy can be cancelled, although the whole group policy can be eliminated).

Mail-Order Companies.   Both individual and group policies may be sold by mail. For group insurance, this may be one of the few reasonable cost methods of notifying members of the availability of this group benefit. For individual insurance, it may be a way to camouflage voids in coverage by making insurance shopping appear easy and inexpensive. Obviously, there is no "free lunch." Therefore, it is imperative to thoroughly investigate the adequacy of any mail-order policies prior to purchase. Begin by checking to see if the mail-order firm is licensed to do business in your state by contacting the State Insurance Department. Most complaints against mail-order firms stem from their minimal benefit payments and maximal exclusions. Although most problems are reported for mail-order sales of individual policies, these group policies require equal scrutiny to be sure they are worth the cost. Many mail-order companies offer indemnity benefits, paying cash directly to you in the event of a claim. But the dollars paid seldom cover the total medical expenses incurred, or even a significant portion of them.

Claim Procedures. The ease of filing a health insurance claim and the expedience with which it is paid are both valid purchasing considerations when a choice is available. The time limits required for reporting a claim are specified in the policy terms. Generally, written notice of a claim is required within twenty days after the policyholder receives medical attention for the accident or injury. If an individual policy was purchased through a local agent, that person can help complete the appropriate paperwork. Under a group plan, one or more group members are generally instructed in this process and responsible for helping other group members properly complete the forms. For mail-order insurance, the claims are processed by mail by the individual claimant.

Insurance companies use various claim forms to be completed by the policyholder, doctor, hospital, or any other suppliers of medical care involved. Under some policies it is possible to "assign" benefits to the hospital, surgeon, etc., involved. By assigning benefits, the insurance company pays the medical provider directly for service rendered. You, the policyholder, are then merely notified that the transaction is complete.

When assigned benefits are insufficient to meet total costs of services provided, the doctor or hospital will bill you directly for the difference between insurance benefits paid and actual charges. In some cases, in order to be certain that assigned benefits will cover total costs, you may have to shop for doctors and hospitals willing to accept this sum as payment in full.

When benefits cannot be assigned, you generally need to complete appropriate company forms for each claim, itemizing a list of covered expenses or attaching actual bills from the hospital, surgeon, physician, pharmacist, and any other covered health care supplier involved. If payments are required when services are rendered, you will have to pay for these services in full and await reimbursement from your insurance company after completing the required forms.

Deductibles and Coinsurance. In order to reduce premiums and focus protection on significant financial losses due to sickness and/or accident, medical insurers require policyholders to share part of the burden of payment for services received. A *deductible* is the sum you must pay before the medical insurance takes effect. Some policies may ask you to pay $75 per person or $150 per household annually before the insurance policy takes over. Others will request higher sums in order to reduce total premiums paid on the policy. Often, receipted bills for these expenditures must be submitted to the insurer to verify payment before the company takes responsibility for additional charges.

The deductible on a major medical policy may equal the maximum benefits provided on your basic medical policy. In addition, the major medical policy may require the policyholder to pay a specified percentage or *coinsurance* of all costs above this amount. Some policies carry coinsurance on all claims while others require coinsurance only up to a predetermined limit. A common example would be for the policyholder to pay 20 percent of costs incurred up to $2,000 to 3,000 before the major medical policy provides full payment.

When evaluating deductible and coinsurance provisions, it is also important to note if these limits apply to each claim filed or to all claims made by the policyholder within a specified period of time. A time factor is usually beneficial to the policyholder although insurers prefer a claim factor. The greater the policyholder's share in payments, the lesser the insurance company's liability.

Prepaid Benefits.   A new approach to medical care needs has come on the market in most areas of the country via health maintenance organizations (HMO's). In an effort to encourage preventive medicine, HMO's have been established as a *prepaid* medical supermarket of services, including physician and hospital needs in lieu of the traditional fee-for-services type of medicine. HMO physicians are generally salaried and may even work in an HMO operated hospital. Cost controls are a high priority to keep expenditures within the limits of prepaid protection purchased by subscribers. Office visits are unlimited, insurance claims nonexistent, unnecessary surgery discouraged, and medical records centralized under the HMO's one-stop medical services program. The selection of doctors is limited to HMO staff physicians.

Costs for HMO coverage may equal or exceed those of a comprehensive medical insurance policy. However, some employers will offer a choice between HMO and medical insurance as a fringe benefit. Many of the exclusions and limitations of traditional medical insurance policies also apply to HMO's, especially in regard to medical history and physical examination requirements.

Despite the advantages, some people cannot afford the cost of medical insurance. These people are generally low income families. Sometimes they are also in high risk categories, like the elderly and disabled, in which case the

GOVERNMENT PROGRAMS

needed insurance is not available or so limited by exclusions that it offers minimal protection. Therefore, government, at all levels, has intervened to offer some medical insurance benefits to these high risk individuals.

The most comprehensive government programs are Medicare (Title 18 of the Social Security Act) and Medicaid (Title 19 of the Social Security Act). Although they both pay the medical bills of qualified individuals, the eligibility requirements for these programs differ significantly.

Medicare. As of July 1, 1966, the Social Security Act was amended to provide both mandatory (Part A) and supplemental voluntary federal government sponsored medical insurance (Part B) for most Americans sixty-five-years-old or over. Rich, poor, gainfully employed, or retired—all receive the same coverage. The primary requirements for eligibility are verification of age, and completion of an appropriate application form. Medicare coverage is even made available to some persons under sixty-five who are disabled or suffering kidney failure.

Part A of the Medicare program is mandatory hospital insurance, including some posthospital care and out patient services. There is no direct charge to the insured for this policy. However, there is a deductible and coinsurance provision that is adjusted routinely to keep pace with inflation.

Part B of the Medicare program is an optional medical insurance policy that helps to pay doctor fees and related medical services such as X-rays, diagnostic tests, ambulances, etc. An annual deductible must be paid prior to obtaining coverage under Part B. Once coverage begins, a coinsurance provision further requires 20 percent of all covered expenses to be paid directly by the insured.

Although Medicare was never intended to be a complete medical insurance package, the total coverage provided to insured people is shrinking consistently. Research has shown that the portion of hospital and medical bills paid by Medicare for insured persons is significantly lower than the coinsurance percentage advertised, especially in regard to nursing home expenses.[4]

In an attempt to reduce this problem for senior citizens, many private insurance companies offer "Medigap" policies designed to fill in some of the gaps in Medicare coverage. A good Medigap policy will usually cover the deductible and coinsurance costs left unpaid by Medicare. However, few of these private policies offer the additional protection necessary in providing coverage where Medicare fails—specifically, long-term nursing home care (especially for custodial needs), and out-of-hospital prescription drugs and medical appliances like eyeglasses, hearing aids, etc. In other words, If Medicare does not pay part of the cost, neither do most Medigap policies. Moreover, if the fees for medical services are greater than what Medicare considers a reasonable sum, Medicare will pay only 80 percent of the reasonable amount, with a good Medigap policy paying the other 20 percent—and the policyholder paying the remainder of the inflated fee!

The largest single void in Medicare and Medigap protection is nursing home care—or the lack of it. While Social Security administration literature about Medicare proudly claims that insured persons have up to one hundred days of coverage in a skilled nursing facility, actual experience is quite different. In 1976, the average skilled nursing facility coverage received nationally was twenty-one days, despite the fact that the average stay in that facility was several months.[5] While it is possible to obtain coverage for one hundred days, the Medicare regulations are so stringent that few insured people can qualify. One condition for full coverage is a steadily deteriorating acute sickness. If the patient reaches a plateau, coverage is denied. The same is true if recovery ensues or if medical needs become predominantly custodial due to physical or mental disability.

Medicaid.   There is, however, some government help for long-term nursing home patients and others drained of personal financial reserves who need to pay for medical services. A program called Medicaid was also instituted in July 1966 for this purpose. This is an assistance program established under cosponsorship of state and federal governments to help people of all ages obtain sufficient health care that they could not afford to buy privately. The primary qualifications for the program are income guidelines.

Persons over sixty-five years of age, or otherwise qualified for Medicare, may also receive Medicaid benefits. For people meeting both sets of eligibility guidelines, Medicaid can pay both the Medicare deductibles and coinsurance. It is actually one of the best Medigap programs available since it also pays for many medical services not covered by Medicare.

DISABILITY INCOME PROTECTION INSURANCE

When accident or sickness strikes, the resultant disability and/or recovery period often means loss of income and mounting medical bills. Therefore, the insurance industry has made it possible for persons gainfully employed to purchase disability income protection insurance as well as medical insurance. Government programs have also determined the necessity of providing income protection benefits to qualified disabled workers. The three basic types of policies sold by private insurers are sick leave, worker's compensation, and long-term disability protection.

BASIC POLICIES

Sick Leave.   Also called "wage continuation plans," these short-term disability policies are generally provided by your employer or purchased at work or through your union or professional association. They pay most or all of your income during a set period of your disability, usually only the early weeks or months. Eligibility for these benefits can begin after a lapse of about seven or more days from work due to accident or illness as described in the policy. Some employer-paid sick leave benefits begin immediately, if you have already worked for the firm for the minimum number of days to qualify for this benefit (usually three months). Length of service to the company may also affect total benefits available under this plan.

Worker's Compensation. Mandated by law, this private insurance program provides disability benefits to persons suffering job-related sicknesses or accidents only. The duration and size of benefits are set by each state. Generally, maximum benefits fall between 60 and 80 percent of predisability wages, up to a state-determined dollar ceiling. Benefits must be paid from the onset of the disability. Unfortunately, this sometimes means retroactive payments since no money is paid until a determination has been made about qualifications for work-related claims and the appropriate sums to provide in compensation. Sometimes medical payments are also made on qualified claims under this type of insurance.

Long-Term Disability Protection. Many people only need income protection insurance if the disabilities they suffer are lengthy. This is especially true when employer-paid sick leave is generous, fixed household costs are modest, and/or the household emergency fund and savings program is sufficient to meet short-term income replacement needs. Long-term benefits generally only begin after approximately six months of disability. Even then, they may be reduced by disability payments received from other sources (like government programs or other insurance policies). Depending on purchasing options, well chosen long-term policies can provide maximum protection for lowest costs since claims occur less often than under short-term sick leave policies. Typical payments approximate 50 to 60 percent of predisability wages, and they can continue for several years or up to age sixty-five when retirement benefits take over.

PURCHASING
OPTIONS

Definition of Disability. Like all other insurance policies, the disability income protection plan you choose is a legal contract between you and the insurance company. Therefore, it is vitally important to understand all of the provisions of that contract. The most important provision in income protection policies is the definition of disability used since this is the deciding factor on when you collect benefits and how much you collect. The most common and lowest price coverage is given for *total disability,* which is generally defined as the inability to work in any gainful employment within five or ten years after becoming unable to follow your regular occupation.

Even that differentiation may differ among insurers, as will the criteria used to verify continuing disability. Some policies deny total disability benefits if the insured person is healthy enough to leave home at all. Others cover only disabilities that occur as the result of accidents only, not sicknesses.

The definition of *partial disability* also deserves careful scrutiny. This can mean the ability to return to work part-time only, or to perform only some of your predisability tasks. This type of coverage is available but expensive in comparison to total disability protection.

Group versus Individual Policies. The differences between group and individual medical policies are very similar to these differences among disability policies in relation to cancellation.

Some group insurance policies offered by employer also provide *pension accrual* benefits to disability claimants. This means that company retirement benefits will be calculated as though the insured person worked during the years of his or her disability. When disability benefits end and retirement benefits begin, the insured will not suffer significant pension losses due to the disability.

Other Restrictions. Benefits paid under any disability policy are paid directly to the insured to spend at will in lieu of regular income. Because of tax exemptions and the reduction in work-related costs, most disabled individuals and their families need only 60 to 80 percent of their predisability earnings to maintain the same lifestyle. This is important to remember when comparison shopping. However, some policies pay a fixed percentage of earnings up to a fixed dollar limit, like $1,000 per month. That may not even meet the 60-percent figure for higher income earners, so be sure to check the policy carefully for limitations.

Benefits paid under a group disability policy are commonly "offset" or reduced in direct proportion to benefits received from worker's compensation, government programs (as discussed later in this section), and/or no-fault auto insurance payments for loss of wages. Some group policies also offset up to 80 percent of earnings received when a partially disabled claimant returns to work in a rehabilitation program.

Guaranteed Purchase Option. Because inflation now seems to be a perpetual drain on fixed incomes, it can be worthwhile to buy a cost of living rider for your long-term disability policy. By so doing, the insurance company will adjust payments made to you during the disability that are in line with a predetermined measure of inflation. While spendable dollars may still shrink, the impact of inflation can be reduced by the guaranteed purchase option. Although an expensive policy addition, if long-term disability strikes, it could prove most worthwhile.

GOVERNMENT
PROGRAMS

State-Sponsored Disability Insurance.   Although granted by a very small percentage of our fifty states, some state governments have mandated disability income protection insurance for their residents who become disabled as a result of sicknesses or accidents that are not job related. Insurance premiums are payroll deductions, with employee contributions required. These are generally short-term disability policies that provide a weekly paycheck until the insured can return to work.

Veteran's Insurance.   Anyone who has served the U.S. armed forces and becomes disabled as a result, whether during war or peacetime, is eligible for disability insurance benefits. These benefits are paid monthly for full or partial disabilities, with the degree of disability determining the size of the check. Benefits generally begin at discharge and continue for the length of the disability, without time limits.

Social Security.   The major disability insurance program sponsored by the federal government is for protection against long-term financial losses due to disability. Qualifications for this program are much more strict than for the retirement program (as described in Chapter 11), but benefits are calculated in essentially the same manner. In other words, a person qualifying for Social Security disability benefits will receive the same benefits as if she or he were eligible to retire now. In addition, sometimes benefits can also be paid to the spouse and dependent children of the disabled person.

Qualifications for the program include a five-month waiting period and medical evidence that the disabled person will be incapable of returning to work for at least one year, or that the disability will result in death. When the length or severity of the disability is questioned, payment can be withheld pending further investigation. Payment will be retroactive if the qualifications are later met. Claims can even be made by the heirs of a disabled person for benefits due just prior to his or her death.

LIFE INSURANCE

NEEDS
ASSESSMENT

One of the primary purposes of life insurance is to protect the dependents of a wage earner against the loss of income that would result from the wage earner's death. The amount of life insurance needed is determined by the number and age of the wage earner's dependents and their ability to be self-supporting in the event of his or her death. A single person may not need life insurance if she or he has enough money saved to pay burial expenses and debts. A retired person whose dependents are now financially independent may have outlived the need for life insurance. Yet a young family with one wage earner and two children under the age of ten may need well over $100,000 worth of coverage.

Donald Schroder and his children from the introductory case study were lucky. Although the loss of a wife and mother is not easy, the insurance compensation received made their financial adjustment to the loss easier. Nancy's earnings had been used for some frivolous family spending and savings for their dream home. There was little dependency on her earnings for the necessities of life. So the insurance benefits received after her death were enough to cover the new child care and housekeeping costs without a significant change in the Shroders' level of living.

If, on the other hand, Donald had died, his survivors would have been in more serious financial problems. At the time of the automobile accident, Donald's insurance coverage was essentially the same as Nancy's, despite the fact that he was the major breadwinner, earning almost twice her salary. If Nancy and the children were forced to live on her earnings plus these same insurance benefits, their level of living would have dropped, resulting in some major lifestyle changes. The insurance benefit totaled only 30 percent of Donald's salary, although they equalled almost 60 percent of Nancy's.

This revelation encouraged Donald to reevaluate his insurance coverage, as did the new circumstances thrust upon him. The basic principle was obvious. Life insurance benefits must compensate for major financial losses based on individual needs if the cost is to be justified.

Lifestyle Costs.   To calculate life insurance need, you must determine what sum of money your dependents would need to live in the lifestyle of your choice if you die tomorrow. This is a very personal decision, although there are some guidelines for calculating this need. A capable insurance agent can be very helpful with this determination, often making computer assistance available at no direct charge to the prospective client.

The two basic things you need to know to calculate lifestyle needs are: (1) the number of years this financial assistance will be required, and (2) the annual spending needs for the survivors. If the survivors are expected to maintain their present lifestyle, annual benefits from the insurance should total about 60 to 70 percent of the insured's earnings.

Since death benefits received from a life insurance policy are not taxable for federal income tax purposes, survivors' income needs are obviously lower than the insured's gross earnings, although the interest earned by the survivors on these investments is taxable whether the benefits are received in a lump sum or in regular installments (except for the first $1,000 in interest paid to a surviving spouse in regular installments). Additional reductions are also possible because of lower costs of household maintenance with one less member to feed, clothe, etc.

Supplemental large expenses that would have been paid from the insured's earnings, like college expenses, are lump sum additions to be included in the lifestyle calculation. Additional money must also be allowed for repayment of debts unless credit life insurance policies (see Chapter 6) are carried to pay these bills. Some money may be needed for funeral and other death-related expenses, including estate taxes (see Chapter 11).

The number of years that benefits will be needed are determined by the age of dependent survivors and their ability to contribute toward their financial independence. Children generally need financial support until age eighteen. In many households this help continues for many years beyond that age. If the surviving spouse works outside the home, help will be needed to cover extra child rearing costs if the children are young. Financial help will also be needed if the salary of the surviving spouse is lower than the insured's. In addition, if the surviving spouse had been dependent on the insured for pension benefits during retirement, provisions must be made to add these costs to the sum of insurance needs.

Net Worth.   It is important for each household to decide how existing assets will be used in the event of a breadwinner's death. Will they be liquidated to provide daily living needs or preserved toward retirement needs or bequested? How much, if any, assets must be liquidated to pay off existing liabilities (not covered by credit life insurance)? If installment obligations, like the mortgage, are assumed by the survivors, is there sufficient income provided to make regular payments in lieu of liquidation?

Once the amount of assets available for survivor's needs has been determined, you should subtract this sum from total life insurance needs. These decisions are very personal, but they must be realistically anticipated in order to yield an appropriate life insurance portfolio. Also, it should be noted that the longer an insured person lives, the less the insurance needs are because she or he is presently providing for all dependents out of current earnings. As assets grow and liabilities shrink, insurance needs can be further reduced.

The biggest unknown in appropriately totaling needs is the effect of inflation on future income needs. This is difficult to calculate. It is also difficult to accurately and realistically estimate the yield on lump sum death benefits wisely invested by the survivors in an attempt to offset inflation.

This is one place in particular where computer projections can be helpful when made available through a life insurance company or other reliable source.

A word of caution is important here. Every company uses their own formula for assessing insurance needs. Be sure it reflects your unique life-style choices before relying on this analysis alone for purchasing life insurance. A fairly common orientation is to focus calculations on the anticipated rise in earnings projected during the life of the insured plus inflation factors. This makes insurance needs seem greater than necessary, particularly when the surviving spouse is trained and willing to work to help support dependents!

Government Benefits. In addition to the career potential of a surviving spouse, some government benefits are available to help protect a breadwinner's dependents in the event of an early death. These should be carefully reviewed along with the net worth statement before any additional insurance protection is purchased.

Social Security benefits are available to the surviving dependents of most American workers during some portion of their lives. These benefits are paid through the Social Security trust funds to which employees, employers, and self-employed persons contribute during their working years. When the Social Security insured worker dies, application can be made by the surviving dependents for a lump sum death benefit (presently $255) for funeral expenses and survivors benefits.

Qualifications for survivor's benefits depend on the deceased worker's eligibility for Social Security benefits at the time of death, and the surviving dependents age and earnings. A worker covered by the Social Security system who earns $50 per calendar quarter (until 1978 and $250 thereafter) continuously for ten years meets the minimum requirements for retirement benefits (see Chapter 11). In so doing, the employee simultaneously makes her or his surviving spouse and dependent children eligible for "surviving family benefits." These dependents can also meet eligibility if the deceased breadwinner earned the legal minimum wage in six of the thirteen calendar quarters prior to death, or one qualifying calendar quarter per year from age twenty-two to death.

The amount of surviving family benefits received once eligibility is established is then calculated based on the deceased worker's average earnings over a predetermined span of time. These benefits are generally equal to 3/4 of the worker's retirement benefit at the time of death, up to a family maximum. Each child receives his or her own survivor's benefit until age eighteen (or age twenty-two if a full-time student). Benefits are paid longer if the surviving children are disabled and if the disability began before age twenty-two.

Benefits are also paid to the surviving spouse. These benefits are paid until the youngest child reaches age eighteen (age twenty-two if a full-time student). This is followed by a "widow's void," in which *no* Social Security benefits are paid until the surviving spouse reaches retirement age and becomes eligible for his or her share of the deceased worker's Social Security retirement benefits. Only if the surviving spouse is disabled does he or she receive lifetime benefits.

Of course, the complete details of elibigility for Social Security benefits are far more complex than this simplified discussion. The best way to determine eligibility is to contact the local Social Security Administration (look under "U.S. Government" in your phone book) for a more thorough explanation of your dependent's eligibility for family survivors' benefits. To do so, you will need to complete a "Request for Statement of Earnings" in order for your local Social Security representative to analyze the benefits due in the event of your death. Once this determination is made, you can subtract anticipated Social Security benefits from your total life insurance needs.

Fringe Benefits.   Some workers are automatically covered by some life insurance through their place of employment. Others have the option to carry this coverage via group membership in a union, fraternal organization, etc. Now is the time to itemize and total the life insurance benefits due to your survivors from these various group life insurance plans, and the likelihood that they will be in effect when you die because you will always maintain group membership.

Worker's compensation will pay a certain amount of death benefits to the surviving dependents of a worker who is killed on the job. The details of this program vary by states and circumstances surrounding the worker's job-related death. Since it is impossible to foresee the cause of anyone's death, these benefits cannot be accurately calculated into an insurance plan. However, their potential to help survivors should be noted here for those circumstances under which they can provide extra protection.

In addition, it is important to review your pension(s) to determine if a "survivorship clause" allows your pension benefits, in all or in part, to be paid to your surviving spouse. The sum total of these survivor benefits should then also be subtracted from your total insurance needs.

Net Supplemental Protection.   After your insurance needs are assessed, with deductions made for assets (which your heirs are willing to dispose of), government, and various group benefits, the remaining dollar figure equals the additional insurance you must purchase in order to adequately protect your family. As you will see in the next section, there are several ways to purchase this coverage at vastly different costs. Depending on the price you want to pay, any of the following policies will protect surviving dependents as long as you can afford to keep the policy in force during your working years.

If you cannot afford the price of this protection, even with the lowest cost options, you and your dependents may need to seriously reconsider your needs versus wants in order to determine how they actually will survive in the event of your death. This may involve consultation with relatives or friends to analyze the resources they have to offer in the event of your death—or a possible change in your present lifestyle to better protect the future. In some cases, a thorough analysis will mean investigating government welfare benefits and their eligibility standards in the event surviving dependents have nowhere else to turn for help.

In addition, it is essential to remember that life insurance protection is primarily needed for household breadwinners only. If the husband is the only worker, he needs adequate protection before any other policies are considered since the household will feel the greatest financial losses if his income stops. If both husband and wife work, both need life insurance protection in proportion to their respective contributions to family income. Obviously, if one spouse's salary is used exclusively for extras, protecting that income would not be as essential as protecting the income that provides the necessities of life. If both incomes are essential to pay basic costs, then both incomes must be protected with equal priorities.

The need to insure the life of a full-time homemaker is a debatable issue. In many cases, significant costs would be incurred by survivors to provide substitute housekeeping and child care services. That would justify modest life insurance protection against these costs. Others argue that the cost of these services would be equal to or less than the cost of supporting a dependent spouse. Either way, insuring the homemaker is a secondary issue.

The lives of retirees and children fall even lower in the hierarchy of life insurance needs. Retired people covered by pension benefits that provide for survivors really do not need life insurance except possibly to cover funeral expenses or preserve their estates from erosion by taxes (see Chapter 11). People without adequate pensions either live off savings and investments which can be passed on to surviving dependents or receive government aid that also provides for dependents.

Children do not generally contribute significantly to household income so their needs are also limited to provisions for funeral expenses. However, it is possible to protect a child's future insurability through the purchase of insurance protection before it is actually needed (with a special provision to guarantee his or her ability to buy more insurance later in life without a medical exam). This can sometimes mean a higher total lifetime cost for insurance. Although rates are lower for insurance purchased at a younger age, paying premiums for twenty extra years can offset that advantage. In addition, the forced savings of a cash value life can also provide the child a low-cost loan source as he or she enters adulthood, or a good start toward paying college costs. Since these are all secondary uses of life insurance, they should only be considered after the breadwinners carry adequate protection.

BASIC POLICIES

When the bottom line of your calculations indicates the need for more insurance protection you can choose from the following types: (1) term insurance, (2) permanent insurance, or (3) endowment insurance.

Term Insurance. As the name suggests, this provides for life insurance protection for a limited period of time—one, five, ten, or twenty years. If the insured person dies during this "term," the *face value* of the policy or the amount of the insurance purchased will be paid to the *beneficiary* or the person named in the policy to receive the proceeds of that policy.

This is temporary insurance. If death does not occur during the term of the policy, the insured person has no further protection unless she or he takes out a new policy. Since the costs of life insurance are based on the statistical probability of your imminent death, as you grow older the rate or *premium* charged to purchase the policy goes up. If you renew a term policy, the premium rises due to your increased age.

Term insurance is the lowest-cost policy available since it is pure insurance and nothing more. It can, however, be purchased with a variety of options to maximize the protection provided. One alternative is the choice of level or decreasing term insurance. Level term maintains a constant face value for the length of the policy. Decreasing term reduces the face value of coverage by a predetermined sum annually during the length of the policy until there is no coverage left. Obviously, decreasing term is cheaper insurance. However, it is only sufficient coverage if your insurance needs shrink proportionately during the years of the policy.

Most, if not all, group life insurance are term policies. Because it provides the most protection for your premium dollars, term insurance is the preferred choice among many consumer advocates and educators.

Term insurance becomes very expensive when the insured reaches age fifty. Some companies refuse to sell it at any price to people over ages sixty-five or seventy. While most insurance companies require the insured to take a medical exam prior to accepting the applicant, term insurance can require additional exams for each renewal.

Credit life policies offered on home mortgages and other installment loan contracts are decreasing term insurance equal to the outstanding balance on the loan. In some cases, a basic term policy to cover all of your indebtedness may be cheaper than several credit life policies bought through the various lenders.

Permanent Insurance. Unlike term insurance, this type of policy provides protection for surviving dependents throughout the insured's lifetime. Premiums for permanent insurance can be paid throughout a lifetime or for a predetermined period of years, but coverage remains constant until the policy is cancelled or until the insured's death. Usually, premium payments remain constant for the length of the policy. A medical exam is generally required to obtain this coverage.

Permanent insurance costs more than term for another very important reason. If you choose to cancel this type of policy, you get some of the money back that you paid in premiums. This is because permanent insurance is more than just protection against financial losses. It is also a savings program. This reserve that accumulates over the years is the *cash surrender value* of the policy or the part that is yours to keep after you cancel the policy. It is also the amount you can borrow (see Chapter 6) at a predetermined rate included in the policy provisions.

A table of cash values is clearly outlined in your policy and will indicate the cash value for each year, generally beginning two to three years after the policy is purchased. The cash value even on a fully paid policy generally equals no more than 50 percent of the face value of the policy. If you should die while a loan is outstanding on the policy, the benefits paid to your beneficiary are reduced by the dollars owed to the insurance company. On a $10,000 policy with an outstanding loan of $1,000 at the time of the insured's death, the beneficiary would receive only $9,000. Moreover, while the policyholder need never repay the loan itself, she or he must make regular payments of interest on the loan or suffer further losses of cash value and still lower payments to the beneficiary.

A growing variety of permanent insurance policies are presently being marketed. The most popular and usually lowest-cost policy is "whole life" or "straight life" insurance. Premiums on this policy are payable until death or age one hundred, when most insurance companies then pay the face value of the policy to the insured, thereafter cancelling further coverage. "Limited payment life" offers the same protection, but premiums are condensed to be paid over a shorter number of years, usually during peak earning periods. Since protection continues for life, premiums are higher for this type of policy since the period for which premiums are paid is reduced. "Modified whole life" is a graduated payment plan for insurance coverage whereby the premiums start low and increase in a predetermined number of years after the policyholder is assumed to have increased earnings to more easily afford the higher costs. In order to provide the face value coverage for the rates paid during the early years of this policy, some of the insurance provided is term and the rest is permanent. When premiums rise to their full level, all of the insurance protection is permanent.

"Variable life insurance" provides a guaranteed *minimum* death benefit plus the possibility of additional monies payable to the beneficiary. This variable rate is achieved through the purchase of common stock with a portion of the premium dollars. If the stocks do well, death benefits would be greater than the face value of the policy. If the stocks do poorly, death benefits will equal face value. A $20,000 variable life policy could pay the beneficiary $20,000 or more, depending on stock market fluctuation.

While this idea has merit, stock market growth does not always equal or exceed inflation. Therefore, it is more prudent to review life insurance needs annually rather than to hope the variable life policy will anticipate your needs. In addition, sales commissions charged on the common stock portion of this policy can legally be many times the rate charged through other stock investment companies, so the net return will be lower due to increased overhead for the purchase and sale of the stocks.[6]

"Adjustable life insurance" is the newest variation of insurance. Like modified life, it also combined term and permanent insurance, although the amount of each purchased is at the discretion of the policyholder. Under prescribed circumstances, adjustable life insurance allows the policyholder to increase or decrease face value of the policy and obtain this coverage through a changeable mix, ranging from term insurance only to a combination of term and permanent insurance to all permanent insurance. The deciding factors are what you can afford to pay in premiums in any given year plus what amount of protection you need. Computer assistance aids in the calculations.

For people with highly variable annual incomes and selected others, this policy can be beneficial in order to allow them to maintain insurance coverage to meet their needs despite fluctuations. But by so doing, the policyholder acknowledges a preference for permanent insurance and its forced savings feature—with one exception. Term insurance buyers may find a greater variety of riders or policy additions available on adjustable life policies than traditional term policies, if they are willing to pay a little extra for these choices.

It should be noted, however, that research indicates the rate of return on the savings portion of a life insurance policy does not justify the expenses. According to FTC chairman Michael Pertschuk, the average yield on this savings feature is zero or less if the policy is cancelled within ten years of purchase and only average 2 1/4 to 3 1/2 percent for policies held twenty years.[7] Newer policies may offer a better return, but only comparison shopping will help you find them.

Therefore, permanent life insurance is a more costly form of protection than term insurance because of the limited return on the investment or savings portion of the policy. However, limited return is better than no return. So the forced savings feature of this insurance may be the only way some people can discipline themselves to save at all. In addition, the rates of interest charged on life insurance loans are lower than most other sources since you are actually borrowing your own money (as in the case of passbook loans). In fact, some policyholders routinely borrow all of their cash value in order to invest these sums at higher rates of return than the insurance company is producing.

Endowment Insurance.   This type of policy is basically a forced savings program with insurance benefits during the life of the policy. It is sometimes called an "insured saving plan." In fact, the savings portion of this policy is so great that the face value of the policy is paid whether the insured lives or dies. If death occurs within the endowment period, or while the policy is in effect, the proceeds will go to the beneficiary; if not, the face amount is paid to the policyholder at the end of the endowment period (maturity). However, when the policy matures, all insurance protection is cancelled. In fact, the insurance included in this policy is decreasing term equal to the difference between savings accumulated in the policy and its face value. As a general rule, the faster the cash value increases, the faster the insurance portion decreases and the more the policy will cost.

People who need a forced savings program are prime candidates for endowment policies. They are commonly used as college education funds or retirement income funds. However, because the rate of return paid on the savings portion is so low, a shrewd investor can produce a greater return by purchasing a decreasing term insurance policy alone and investing the difference somewhere else—even in an automatic payroll deduction program or a comparable forced savings mechanism.

Individual versus Group Policies.   Group life insurance policies are the least expensive form of life insurance. Therefore, it is always wise to seek out all group policies for which you are eligible and buy them up to the maximum levels available before you purchase any individual policies. Total premium dollars paid will be lower for this term insurance protection.

In order to do this you must maintain membership in the groups offering this benefit and pay premiums promptly. Since many group policies limit protection available to $25,000 or $50,000 per policyholder, some peo-

PURCHASING
OPTIONS

ple will need to carry several policies—and remember to keep them all current. The policyholder will also have to be very careful to list all of these policies and inform beneficiaries or the executor of his or her estate of their whereabouts so all of the proceeds can be properly claimed in the event of the death of the insured.

Participating versus Nonparticipating Policies. The rates set for life insurance are determined by actuarial tables on mortality or the statistical probability that a certain number of policyholders will die during the year for which premiums are paid. Much of the data used in this analysis is from the insurance industry's actual experience in earlier years. While this mathematical guessing game is usually a close approximation of reality, accurate figures cannot be tabulated until that premium year has ended.

In an attempt to work toward a more equitable premium rate based on these facts, some insurance companies pay dividends, or return some money, to their policyholders of "participating life insurance" to reflect the difference between premiums charged and actual experience. The original premium rate is set at a rate that will provide some margin over the anticipated cost of insurance protection. So while the initial annual outlay for insurance is higher than for "nonparticipating policies" (those that do not pay dividends), the net cost may be lower. Over the past twenty years, participating policies have usually been a better buy.[8] Moreover, no income taxes are levied on these dividends since they are considered an overpayment of premium rather than return on an investment.

Usually mutual life insurance companies only sell participating policies. Stock insurance companies sell nonparticipating policies primarily, although a few issue participating as well.

Policy Options. Within the framework of each insurance policy are usually one or more choices for the policyholder to make in relation to lifestyle preferences. These policy options seldom add to the cost of premiums. Any type of insurance policy can offer the beneficiary "settlement options" or choices in how benefits will be paid.

Riders. These are amendments to the insurance policy. Since they add to the basic policy provisions, they cost extra. Some are well worth the added cost. Others are not.

"Double or triple indemnity" riders pay the beneficiary two or three times the face value of the policy if the insured dies due to accidental causes. Since the surviving dependents' financial needs are the same despite the cause of the insured's death, this rider is not a wise investment.

"Guaranteed insurability" riders promise that the insured can purchase additional permanent insurance coverage at specified times during her or his life without medical exam. That means at three-year intervals or significant lifetime events (like marriage or the birth of a child) the insured can buy more insurance at a rate based on her or his state of health at the time the original policy was obtained—despite any subsequent health problems that would otherwise raise rates or deny coverage.

"Guaranteed renewable" coverage is a similar rider applied to term policies. It promises that the insured will definitely be able to buy successive term insurance policies, despite health conditions. However, the rate will go up based on mortality tables reflecting age and health changes.

"Waiver of premium" riders provide that the insurance company will keep an existing insurance policy in force without further payment of premiums by the policyholder. This is generally used only in cases where the policyholder becomes totally or permanently disabled. In other words, the insurance company will pay premiums during a policyholder's disability period. However, the definition of disability used for determining eligibility varies by company. This rider is usually cheaper than carrying extra disability coverage to pay life insurance premiums in the event of the policyholder's total disability.

"Convertability" is another term insurance rider. It allows the policyholder to transfer coverage from term to permanent insurance without a medical exam. Most companies allow conversion up to age fifty-five or sixty, even though term coverage can often be carried to age sixty-five or seventy. Premium rates are calculated at the time the age conversion is requested.

SPECIAL POLICIES

Insurance companies have developed a host of special policy plans to entice the buying public. Most have been developed to build on certain emotional needs of the prospective customers.

Home Service Insurance.   This is the most offensive and expensive special policy. It is essentially burial insurance, with the face value of policies ranging from about $1,000 to $3,000. The most unique feature of the policy is that it is sold door-to-door with premiums paid weekly or monthly and collected by the door-to-door salesperson. "Industrial insurance" was its original form with the smallest policies (up to $1,000 in face value) paid in weekly installments. "Monthly debit ordinary" carries a face value of $3,000 or so with premiums collected monthly. These are both forms of permanent insurance and can be purchased without a medical exam. The problems they generate are high cost with low return. Since most of these policies are sold to low income families, they do little to provide adequate coverage for their needs. Persuasive salespeople and frequent collection of small premiums makes these home service policies targeted to the people that can least afford them.

"Savings Bank Life Insurance."   This insurance is a good buy for all purchasers of this low-cost term and permanent insurance if they know what they need. Sold exclusively by mutual savings banks in Connecticut, Massachusetts, and New York, it is available only to residents of these states or persons who work there regularly. Each state sets its own limit to the maximum insurance an individual can purchase from one institution. The policies are generally all participating insurance.

"Family Policies."   These are packages of life insurance protection to cover all family members under one policy. Coverage will usually include permanent insurance (usually whole life) at a set face value for the father, with temporary insurance in smaller amounts for the mother and all children. The wife's policy might mature when her husband reaches age sixty; the children's policies when they become eighteen or twenty-one. These maturity dates are selected to coincide with the age at which children become financially independent and parents no longer have child care responsibilities.

This type of policy can effectively meet the needs of some young families who want this mix of protection. It is only suitable insurance if the coverage on the father as major breadwinner is truly adequate to care for surviving dependents and if burial expense policies are needed on other family members due to a lack of savings to offset this possible emergency. Dual income families need adequate protection on both breadwinners, so a modified family plan would be needed.

"One-Parent Family Plans" also provide permanent insurance on the parent and term insurance on the children. In some cases, dual income families need to buy this coverage plus a separate permanent policy on one parent in order to provide both spouses with permanent insurance and include term insurance for the children.

It should, however, be remembered that life insurance is needed to protect the loss of income resulting from the death of a breadwinner. That has to take priority in wise planning before insuring the lives of dependents. Funeral bills can eventually be paid if a surviving breadwinner continues to earn. Surviving dependents can not often provide for their own financial needs upon death of a breadwinner. Insuring children and dependent spouses has to remain secondary to insuring the breadwinner!

SWITCHING POLICIES

After studying the principles of better buymanship, some people may decide to cancel one policy and buy a more economical one. With most forms of insurance this is a wise move, provided the policyholder maintains the original policy until the new coverage is protected by successful completion of the new company's medical exam or waiting period, etc. However, with life insurance policies, this type of switching may not always be advantageous since premiums rise with age. This is especially true among permanent insurance policies that carry high first-year sales commissions and no cash value for three years or so. Careful scrutiny is essential to avoid financial losses. However, if you are willing to dig up the necessary facts, some experts are confident that swapping policies can pay because inflation has driven dividends up over the years and premiums down,[9] thereby offsetting some age differences and longer term interest payments on cash value accrued.

PROFESSIONAL GUIDELINES

Insurance protection is an essential household need for most American families. The complexity of products on the market plus their diversity of costs make wise insurance decision making a challenge to most purchasers. Professionals in the field of money management must help their clients to better understand the basic principles of insurance without the high pressure sales tactics common to much of this industry.

The first step in helping clients is to assist them in analyzing the adequacy of their existing coverage in relation to their greatest needs. That means reviewing their existing policies to determine their present level of coverage, then comparing them with a calculation of needs as defined in this chapter. When significant voids in coverage appear as a result of this analysis, general recommendations should be made about the amount and/or type of additional coverage to buy. Referral can also be made to competent local insurance agents to help clients locate appropriate policies within their income guidelines.

Some clients will be "insurance poor." They will need guidance in determining how to reduce their insurance coverage by trimming the extras and concentrating on priorities. Other clients will be too poor to afford private insurance. These people need to identify and use all government services for which they are eligible, including Medicaid, Medicare, and welfare services. Ignorance of these programs or the application process for them can sometimes make a considerable difference in the quality of life. While it may be difficult for all money management professionals to stay continuously up-to-date on program changes, it is imperative that they maintain good referral relationships with capable government employees working as service providers. Follow-up is essential to be sure the clients have been appropriately matched to needed services, just as feedback from clients about program assistance is vital to beneficial future agency referrals.

After all, insurance benefits can make the difference in a relatively comfortable adjustment versus a debt-ridden adjustment to catastrophe. Therefore, it is essential for money management professionals to develop their insurance expertise so to at least be able to make *appropriate* referrals as needed. While that is no small task, it is an essential career goal in this field.

ENDNOTES

1. Howard S. Shapiro, *How to Keep Them Honest* (Emmaus, Penn.: Rodale Press, 1974), pp. 11–12.
2. Despite the fact that this type of property damage liability insurance covers most types of roadworthy motor vehicles, it is commonly referred to as auto insurance.
3. Casualty and theft losses over $100 are deductible on federal and some state income tax returns. The out-of-pocket losses incurred are actually reduced by an amount equal to your tax bracket, if you itemize.
4. "Filling the Gaps in Medicare: Health Insurance for Older People," *Consumer Reports* (January 1976): 27.
5. Eugene Schiller, "Medicare: Promise vs. Practice." Unpublished paper, University of Connecticut, 1977, p. 4.
6. Richard Guarino and Richard Turbo, *The Great American Insurance Hoax* (Los Angeles: Nash, 1974), p. 161.
7. Joseph S. Coyle, "How to Save $7000 (Or a Lot More) on Your Life Insurance," *Money* (July 1978): 82.
8. "What's Happening to Life Insurance Dividends?" *Consumer Reports* (November 1976): 662.
9. Coyle, "How to Save $7000," p. 75.

NINE

Cash Substitutes and Storage Facilities

"Some people certainly do watch their pennies," mumbled Jessica as she walked away from #76 Congress Street. The Gerards who lived there used three different banking institutions to take advantage of the most economical services of each. They had a free checking account at Silver City Bank and Trust Co., which had a branch located en route to Ben's job. It was convenient and inexpensive so they could write many checks to aid their household recordkeeping without concern for the cost of this service. They didn't like extra money to lay idle in this account since it paid no interest, so they opened a NOW account at a savings and loan association about thirty miles from home. This account held the money set aside to meet annual expenses plus a small emergency fund. While they often had to pay postage to mail in monthly deposits, the price was well worthwhile considering the interest paid and the ease of withdrawal when the money was needed. Savings accounts were maintained in still a third institution—the credit union at Ben's place of employment. Interest rates paid were one-fourth percentage point higher than local banks, and payroll deduction certainly made saving easier!

While the Gerards' attitude toward careful selection of banking services was most practical, it was quite a contrast from Jessie's previous interview. Daniel Hansen and his wife used one bank only. It was the largest commercial bank in the area with branches everywhere and all kinds of new services. They had a debit card on their checking account, an ID card for instant check cashing, direct deposit of Dan's payroll check, and telephone transfer from one account to another. The bank's computer would even pay some of the Hansen's routine bills when authorized to do so. What could possibly be more convenient? After all, time is worth money, too, in our fast-paced society. And it was certainly important to establish a good working relationship with a financial institution to assist you in successful borrowing when these services of the institution are also needed.

Both sets of arguments were rational to Jessica. Coming from people with similar incomes, it was difficult to believe that one was right and the other completely wrong. There must be some other elements of decision making that were not yet obvious. There had to be a logical explanation. A closer look at these choices would probably provide the missing information.

TYPES OF BANKING INSTITUTIONS

COMMERCIAL BANKS

The widest variety of specialized services is offered by commercial banks. Since they try to meet the needs of business, industry, and individual consumers, these banks stress "full-service banking" to meet all needs under one roof. Some of these services may include: (1) checking accounts; (2) NOW accounts (interest-bearing checking accounts); (3) savings accounts and certificates of deposit; (4) certified, cashier, and traveler's checks; (5) safe deposit boxes; (6) personal and business loans; (7) home mortgages; (8) estate planning and trust management; (9) credit cards; and (10) electronic funds transfer systems.

Commercial banks are owned by stockholders and operated for profit in much the same manner as any other business corporation. Stockholders buy shares in the bank corporation and receive a portion of the profits as "dividends" on their stock. The people who own stock in a commercial bank do not necessarily have any money on deposit in the bank.

SAVINGS BANKS

These nonprofit thrift institutions exist in only eighteen states. They are owned by their depositors on a mutual basis and are therefore often referred to as "mutual savings banks." Although services have grown to be quite diverse in these institutions, they were first established to promote home mortgages, a task which commercial banks did not like to undertake. Presently services may include: (1) savings accounts and certificates of deposit, (2) home mortgages, (3) checking and NOW accounts (in some states), (4) low-cost life insurance policies (where state laws permit), (5) passbook and some personal loans, (6) traveler's checks, and (7) safe deposit boxes.

Because of their priority to home mortgage lending, government regulators have allowed savings banks to pay a slightly higher rate of interest to depositors than commercial banks. That is why some depositors, like the Gerards, may choose to use the services of several financial institutions in order to maximize the benefits received.

Located from coast to coast, savings and loan associations provide very similar services to the savings banks, with an equal or greater priority given to home mortgage lending and home improvement loans.

SAVINGS AND LOAN ASSOCIATIONS

Deposits in savings and loan associations are represented by shares of ownership in the organization. The depositor is referred to as a "shareholder" and the earnings on deposits are called "dividends," rather than interest. As in the case of the mutual savings banks, dividend rates are generally higher than interest rates on commercial bank savings accounts for the same reason.

Credit unions are essentially banking "cooperatives" in which members pool their savings in order to make loans to each other. Membership in a credit union is restricted to those people who share a specified common bond; for example, employees working for the same employer, or members of a union, church, or fraternal organization. Loans are made only to members and are often limited by law to relatively short terms and specific maximum amounts. Costs of borrowing money are ordinarily lower than at commercial banks, and dividends paid on savings are frequently higher than those available at other types of thrift institutions. Depositors own a credit union by purchasing shares of its operation. Usually, one share is equal to every $5 on deposit with the credit union. Accordingly, shareholders are paid annual dividends rather than interest on their dollars deposited.

CREDIT UNIONS

In recent years, federal and state regulatory agencies have allowed credit unions to expand available services to include: (1) long term mortgages, (2) certificates of deposit, (3) credit cards, and (4) share draft accounts (or interest-bearing checking accounts).

While this potential to expand services makes credit unions more competitive with other financial institutions, it may also raise their costs of operation as they draw more customers. In turn, that may put the credit unions at a disadvantage if it means raising lending rates and reducing saver benefits to meet higher costs. Even the uniqueness of payroll deductions for savings or loan repayment is presently beginning to be met competitively by those financial institutions that offer direct deposit on payroll checks coupled with automatic bill paying, etc.

SAFETY PRECAUTIONS

CHARTERS

Banks and savings institutions, including credit unions, are chartered or licensed to do business by either the state or federal government, depending on the criteria they choose to meet. All states permit chartering of commercial banks, savings and loan associations, and credit unions. Only select states on the East Coast will charter mutual savings banks.

From the depositor's perspective, it matters very little whether the bank's charter originates from the state or federal government. However, unless otherwise limited by state law, it is possible for state-chartered banks to pay higher rates of interest to depositors than allowed under federal regulations. Few financial institutions use this privilege, though.

OTHER
GOVERNMENT
SUPERVISION

The level of government that charters each financial institution also supervises and regulates that institution's methods of doing business in many aspects. Restrictions are placed on the percentage of deposited funds that can be loaned at any one time, the type of investments made by the institution, the type of savings and checking accounts available to customers, and the rate of interest returned to depositors with various types of accounts.

The Federal Reserve Board is the primary supervisor for federally-chartered commercial banks. The Federal Home Loan Bank Board takes essentially the same role with federally-chartered savings and loan associations. Mutual savings banks and other state-chartered institutions are supervised by their own state banking department. Credit unions are also regulated under state and federal law, depending on their charters. However, aside from reserve requirements, or cash on hand to meet depositor needs, and an annual audit, credit unions are less restricted than other financial institutions on their investment policies, rates of interest paid to savers, etc.

A host of other federal agencies also join these primary supervisors in determining institution compliance with the multitude of consumer protection laws, particularly in regard to credit granting. At the state level, the same type of team effort in regulation may occur, or all banking functions may be handled by the same department, depending on the structure of government in that state. Each state has the right to monitor their own financial institutions in the manner in which they choose. To simplify complaint handling, it is generally acceptable to contact the nearest regional Federal Reserve Bank about problems with a federally-chartered institution, and the state banking department about problems with a state-chartered institution.

DEPOSIT
INSURANCE

Participation in the federal deposit insurance program is mandatory for federally-chartered institutions. It has been made available to these and other financial institutions in an effort to provide peace of mind to depositors. The specific purpose of the program is to protect depositors against any loss of their savings in the event of bank failure. While some banks carry private insurance for depositors against this same risk, this is not generally considered as reliable as the government programs.

The federal government offers three insurance programs to the financial institutions which it charters. The Federal Deposit Insurance Corporation (FDIC) offers $100,000 of insurance protection per depositor in member commercial and savings banks. The Federal Savings and Loan Insurance Corporation (FSLIC) offers the same protection to depositors in member savings and loan associations, as does the National Credit Union Administration (NCUA) for member credit unions. Essentially these insurance programs all boil down to a promise by the U.S. Treasury to pay to all depositors at federally-insured institutions. In fact, the program is considered so secure that the federal government frequently brags that "no insured depositors have suffered losses since governmental insurance programs became effective."

State-chartered institutions may participate in comparable insurance programs backed by the state treasury. These are generally recognized with the same respect given to their federal counterparts, although their ability to adequately protect depositors can only be verified through each state banking department. Some state-insured programs offer higher limits of protection per depositor than their federally-chartered counterparts.

The deposit insurance programs that require the most thorough investigation are those made through private insurance companies. This is simply because these insurance programs can be as unique or complex as they choose since the insurance is not required. When several privately-insured savings and loan associations in Maryland failed in the early 1960s, some of the depositors sent claims to the private insurer which turned out to be a "poorly funded one-room operation in Tangier."[1]

The type of financial institution to completely avoid making deposits with is the one that carries no insurance at all. After all, there is no incentive to risk losing your deposits in this manner. The uninsured institutions do not offer higher interest payment than their insured competitors.

There are ways in which depositors in federally-insured institutions can reduce their losses even when more than $100,000 is deposited in one account. If the institution where these deposits are held does fail, the government will intervene to equitably distribute any assets among uninsured depositors. Although the process may take up to seven years, as compared to one to three weeks for reimbursement on federally-insured accounts, the results may still be worth the wait.

The simpler way to handle this dilemma is by avoiding it altogether. Insurance regulations are such that a person may have an account with

$100,000 in his or her own name, plus another account held in joint ownership with another person for $100,000 in the same bank, and both would be fully insured. Because the joint account is considered to be owned equally by both parties, its legal owner is different from that on the first account. However, both checking and savings accounts held in the same name are included in the $100,000 limit per depositor.

A couple could maintain accounts of up to $400,000 in one bank and be fully insured. This amount would be equally divided so that one account was in each partner's name alone, and one held jointly. Additional options are also available through trust accounts which can bring the insured limit on deposits for a family of four up to $1,400,000 per institution.

If a depositor has money to be held by a financial institution above these limits, he or she must use two or more different savings institutions in order to be assured of full insurance protection.

SERVICES AVAILABLE

The types of services offered by the financial institutions previously discussed are multiple and diverse. Only savings plans and home-related loans are available at all four types of institutions. Even then, the rates of interest differ among them. It's no wonder this smorgasbord of choices convinced the Hansens to save time rather than money by using only one institution. This type of simplification of alternatives is sometimes essential for peace of mind, but it is not the most economical. Some general guidelines on types of services and their availability may, however, help reduce the choices among banking centers to maximize their utility and investment return without requiring an exorbitant time commitment for the selections.

When someone deposits money in a bank, etc., she or he agrees to let that financial institution lend the money to qualified borrowers until the depositor chooses to withdraw it. In exchange, the financial institution promises safekeeping for all sums on deposit and generally some monetary reward for use of the money.

The value of the monetary reward varies with the liquidity of the funds on deposit—or the speed with which they can be turned into cash and withdrawn from the institution. The more liquid the deposit, the lower the monetary reward (the interest paid by the financial institution for use of the money). The more easily deposits can be withdrawn, the less time the institution has to use the deposits for lending. In reverse, these same institutions will pay much higher rates of interest on funds that are guaranteed to remain on deposit for several years because the institution's opportunities to use these sums for lending are greatly increased.

An analysis of the liquidity and function of various banking services will show the common tradeoffs between depositors and financial institutions to enhance their respective needs. Let's take a look at the options presently available.

The most liquid account available is a checking account, also referred to in bank terminology as a "demand deposit." Funds on deposit with that financial institution may be withdrawn immediately (or on demand) by writing a check. These accounts were developed to provide a safe, convenient method of payment that can also serve as an accurate recordkeeping device for basic budgeting, income tax deductions, etc. Because of the recordkeeping services rendered on this account and the magnitude of transactions that may be involved, as well as the liquidity of the account, many banks charge a fee for checking account services rather than paying a return on this investment. Therefore, you will probably want to shop around to find the best and cheapest checking account to meet your needs.

CHECKING
ACCOUNTS

How do you shop for a checking account? First of all, you should be aware that most banks offer at least two kinds of checking accounts. The first, a special or activity checking account, charges a per check fee for processing plus a monthly maintenance charge on the account (even if you don't write any checks that month). Each check may cost 10¢ to 15¢ plus 25¢ to 75¢ monthly service charge. That means if you write thirty checks per month, at 10¢ a check plus a 50¢-monthly service charge, you would be spending $3.50 per month for the privilege of using that checking account. Multiply $3.50 by 12 to get an annual cost for this service to simplify comparison shopping.

The basic alternative account works quite differently. It levies no monthly or per check charges, provided you maintain a mutually agreeable monthly minimum balance in your account at all times (money that you promise not to use without penalty). Generally, this minimum runs from $100 to $500. If your balance ever drops below that minimum balance, you agree to pay a penalty service charge, often as high as several dollars, each time this occurs.

Even if you faithfully maintain this minimum balance, your checking account is not free. To determine its real cost, you must consider the earnings that the $100 to $500 minimum balance would provide for you if it were placed in a savings account. If the savings account earned 5 percent per year, you would be paying $5 per year per $100 of minimum balance for the use of the checking account—unless the bank you choose to do business with allows you to maintain the minimum balance in either a checking or savings account in their institution. This practice is growing in popularity among many highly competitive banks.

The deciding factors in comparing checking account costs are the number of checks written each month and the unused balance regularly maintained in the account. The more work demanded of the institution in processing checks, the higher the cost of the account to the depositor. An exception occurs when the size of the deposit left idle in the checking account is large enough for the banking institution to trade "free" checking services for "free" use of the idle deposits for lending.

Some financial institutions offer free checking accounts as a customer service to draw other business to that institution. To be really free, the checking accounts must *not* require any monthly maintenance fees, per check charges, or a minimum balance. Sometimes these are restricted to special groups like senior citizens, students, or persons doing specific other business with that institution such as credit card holders.

However, even free checking accounts charge a penalty if you *overdraw* your account, or write checks for more money than you have in the account. They also charge a fee if you want your address stamped on your checks or if you choose checks with special designs, fancy checkbook covers, etc. These services are widely available, but they all cost money. So if you expect to use them, they should be included in your cost comparison figures.

Although it further complicates decision making about checking accounts, it is also advisable to compare costs of supplemental checking account services, including overdrafts, stop-payment orders, and banking by mail. Mathematical calculations alone sometimes cause the most careful people to overdraw their checking accounts or write checks for more money than the account contains. Whether this was done intentionally or not, when an overdraft occurs the financial institution must return the check for replacement with cash or a check adequately backed by funds in the checking account. Besides sometimes causing some embarrassment to the account holder, an overdraft increases bank handling costs which are then in turn passed on to the account holder. These costs and the processing of overdrafts may vary among institutions. Some institutions also apply a service charge to your account when someone else's check is refused for insufficient funds upon deposit in your account. Others charge a fee just to notify you of an overdraft before "bouncing" your check. Therefore, it is wise to discuss the costs and procedures of handling overdrafts with each institution as you complete comparison shopping for a checking account.

To reduce the embarrassment of overdrafts and the human element in processing them, many banks offer creditworthy customers special overdraft privileges on their checking accounts. These privileges automatically process a personal loan to cover the overdraft so there is no need to return the check, etc. Any customer interested in this service must request it and complete an appropriate credit application to determine eligibility. While there is generally no charge for obtaining this privilege, the account holder must pay interest on the amount borrowed from the day the loan was made until it is paid off. The specifics of this arrangement and the rate of interest (usually 12 to 18 percent per annum) are determined by the institution and explained in the credit contract covering this special lending process.

Stop-payment orders may also carry a supplemental checking account charge. For this service, the account holder asks the financial institution to refuse payment or invalidate a particular check drawn on that account often because it was lost, stolen, or inaccurate in some way. Again, the extra cost is a result of extra processing time.

In selecting diverse institutions among which to compare checking account costs, the wise shopper should choose institutions of various sizes and types. Several studies of checking account costs have shown that smaller institutions very often charge less for checking accounts than the larger, more well-known financial institutions in the same community. This is because economies of scale do not apply to banking services beyond a certain size.[2] However, larger banks often have more checking account customers because of their greater publicity, convenient locations, greater choice of services, etc.

Until a few years ago, the only financial institution allowed to offer demand deposit accounts were commercial banks. That meant anyone wishing to earn maximum interest on savings was forced to use two financial institutions if she or he also wanted checking account privileges. This was true because savings and loans and mutual savings banks and credit unions can legally pay a higher rate of interest on savings than commercial banks. Those persons preferring the convenience of one-stop banking could maintain checking and savings accounts at a commercial bank only if they were willing to accept a rate of return on their savings that was at least 1/4 percent below the legal maximum payable on savings accounts at savings institutions.

INTEREST-BEARING CHECKING ACCOUNTS

An ever-growing number of states have recently passed legislation to change this by allowing their thrift institutions to offer checking accounts just like the commercial banks do. That has satisfied many customers who now have a choice of institutions for one-stop checking and savings. The variety and cost of checking accounts at these thrift institutions is comparable to those offered by commercial banks in the same region.

However, with the clamor for change in banking regulations, some people began to wonder why checking accounts could not pay interest on the funds left on deposit or, in reverse, why savings accounts could not have checks drawn against them for easy withdrawal of funds. When no satisfactory response could be made for denying this request, a new type of demand deposit was introduced. Called a "Negotiable Order of Withdrawal," or "NOW" account, these demand deposit accounts function as checking accounts that pay interest on the funds remaining on deposit. The idea was born at the Consumer Savings Bank of Worcester, Massachusetts. After court battles in Massachusetts and the U.S. Congress, NOW accounts are now legal in all six New England states and New York in all four types of financial institutions. (They are called "share draft" accounts in credit unions.) Effective January 1, 1981, legislation will expand this service nationwide via a permanent change in banking law.

While the idea of NOW accounts is a very sound one, this type of demand deposit account is not always the most economical. The costs of this service must be compared with checking accounts to find the lowest cost demand deposit to meet individual needs. While some NOW accounts are free of minimum balance requirements, service charges, etc., this is rare. In addition, the interest paid on NOW account deposits may not be at the legal maximum for savings at the institution. Therefore, it is important to carefully compare costs between checking and NOW accounts.

Generally, when minimum balance or service charge requirements are levied on a NOW account, they become preferable only for people who:

1. Choose to keep a generous cushion of regularly unused money in their checking account.
2. Make few and perhaps infrequent withdrawals from the account.
3. Want the convenience of one account for checking and savings.
4. Live in an area where checking accounts carry the same costs as NOW accounts without paying interest.

Since most financial institutions lose money by offering free checking and NOW account services, the irony of increased competition for demand deposits may be that consumers will soon pay out in service charges the equivalent of what they earn in interest.[3] If or when that occurs, the purpose of NOW accounts will be defeated to be replaced only by high-cost record-keeping to maintain this status quo.

SPECIALIZED CHECKING SERVICES

Many merchants, etc., will not accept a check drawn against an out-of-state bank. Other times, even local merchants want to be sure there is enough money in your checking account to make certain your check doesn't bounce. Yet because of theft and loss problems, few people are willing to return to paying cash for all of these purchases. Aware of this problem, the financial institutions offer three types of special checks to help resolve the dilemma. They include certified, cashier's, and traveler's checks.

A certified check is drawn against your own checking account and guaranteed by the financial institution that there are sufficient funds in your account to cover payment. But because the institution certifying the check accepts liability for it, they may choose to keep the cancelled check, in which case the account holder would not have a receipt for the transaction. Usually there is no charge for a certified check, although the service is limited to the institution's own depositors.

A cashier's check is purchasable by nondepositors as well as depositors because it is drawn on the bank's own checking account. Often this service is free to depositors, especially when this is used as the method of payment on a withdrawal from a savings account. While a carbon copy of the cashier's check is given to the purchaser, there is no receipt proving that this check has been cashed and cleared.

While both of the previously mentioned types of checks must be written to a particular person or agency for safe transport, traveler's checks are countersigned by the owner to verify use by the proper person. Uncashed checks can be replaced if they are lost or stolen if the proper records are kept on the serial numbers of missing checks. Moreover, there is no time limit on their use. The cost is generally $1 per $100 of checks, although some institutions offer them free to all or some customers.

Bankers refer to savings accounts as "time deposits." In ordinary banking practice, conventional savings account funds can usually be withdrawn without notice. But legally, the bank has the right to require thirty days' notice before honoring a request for withdrawal. Regulations governing withdrawals are printed on the inside of the back cover of the passbook or on the savings account agreement. Read through the regulations carefully to find out what restrictions the bank places on withdrawals and ask how strictly they are generally enforced.

In addition to the conventional savings account, most banks offer special higher-interest-bearing "notice accounts" that require 60, 90, or 120 days' notice before a withdrawal is allowed. As a general rule, the savings institutions adhere very strictly to the required number of days' notice stipulated in the savings account agreement.

Savings certificates, also called "certificates of deposit," are another savings method made available by banks. The depositor agrees to leave his or her money in the bank for a specified period of time in return for a higher interest rate than that offered for regular and notice passbook savings accounts. While banks may require a $500 to $1,000 minimum investment before issuing a savings certificate, this is no longer required by law. The interest rate is guaranteed throughout the term of the certificate—which may range from as short as thirty days to as long as ten years. If you cash in the

SAVINGS ACCOUNTS

savings certificate before the maturity date, you will be penalized three months' interest on CD's issued or renewed after July 1, 1979, and six months' interest on CD's issued earlier. In other words, you must hold the certificate to maturity in order to reap the benefits of the greater rates of interest they offer. Savings certificates may be insured by the federal government in the same fashion as other bank deposits.

How do you know which account to choose? First, you must determine how much money you have to save (in case your first choice account requires a minimum balance), and then you must decide the liquidity you will need. Do you need some of these funds available immediately in case of emergency, or is this account for long-range goals like the property you'd like to buy in ten years? Remember, there are penalties for premature withdrawal on some accounts. And last, but certainly not least, you must compare the interest earned on each type of account to see which gives you the most for your money.

Interest rates are controlled by federal and state laws. These regulations set the maximum amounts that the different types of financial institutions are allowed to pay on savings deposits. In general, savings banks, savings and loan associations, and credit unions are permitted to pay higher interest or dividends than commercial banks. Similar kinds of banks located in different parts of the country may, at times, be allowed to pay higher rates than those located in other areas.

It should be noted that federal regulations permit savings institutions to pay up to a maximum rate of interest but do not *compel* them to do so. In other words, banks cannot pay more than the legal interest limit, but the regulations do not prevent them from paying less than the maximum. Therefore, not all banks of the same type automatically pay the same interest on savings accounts.

The rate of interest paid on savings may be calculated by two methods. The *nominal rate,* or simplest form, reflects the rate paid, without consideration for how that rate is calculated by the individual institution. The *effective annual yield* includes: (1) the interest paid, (2) how frequently it is compounded (or computed on previous interest earned), (3) the effective date of deposit, and (4) the amount of deposits on which the interest will be paid. Therefore, the latter figure is far more comprehensive for comparison shopping.

"Compounding" also affects the manner in which your savings grow. Compounding is a system of paying interest on money that has previously been paid as interest. For example, if you deposited $100 in a bank at 5 percent annual interest, at the end of one year the passbook balance is $105—your original deposit of $100 plus $5 earned as interest. Let us assume that you make no further deposits to the account during the next year.

At the end of that year, interest is calculated on the total $105 and results in a new balance of $110.25. Interest has been paid on interest which you have previously earned. This process speeds the rate at which your money accumulates.

Your savings fund will grow even faster if interest is compounded more frequently than once a year. Thus, if two banks provide the same interest rate, but differing frequencies of compounding on savings, it pays to place your savings in the bank that compounds interest more often. Today that usually means an institution that compounds daily or continuously.

The third factor that influences the rate at which savings accumulate is the "effective date of deposit." Financial institutions have varying policies concerning the date on which deposits begin to be eligible for interest payments. Some figure interest for the month only on money that has been deposited to your account by the first of the month. Some calculate monthly interest only on deposits received before the tenth day of the month. And some pay interest from the day of deposit to the day of withdrawal.

The "day of deposit to day of withdrawal" system provides the largest base upon which interest can be calculated. You do not have to meet any bank deadline in order to have your money bear interest for thirty-five days, and there is no penalty for making the deposit after a specified day.

Last, you should be aware that the financial institution may choose to compute your interest at the beginning or end of the interest period or on any other basis they choose. For example, some institutions compute interest based on the "highest continuous balance," or the largest amount that remained in your account for the full period, which could be a full year if interest is paid annually. This means if you made monthly deposits of $50 into the account, you would have saved $600 in the first year but only earned interest on the first $50!

Other institutions are more generous and pay interest on a formula called LIFO—"last in, first out." Your interest is computed on the balance remaining in the account on the date interest is computed. Any withdrawals made against the account are counted against the dollars last added to that account—or those drawing the least interest. Therefore, very little interest is deducted.

Since this determination in regard to withdrawals is also at the institution's option, your interest may be computed on the balance remaining in the account at the end of that period under a formula called FIFO—"first in, first out." Under this method, your withdrawals are assumed to be taken against the funds first deposited in your account, so you stand to lose more earnings, of course!

How do you ever compare all these factors? Since there is presently no Truth in Savings disclosure law available to help, you will have to learn to ask questions about these four factors that influence savings accounts and then draw your own conclusions. Effective annual yield rates will be helpful, but the factors incorporated in this computation are left to the discretion of the individual banks.

Does it ever cost money to maintain a savings account? Yes, it can. This is a possibility if you choose to prematurely withdraw from a Certificate of Deposit account as described earlier, or if your bank chooses to impose a fee. It may do so for: (1) a minimum balance before interest is paid, (2) closing the account within one to twelve months after it's opened, (3) "excess" withdrawals during an interest period, or (4) service charges and the discontinuance of interest payments on inactive accounts that have not been touched from five to 15 years. So, be sure to inquire if your bank charges any or all of these fees when completing your comparison shopping.

SPECIAL PURPOSE THRIFT ACCOUNTS

Special thrift or savings accounts are also available at most financial institutions to meet individual needs. These encourage savings by requiring regular weekly payments into the account. Reminders in the form of coupons are provided to help foster completion of this program. They resemble the coupon books used for loan repayments. While these accounts now pay interest to the depositor, it is a rate that is generally lower than the institution's regular savings accounts. These special accounts are most commonly used as Christmas or vacation clubs.

Employer-based credit unions offer a similar program to all interested members via payroll deduction. Therefore, no coupon books are needed to remind the account holder to save regularly. At the credit union, the rate of interest paid on savings accumulated in this manner is equal to any other savings plan at that institution.

U.S. SAVINGS BONDS

Many financial institutions also sell certain U.S. government bonds, if that is your preferred method of savings. Savings bonds are certificates evidencing a loan to the federal government. The bond symbolizes money on deposit with the government in much the same manner as the savings certificate is evidence of money deposited in a bank. Many different types of U.S. savings bonds can be purchased through various types of financial institutions. (See Chapter 10 for details.)

SAFE DEPOSIT BOXES

Safe deposit boxes are another banking service. These are essentially "mini-safes" rented to interested parties. They are located within a bank vault and are offered for use to protect valuable papers, etc., from fire and theft in your home or office. They come in various sizes, may be rented individually or jointly, and require proof of identification to gain entrance. However, some things should *not* be stored here because of legal restrictions. Check the box lease for details, including insurance protection provided to the boxholder by the institution.

The growing computerization of banking services has begun to have impact on some of the traditional consumer dealings with financial institutions, particularly in relation to the deposit and withdrawal of funds. As explained in Chapter 2, it is now often possible to deposit or withdraw funds or borrow certain amounts of money from a financial institution twenty-four hours a day. This has been made possible by the introduction of: (1) automated teller machines located at banks or in shopping centers, and (2) computerization responsive to direction from the varying signals given by touch-tone telephones.

In addition, debit cards have been implemented that are intended to replace checks and ordinary credit cards. The debit cards are used in stores linked by computer to the issuing bank. When a purchase is made with the debit card, the computer at the store validates the card to be sure there is sufficient money in the checking account to cover the purchase. Later the purchase is deducted directly from the checking account balance. It is intended that future developments will streamline this procedure to make instantaneous electronic transfer of the purchase price from the buyer's account to the seller's.

Other institutions offer telephone banking where no plastic card is needed. Transfers from one account to another and bill paying to participating merchants, etc., can be accomplished by dialing the correct numbers on a touch-tone phone. Dial-phone users may participate in this service, too, via a teller's "translation" of their directions to the bank's computer. However, unlike debit card users, pay-by-phone customers do not get receipts. They do receive a monthly statement and a payment register book to keep near the telephone.

Although these services are intended to make banking more convenient, EFTS programs are not problem free. Consumer protections available to credit card users now apply to debit cardholders with some less benefits. No stop-payment orders can be written on a debit card purchase because the direct electronic transfer of funds make EFTS work like a cash transaction. Equally significant is the loss of "float" through EFTS.

Normally it takes several days for a check to clear or several weeks for a credit card purchase to be due on your account. This time lag between the actual purchase and the deduction of that sum from your account is called *float*. With credit card purchases, it amounts to an extended grace period of thirty to sixty days or so that are interest free. On checking accounts, the time period is less, but the float can be equally valuable in coordinating deposits and withdrawals to meet bill payment deadlines, etc.

RETIREMENT PROGRAMS

Savings accounts and certificates of deposit are IRS-approved investments for Individual Retirement Accounts (IRA) and Keough Plans (explained more fully in Chapter 11). They offer convenience, safety, and no service charges. These retirement accounts pay the same rate of return as other savings accounts—sometimes with added advantages. For example, some institutions allow deposits below the minimum on long-term savings certificates if the total deposited during that year will meet or exceed this minimum.

LIFE INSURANCE

Mutual savings banks may sell low-cost life insurance to all interested persons who live or work in the state where the savings bank is located. A variety of types and amounts of life insurance are available up to a predetermined limit set by state law. Costs are low for these policies because there are no commissions paid. The sale of all policies is made at the bank, either in person or by mail. However, only mutual savings banks in Connecticut, Massachusetts, and New York offer this particular service. Most other financial institutions offer only credit life insurance on outstanding loans.

TRUST AND ESTATE PLANNING

Commercial banks may offer trust and estate planning services to community residents. These are specialized services to help individuals and families organize their financial affairs to protect their heirs (for more details see Chapter 11.) Depending on the nature of the services used, there may be a fee charged by the bank. You do not have to be a depositor to use this service, nor do your investments need to be held in accounts at that institution.

FINANCIAL COUNSELING

Most financial institutions will readily answer customer questions in banking-related aspects of money management, including budgeting, housing cost factors, credit, etc. If and when this advice can mushroom into actual counseling for the customer on improving her or his own money management will depend on the institution and the qualifications of staff. While the average banker trained in business administration may have limited skills in personal financial counseling, a growing number of financial institutions are hiring or training staff to provide this service for customers and/or the general public.

Therefore, anyone seeking these services of a financial institution should first investigate the background and training of the counselor to be sure that her or his experience in personal finance includes the problems for which counseling is being sought. In mortgage financing and/or debt management counseling, it is also important to determine if the counselor puts the client's needs first or the financial institution's.

BANKING BY MAIL

Sometimes the financial institutions offering checking account services at the lowest price are inconveniently located in relation to home and office. Driving thirty miles out of your way each time you need to deposit money into your checking account is seldom worthwhile. Banking by mail may, however, solve this problem if the timing of your financial transactions can accommodate the time lag caused by mailing. In more and more places, this is being facilitated by such services as direct deposit of payroll checks, etc. In addition, many financial institutions offer free postage both ways to entice potential account holders to use their services despite the distance. Postage-free banking can prove most economical, especially for less active accounts like the one that holds the money for annual expenses, etc. It is particularly expedient for checking accounts since only deposits need to be handled by mail.

PROFESSIONAL GUIDELINES

Helping clients to understand and use various banking services economically and efficiently can sometimes be quite a challenge. This is particularly true for low literacy clients who would have difficulty with the written communications involved, or individuals distrusting of institutions or their computers. Therefore, it becomes imperative for helping agency professionals to tactfully ascertain the reasons behind a client's hesitancy to try new things of this nature. The solution then becomes finding a compromise that fits comfortably into the client's lifestyle.

For example, a client needing guidance to live within his or her income may have difficulty keeping a checking account balanced. So that person may function better with several savings accounts earmarked for different purposes. Then in order to spend the bill-paying money on other things, the client would have to make a special trip to the financial institution to make a withdrawal. The extra effort may be enough of a deterrent to eliminate the problem and make budgeting easier. Other clients may need the discipline of paying for virtually everything by check to better observe where their money really is being spent. Under these circumstances a free checking account would prove most economical.

Aware of the advantages and disadvantages of commonly used services, the professional can then aid clients in selecting the most appropriate services to meet their unique needs. This may reduce client frustrations and assist in strengthening his or her coping skills for our technological age and its future developments!

ENDNOTES

1. Paul S. Nader, "When Banks Run Out of Money," *Money* (September 1974): 80.
2. "A Guide to Banking Services," *Consumer Reports* (January 1975): 33.
3. Urban Lehner, "How NOW? Interest Bearing Checking Accounts Gain Support, But Fate in Congress is Uncertain," *The Wall Street Journal,* May 6, 1977, p. 40.

TEN

Putting Your Assets to Work

"It must be nice!" Jessica thought as she left #239 Congress Street. Yes, she was jealous of the accumulated assets Emil Jacoby had invested as a nest egg to cushion his pending retirement. After thirty years of hard work and sacrifices Emil was proud of his accumulated wealth. His mortgage was paid off on his home which was valued at $60,000. He had $30,000 at the local savings and loan in certificates of deposit and $65,000 in various stocks and bonds. Income from the latter two sources alone generated $7,000 annually. That plus pension benefits should allow him and his wife to live comfortably for many long years of happy retirement—before they even have to touch the principal!

Yet at the same time, Jessica was apprehensive for them. At age eighty-nine, Angela Beloin from #245 Congress Street, was living proof that Emil's dream of lifelong financial security could easily burst. She and her late husband had followed a similar lifestyle, saving every extra penny toward their later years. Cautious in their investment decision making, they weathered the Depression Years of the 1930s well and watched their assets grow slowly and steadily during their working years. But twenty-five years of retirement saw mushrooming inflation eat away at their once generous stockpile of funds. Interest earnings on their U.S. savings bonds and bank deposits fell behind the rate of inflation. Stocks were viewed as too risky to protect the principal. Gold and diamonds in Angela's beloved jewelry were her salvation now. Once planned to be their children's legacy, these precious jewels were the only remaining investments she could use to maintain her financial independence. Rapidly rising prices had wiped out everything else! This was something she would never have anticipated during all those years of scrimping and saving. Inflation just wasn't exerting the same economic impact during those times.

So, while Jessica wished she, too, could have Mr. Jacoby's wealth at his age, she would hate to watch it shrink into worthlessness over the years. There had to be another way! But her knowledge of investment decision making was so limited, she didn't know the answer. She only hoped Emil and the others that had worked so hard to accumulate some small wealth would discover the answer. But where do they begin?

The relationships among factors affecting investment decision making have changed significantly in the last decade or two. Economic conditions, plus the government intervention used in an attempt to control these conditions, have had a marked influence on the appreciation or growth of most investments. Inflation seems to be here to stay, outpacing the earnings of most savings accounts and many other investments that assured safety of principal plus a modest return. So the meaning of safety has begun to be defined in relation to the effects of inflation. The world of investments now need to be viewed in a much broader sense. Risks have increased; so have the number and design of investment instruments. In order for Emil Jacoby and his counterparts of any age to truly benefit from their investment returns, they have much to learn and many changes to implement in line with fluctuating economic conditions and related variables.

INVESTMENT READINESS

The attitude that inflation is here to stay has become an increasingly popular philosophy in recent years. A considerable amount of mass media coverage is addressed to this issue, including coping mechanisms to beat inflation—or at least keep abreast of it. Wage increases tied to cost-of-living indexes are a primary vehicle in this defense. Better buymanship is also acclaimed as a real dollar stretcher. One popular author on the subject claims that a $500 annual savings due to careful shopping is equivalent to the interest earnings on $11,364 held in a 5 1/2 percent savings account (for someone in the 20% income tax bracket).[1]

Other experts claim that the best strategy is to borrow to your credit limit, paying back these loans in cheaper dollars as inflation takes its toll. Yet the resulting increase in personal indebtedness among Americans, coupled with our growing government debt, is viewed as worrisome to some economic analysts. The past records of runaway inflation at 30 + percent in other countries around the world adds further stress to the fear that this problem will also occur here. The trend reversal to a rapid and sudden deflation with prices plummeting downward can neither be eliminated or realistically predicted. That leads to confusion and controversy in market place strategies and investment decisions. It has prompted some analysts to promote a doomsday theory of severe economic losses in a forthcoming deflation, with food shortages, chaos in the cities, and virtually worthless paper money.[2] Others have found recent economic trends to temper their despair of monetary conditions and lessen their doomsday view—at least for the next decade or so.[3] Still others feel inflation can be beneficial and that we need merely learn new strategies to live with it amiably and profitably.[4]

Needless, to say, no one has a crystal ball that can accurately and realistically predict the future. The world is too complex and the variables only minimally controllable. Therefore, the logical approach is to develop at least a basic understanding of economics in order to appropriately adapt to changing economic conditions. Then the key to effective coping becomes learning when, why, and how to change your purchasing and investment strategies to maximize the benefits in light of present circumstances. Few of the traditional principles have been negated. Instead, they are merely analyzed in light of inflation's effects as well as your own values and goals. The big difference is a need for more frequent reviews and reassessment to keep pace with change.

BASIC NEEDS

The first principles of investment decision making is that the money used to make more money be the extra funds remaining after your priority needs are met. That means that you should evaluate the spending plan and net worth statement to determine your investment readiness. Are there funds available from your present income that are regularly "left over" after food, clothing, shelter, and other needs are met? If so, are you willing to sacrifice discretionary spending with these extra sums in order to put these funds to work to multiply their value? If the answer is affirmative to both questions, you have reached the first step in investment readiness.

DEBT LOAD

Despite the fact that these extra funds remain after monthly installment obligations are calculated, it is imperative to review your liabilities as the next step. What is the interest rate charged on each of your outstanding loans? How does this rate compare with a realistic return on the sums you plan to invest? If you owe 18 percent per annum on charge account balances of $1,000 and could only get a 10 percent return if the same sum was invested, what is the logical use of that money? Obviously, under these circumstances it would be wiser to pay off the bills before you consider investing (depending on your tax bracket and the use of the zero bracket deduction versus itemizing on your federal income tax return; see Chapter 3 for details).

However, when the value of your property being purchased on credit can be expected to rise at a rate equal to or greater than inflation (or other available investments for which this sum of money could be used), it may be wiser to retain your borrower status—or even increase it. In recent years, homeownership has certainly been a leader in this category. With 0 to 25 percent down payment usually required to make the purchase, homes have returned a 10 to 15 percent appreciation annually in some areas of the country. Since this figure is applied to the selling price of the home rather than the down payment, the dollars invested have actually multiplied many times this percentage. Although the mortgage interest rate charged on this installment obligation may equal or exceed many investment dividend or interest payments, the rising value of the property makes the effective yield significantly higher, if the home is sold under these favorable circumstances.

For example, if you were to purchase a $60,000 home with a $12,000 down payment at a mortgage rate of 10 1/2 percent, you would need a return on your investment greater than the cost of borrowing to come out ahead. If that house was sold in four years for $79,200, the gross profit on the investment would average $4,800 per year or 40 percent of the $1,200 invested, as opposed to 8 percent of the purchase price. Of course, net profit is the only money really earned on the investment. Yet, when all expenses related to the out-of-pocket cost of homeownership are calculated, including purchase and sales costs, profits can still exceed credit costs. Assuming the rental of a comparable dwelling, a conservative net profit figure could still yield a return of approximately 20 percent per annum on the $12,000 invested. So, in favorable market conditions, borrowing to invest in this manner could prove profitable.

Few durable goods appreciate in value like real estate so it is important to adjust your debt load to maximize your return. Cars, recreational vehicles, furniture, etc., all depreciate in value over time unless or until they become "collectibles," the values of which vary with supply and demand. In some cases, it is possible and profitable to borrow money for investment purposes and reap a reasonable reward. The key to success is evaluating the related variables.

PROTECTION FOR DEPENDENTS

One of the primary goals for many investors is to attempt to ease the financial strains of the future, both due to inflation and individual needs and wants. College education, homes, vacation trips, etc., can be expensive. If income set aside for these purposes can be invested to expand the dollars available for these goals, they can be achieved more readily.

Yet, because the future is somewhat unpredictable, before you work exclusively toward making dreams come true, your first priority should be to protect dependents from financial losses due to unanticipated events like the death of a breadwinner. That makes it essential to get all of your insurance programs in order before you invest. Analyze existing insurance policies to be sure they meet priority needs.

When cash value life insurance is part of this protection package, assess its investment value in much the same way as you evaluated debt load. In some cases, the forced savings of cash value insurance can build a nest egg in that policy with which to begin or expand an investment program that can offset the low rate of return inherent in the basic policy. In other cases, this and other types of insurance must be reviewed and revised to maximize their protection benefits and free appropriate sums for investment purposes. (See Chapter 9 for details.)

EMERGENCY FUNDS

The money set aside to meet unexpected demands not provided for in your monthly spending plan is called an "emergency fund." It is money you can get to easily and quickly when needed—to pay for repairs on the water pipe that burst, or travel expenses to care for a sick relative who lives half-way across the country, etc. The specific uses of the fund will vary with individual circumstances. What ever the uses, this money must be immediately available and *liquid,* or easily converted into cash so it can serve its intended purpose.

Not all good investments are liquid, nor do they need to be. However, since the sum of extra funds earmarked for emergencies must be highly liquid, appropriate investment vehicles are somewhat limited. Generally, realistic alternatives include NOW accounts, regular savings accounts (at banks, savings and loan associations, and their credit unions), as well as the relatively new money market funds which will be explained later in this chapter. Checking accounts and home safes are other places to store this cash. But since they offer no investment return, they are generally not recommended when investments of comparable liquidity are available with the addition of some yield on the dollars held.

GOALS

Before appropriate investment instruments can be selected, you must analyze your investment goals carefully. What do you realistically hope to achieve with this investment program? On what schedule do you need to meet these goals? As you will note later in this chapter, timing is a critical component of investment decision making. Sometimes the best yield from an investment will be produced only if the investment is held intact for one year, five years, etc. Can you afford to wait this time period out and still meet your goals? If not, you need to select another investment more appropriate for your own unique time schedule.

In addition, you need to estimate if the stated or projected rate of return will provide the required dollars needed to attain the goal by the scheduled time. If not, do you prefer to select a different investment or change the target date? Again, the choice is highly individualized. The alternatives for decision making can often be clarified by expanding your knowledge of investments, beginning with the variables that differentiate investment instruments.

INVESTMENT VARIABLES

Investments vary in *safety,* or risk of loss, *liquidity,* or ease with which they can be converted into cash, and *yield,* or the rate of return. Cash stored in a safe deposit box would be very safe and liquid, but it would be a low yield investment. Homeownership would be less safe, since the value of the property could decline. It would be less liquid because you have to find a buyer able to exchange cash for the house, but provide a greater yield because of the present appreciation in real estate values.

Obviously, there is a tradeoff to be made in all investments in relation to their safety, liquidity, and yield. To make an informed decision in this regard, you must know these characteristics of various investments and your personal priorities in these areas.

SAFETY VERSUS RISK

Once you have accumulated a sum of money for investment purposes, you have to decide how much, if any, of that sum you are willing to lose in your quest for profits. The bigger the risk, the greater the return—and the greater likelihood of incurring losses if your investment choices don't accurately predict the future. Sheltering your principal, or the original sum to be invested, from losses produces the reverse effects—low risk of loss and low profits from the investment. Investment instruments are availabe to meet either priority. Before deciding the acceptable level of risk, it is important to understand the risks involved. These risks focus on the following variables:

1. The ability of investment managers to conduct business profitably.
2. The rate of inflation, specifically as it is related to investment yield.
3. Changes in investor attitudes as they influence investment values.
4. The impact of economic and monetary policies on investment return.

LIQUIDITY

As a general rule, in order to use your investments to reach specific goals, they have to be liquidated, or converted into cash on short notice. The ease with which this can be done varies with the nature of the investment. Even when dealing with the same institution, liquidity can differ; for example, checking and savings accounts are more liquid than certificates of deposits from the same institution. While you have to agree to absorb a reduction in yield, you can, however, liquidate a CD faster than some parcels of land, debt obligations, art objects, and other investment instruments.

Liquidity is attained in the investment world through marketability and careful selection of transaction dates. Marketability means that a continuing demand exists for your investment so that there are always buyers interested, if the price is right. If you build a one-room house, its liquidity will be relatively low compared to other dwellings because the housing demand is greater for multiple-room houses. They are more marketable. This factor would be particularly important to you if you bought the house as a hedge against inflation and later wanted to use the assets invested to start a business. Timing could be critical on this business purchase. By making it contingent upon the sale of this illiquid one-room house, you stand to lose out if you expect to time the sale of the house and purchase of the business in close proximity. Low liquidity plus a probable mismatch on transaction dates are the causes.

The rate of return on an investment is called the yield. Calculating the actual yield means considering all of the variables that affect purchase and sale prices. These include all expenses of buying, owning and selling the investment including the effect on taxes paid by the investor.

YIELD

While the rate of return generally rises with increased risk and reduced liquidity, the other variables mentioned can also have an important impact. That is why it is essential to understand the interrelationships among these three primary investment variables and their secondary considerations. The best starting point for clarifying these interrelationships is with a discussion of common investment alternatives and how they are affected by these variables.

GENERAL TYPES OF INVESTMENTS

Aside from the variety of savings accounts offered by financial institutions, debt instruments are the most widely accepted type of *fixed return* investment. A fixed return investment has a predetermined yield that is promised to you at the time of purchase and will not change if you hold the debt instrument to maturity. These debt instruments are contracts under which a corporation or government unit borrows a predetermined sum of money from another party to be repaid at a mutually agreeable date and rate of return. Depending primarily on the length of that loan, these debt instru-

DEBT INSTRUMENTS

ments are called bonds, notes, or bills. Mortgages also fall into this category of investments (when the investor is the creditor and lends the money).

Because a debt holder is in all cases a creditor, this investor has a good probability of receiving a full return on principal if the borrowing agency wishes to maintain its credit rating. Also, in a bankruptcy action, the creditor has priority access to the debtor's assets. That makes an investment in debt instruments quite safe but relatively low yield. Liquidity is variable, fluctuating with market conditions and length of the debt contract.

Bonds are traditionally defined as debt securities with an original maturity date of five or more years into the future. *Notes* and *bills* have shorter maturities. They pay interest periodically and are readily negotiable in the market. Treasury bills are auctioned weekly by the Federal Reserve Banks. Most commonly, they mature in three or six months. Although they are considered to be of maximum safety and liquidity, they are unavailable to numerous investors because of the $10,000 minimum investment required. However, investors can now pool their assets to reach this minimum on selected Treasury bills.

Profits on bonds are calculated partially on the rate of interest paid during the term of the loan. Profits are also made from bonds by purchasing them *at discount* (below face value) and selling them *at par* (face value) or *at premium* (above face value). For example, a $1,000 Company X bond with maturity in 1985 may sell today for $950 with a 7 percent interest. The bond holder making this purchase would thus receive interest payments at the rate of $70 per annum or 7 percent of $1,000. This is called *coupon or nominal yield* of the bond. But the effective rate of return is higher because the purchaser paid only $950 for a bond maturing at $1,000. Therefore, it is more accurate to calculate profits passed upon the bond's *yield to maturity*. This calculation considers present market price of the bond, coupon yield, years to maturity, and par value in determining bond yield. For discount bonds, it generally means a yield higher than that stated by the coupon yield. The *current yield* falls between these two extremes. It is an interest calculation expressed as a percentage of the present market price, whether at par, discount, or premium.

To avoid confusion in comparing bonds, it is advisable to use yield to maturity figures whenever possible. Although U.S. Treasury bonds are always sold on this basis, corporate and other government bonds are not. However, the information is generally available from the seller.

Because they are fixed return investments, the greatest risks carried by bondholders are purchasing power and interest rates. If inflation exceeds bond yields, these investors lose money. Accordingly, if interest rates paid on new bonds rise during the years until maturity, bondholders also reduce their potential profits. However, it should be noted that most bonds are saleable prior to maturity at the prevailing market rate.

While marketability is significantly determined by economic and monetary policy, it is also affected by the stability of the bond issuer and investor attitudes. The perceived ability of the bond issuer to repay these loans plus interest as scheduled is available to investors via several companies whose business it is to make these assessments as a measure of financial risk. The two most popular rating services are Standard and Poor's Corporation and Moody's Investor Service, Inc. Both agencies use similar rating systems, ranging from a high of triple A (AAA) to single C (C). However, Standard and Poor's continues with single to triple D (D to DDD) ratings for bonds in default, while Moody's rates these same bonds in the C range. For both agencies, bonds rated BBB or better are considered to be of investment grade with good safety of principal. The two rating services do not always agree on the rating of a particular bond issue nor do their ratings remain constant over the years.

Higher grade bonds are generally more easily marketable because of their greater safety. For this same reason, they often produce a lower yield. However, when corporate or government financial difficulties make news, investors' confidence shrinks and bond yields to maturity generally rise despite high grades. Usually this occurs through deeper discounts from par rather than reissue at higher coupon yields. That is why yield to maturity is such an important factor in bond investments.

Three basic types of bonds are common debt instruments held by individual and institutional investors alike. These include corporate, municipal, and savings bonds.

Corporate Bonds.   These generally pay the highest coupon yield on the bond market. They are loans made to corporations for various purposes. Corporate bonds provide greater return for greater risk than many other bonds. However, profits on bond earnings are fully taxable although earnings from a difference in purchase and sales price (generated from buying at discount) are taxed as capital gains or losses.

Municipal Bonds.   These are debts incurred by city, county, or state governments or agencies within these levels of government. They are also sold for multiple purposes. Municipals carry a much lower yield than corporate bonds because of compensating benefits. The interest earned from coupon clipping on these bearer bonds are tax free to the bond holder on federal and most state income taxes. Profits from the difference in purchase and sale prices are, however, taxable as capital gains or losses. Therefore, taxable income can be the deciding factor in selecting between two bonds of equal grade and maturity dates. Tables are available from investment brokers, etc., which compare net yield between taxable and tax free investments as determined by your tax bracket. This information can be very useful in investment decision making. As a general rule, the higher your tax bracket, the more lucrative a tax free investment becomes.

Savings Bonds.   In order to encourage the small investor to participate in the creditor financing of some government operations at the federal level, the U.S. government has made bonds purchasable for $25 or more. Devised as a savings vehicle primarily, these Series EE and HH bonds issued by the U.S. Treasury are very safe investment vehicles offering maximum protection of principal, limited liquidity, and modest returns.

As of January 2, 1980, Series EE bonds allow a maximum annual investment of $15,000 at par in units of $25 or more. These will be purchased at 50 percent of par value with maturity in eleven years and nine months. Interest earning will average 4 percent during the first five years and 6 ½ percent thereafter. The minimum holding period is six months before they can be redeemed.

Series HH bonds allow a maximum $20,000 annual investment at par with average interest rates of 6 percent from purchase to maturity in ten years. HH bonds are purchased at par value with interest payments made semi-annually to the registered owner.

While interest earned on all U.S. government securities are fully taxable by the federal government, investors may choose to pay taxes on Series EE bonds in the year it is earned or when the bond is redeemed. Under certain circumstances, taxes can also be deferred by exchanging EE bonds for HH bonds. No state income tax is due on the interest earned by these bonds or the older Series E and H bonds which are no longer being sold, although many are still being held to maturity.

SHARES OF OWNERSHIP

Stocks are shares of ownership in a corporation. Therefore, the profits or losses from this investment will rise and fall with corporate profits and investors attitudes. Therefore, the rate of return fluctuates with financial risk of the corporation plus market conditions. That increases uncertainties about investor profits but it simultaneously reduces purchasing power risk because stocks have the potential to match or exceed inflation rates. While potential returns are essentially unlimited, losses are limited to the dollars invested even when corporate liabilities exceed total stock value.

There are two types of stock available; both are purchased through brokerage houses with prices set by supply and demand.

Preferred Stock.   Although actually shares of ownership, preferred stock resembles bonds in that it pays a predetermined dividend or share of the profits as set by the Board of Directors of the corporation. While a corporation is not legally required to pay dividends to any stockholder, preferred stockholders must be paid their specified dividend per share before other stockholders are paid any dividends (but after bondholders are paid in full).

Common Stock.   The stockholders who share in the ownership and profits of a company without a promise of fixed returns or dividends have purchased *common stock*. These investors receive profits through an increase in the market value or selling price of their stock and receipt of dividends paid annually (or quarterly) to shareholders. Since corporate profits can be reinvested by the firm for future growth and/or paid to stockholders, dividend payments will vary based on corporate policy. When dividend payments are made to stockholders, they can be in the form of cash, stock, or both. Dividend payments are the only profits paid to stockholders during their stock ownership. Because these dividends are fully taxable (with some exclusions), some investors prefer to purchase equity in *growth* companies that reinvest most profits rather than *income*-oriented stocks that return maximum profits in the form of dividends. Appreciation, or the increase in market value, of a stock is taxed as a capital gains.

Because the rate of return on common stock is not fixed, it is very difficult to predict future profits. While various aspects of the stock's past history are frequent tools of stock analysis, it is unlikely that the future will repeat the past. Standard and Poor's as well as other firms publish gradings of many common stock, but these grades are not as useful in aiding investor decision making as they are for bonds. Bond ratings are designed to reflect financial risk of the investment. Stock ratings analyze companies for overall financial strength. Other risk factors are of equal importance and often harder to predict.

The key is to invest in companies whose intrinsic or natural value is above the market price with good prospects for future growth in that industry as a whole and that company in particular. Finding this information is no small task. It takes careful study of economic trends, government actions, industry progress, and the corporate balance sheet. Numerous aids are available to help in this decision making although their individual value varies significantly among the experts. Key factors to watch presently are the federal money supply as it affects interest rates, industrial growth as projected in light of proposed economic and environmental conditions, and individual corporate policies. (Sources of this information will be presented later in this chapter.)

It is essential to recognize the need for this type of analysis prior to purchase. It is equally essential to note that professional advise on stock selection is readily available through most brokerage firms that execute the purchases and sales orders for stock as well as independent investment advisors. Independent advisors have no stake in your selection since they sell advice only rather than investments. However, in either case the advice given is only as good as the person providing it and the probing abilities of the advice seeker. The wise investor does best by using professional help as an aid in his or her personal investment analysis rather than as a substitute for it.

Convertibles. Some people want the advantages of both stocks and bonds in one investment. So they will choose convertibles which are available in both the stock and bond markets. Several companies sell their preferred stock with the option to convert it into a predetermined number of shares of common stock at the owner's discretion. Some corporate bonds also provide the option for exchange into that company's common stock. While there is no direct fee for the conversion, the cost of convertibles is slightly less advantageous to the buyer than the direct purchase of the same common stock. For this small difference, an investor can easily work to reduce purchasing power risk with the same investment that he or she selected when other risks were given greater priority at the time of investment selection.

INVESTMENT COMPANIES

Investment companies operate for the purpose of investing other people's money at a profit for the investors and the company. Their basic operating procedure is to combine the funds of numerous small investors to increase the yield and afford to buy the services of capable investment advisors to also aid in reducing the risk. That makes the key to selecting a good investment company focus on the firm's management abilities to reach these and other stated goals.

Closed-end Funds. The first type of investment companies were much like the corporations in which they invested. Called "closed-end funds," these corporations issued a set amount of stock that could be bought and sold on the market but not readily increased over the original number of shares provided. Purchasers and sellers had to be located and matched by brokers, as in traditional stock transactions, with comparable cost incurred for this service. The only difference between closed-end investment companies and other corporations is that profits come solely from the proceeds of investments rather than the sale of products or services.

Mutual Funds. In order to provide greater liquidity to investors and draw more dollars into their firm, some investment companies took a different approach concerning the total shares of stock they would issue. These mutual funds increased the number of shares of stock available to meet investor demand and made them redeemable on any business day. Although these mutual funds can be bought and sold through brokers, they can also be traded directly with the mutual fund company. Some mutual funds charge a sales commission called a "load." Those that do not are called "no-load funds." Both are generally available from a broker although many mutual funds can also be purchased directly from the company. This is especially true of no-load funds. Usually the mutual fund manager decides if the fund is to be sold as "load" or "no-load"; it is not an investor's option. Similar investment opportunities are available in both kinds of mutual funds. However, net profits must be compared rather than gross profits in order to account for load charges plus administrative costs that may be incurred on either fund.

Mutual funds are available with an investment mix of stocks and/or bonds geared to your own priorities among the investment variables of risk and return. Liquidity is comparable to common stock since your investment can be easily converted to cash, but no guarantees can be made that the principal will be preserved. Even when mutual funds invest exclusively in bonds and/or preferred stock, shareholders do *not* receive a fixed return on their mutual fund investment, although they may elect this type of fund in an attempt to preserve their principal.

While mutual funds in the stock and bond market offer diversification and professional management, *money market funds* offer one more unique feature. These mutual funds invest in large denomination bank CD's and short-term debt securities primarily of the U.S. government. While few individuals can invest $100,000 or more to obtain high rates of return, the money market funds can pool the shares of numerous small investors to obtain this rate plus low risk of the debt instrument investment. To make this type of mutual fund even more enticing to investors, many money market funds have offered speedy withdrawal procedures, including limited check writing privileges to shareholders to increase liquidity. (Unlike bank accounts, however, money market funds are not insured against losses by FDIC or a comparable insurance protection plan.) Of course, returns are not fixed, so profits fluctuate with interest rates. But the opportunity exists for small investors to choose an otherwise unavailable vehicle for their extra dollars with sufficient liquidity and yield to out perform many investments of comparable safety.

When a fixed rate of return is preferred in the bond market coupled with diversification and professional management, investors may choose a "unit bond trust" which differs somewhat from a mutual fund dealing in bonds. Large brokerage houses usually sponsor these trusts by purchasing a selection of bonds and reselling them in $1,000 units to interested investors at a stated yield which will be paid in full if the bonds are held to maturity by the investor. The yield reflects a deduction for sales charges to the investor so no additional purchase fees are involved. However, losses of principal can occur if the investor sells these prior to maturity and current interest rates are higher than those paid when the trust was established. Unlike a mutual fund, the unit trust cannot trade bonds in its portfolio in order to compensate for market changes. Interest on the bonds held are usually paid monthly. Return on the principal is paid each time a bond in the trust reaches maturity until all bonds have matured and all funds are returned to their investors. Unit bond trusts are available for corporate, municipal, and U.S. government bonds in terms from six months to twenty-five or more years.

DIRECT BUSINESS INVESTMENT

Some people prefer to rely on their own management abilities in business dealings. Rather than buy shares of someone else's corporation, these investors may prefer to buy their own business. Success and profits depend on: (1) market demand for the product or service, (2) money available to begin the enterprise, (3) operational efficiency in relation to competition, and (4) management abilities to adapt to changing economic conditions and other factors that affect business.

Advice on this investment can be obtained from the Small Business Administration, a federal agency with district offices nationwide established for this primary purpose. Other sources of help include commercial lenders who will probably be approached to help finance such a venture. An accountant can also provide the prospective business investor information on tax advantages (including depreciation) which are reaped even if a business does poorly.

Common problems encountered with this type of investment are: (1) insufficient market for goods and services, (2) difficulty in repaying the initial capital for business start up, (3) inefficient operations and limitations on the business owner to manage effectively, and (4) limited liquidity and loan value.

One of the strong forces needed to be overcome by the small business owner is competition from large sellers who can take advantage of economics of scale. One way to eliminate that problem can sometimes be handled through franchising—a marketing method that joins a large corporation with buying power and management experience with a small investor willing to trade dollars and sweat equity for a share of corporate profits. Usually, a modern franchising arrangement involves a sizeable dollar investment for the privilege of selling corporate products or services. There are also fees for licensing, advertising, training, and establishing the "branch" operation at a mutually agreeable location. While the idea has merit with widespread corporate acceptance as an easy vehicle for expansion, there are many complaints from investors. Most frequent concerns include "misrepresentation of long work hours, low initial profits, dangers from competition and shaky financial condition of the parent company."[5]

Recent studies have been made to improve the quality of the franchising arrangement by the prolification of voluntary and mandatory disclosure requirements to provide adequate information to prospective buyers as an aid in decision making. Voluntary compliance is encouraged by the International Franchise Association established in 1960 to represent firms in various industries that choose the franchising method of distributing their goods and/or services. Numerous states have enacted comparable and sometimes more comprehensive legislation to require full disclosure by franchisors who want to do business in their states. The Federal Trade Commission is also considering a similar national mandate under a proposed trade regulation rule.

REAL ESTATE

In addition to ownership of their primary residence, many investors are drawn to the real estate market as a vehicle for multiplying their extra dollars. As homeowners, they feel somewhat knowledgeable about the management of this type of investment, so they are more confident in their decision making. In many cases they also believe that they can use sweat equity via their own labor for repairs and improvements to yield a larger dollar growth in profits at resale.

Real estate investments usually do require significant amounts of time and energy devoted to management, besides the possible demands via sweat equity. Because taxes must be paid and properties adequately maintained, real estate also entails sizeable out-of-pocket costs during the investment period, in addition to possible sales charges if the services of a real estate broker are used to help execute a sale. Not many investors can afford this type of commitment—nor can they rely solely on their own ability to assess market conditions in relation to the profitability of each unique piece of real estate since location plays such a critical factor in determining value. This problem is compounded by a decided lack of statistical data available on the past histories of investment properties to aid in decision making. Even though real estate investments do carry substantial financial risks, there is a good probability of outpacing inflation with proper location and timing.

While some of these management commitments are lessened with investment in raw land, the uncertainties of its future use affect market value. Also, there is no income to offset direct costs like property taxes. When investors buy tracts of raw land in areas of limited development, growth patterns may be unclear, or costs of preparing the land for development are so high that they have a neutral or negative affect on appreciation. Zoning changes and tax rate increases may also take their toll.

One of the biggest drawing cards of real estate investment is the tax advantage offered in the form of *depreciation* on the value of buildings owned *and* rented out to others. Since all buildings are calculated to have a limited useful life, the federal government allows investors to calculate the costs of this useful life and deduct a portion of this value from taxes owed annually during that period. Even if this depreciation exceeds income earned on the property, it is an allowable deduction! Depreciation is *not* allowed on raw land or the home you live in (except for the rented portion of a multi-family dwelling). It can, however, make a seemingly unprofitable real estate investment very worthwhile, particularly to investors in high tax brackets.

Mutual funds and limited partnerships are also available vehicles for real estate investments. Both allow small investors to join together to buy large (generally commercial) properties. Professional managers are hired to handle rental, leasing, and maintenance matters; hence, the investors need spend little time and energy on these investments after a careful analysis to aid in selection of the appropriate fund or partnership. Profits and tax advantages are passed on to the many small owners while losses are limited to the dollars invested by each.

The risks involved with real estate investment vary with its location and the nature of the market. Liquidity is relatively low because it takes time to find a buyer and await a decision on that person's ability to finance that portion of the purchase price he or she cannot afford to buy for cash. Outpacing inflation, however, is quite possible with good quality real estate investments if demand continues to exceed supply.

COLLECTIBLES

Paintings by famous artists, antiques, jewels, etc., can appreciate in value through the years. Therefore, any or all of these "collectibles" could be viewed as an investment because they often sell for significantly more than their purchase price when demand exceeds supply. This is contrary to the value of ordinary household goods that lose their value through the years.

Many collectors buy only what they enjoy owning and appreciate aesthetically. In so doing, they derive some satisfaction from these possessions even when their demand as an investment is low. For those people who collect various articles purely because they should rise in value, disappointments may dominate these investments. Besides a very changeable market demand, there is stiff competition from dealers and large sales commissions, as well as the possibility of storage costs and added homeowner's insurance premiums to protect the collectibles.

Liquidity can be low depending on market conditions at the desired time of sale. Risk is great because of market volatility and the possibility of damage to the investment itself. Safety of principal is also low because of the limited intrinsic value of many of these items. In addition, government protection for investors in collectibles is virtually nonexistent.

Agriculture is big business today. When a typical crop yield per farmer could be 10,000 or more bushels of a particular crop, a penny or two difference in the unit price paid at market could significantly affect farm profits. The same is true for the mining of precious metals like gold and silver. The costs of production in these and other areas heavily dependent on raw materials can be staggering. To reduce the impact of negative conditions that might cause a selling price to fall below costs incurred, producers in seventy different types of commodities will sell future contracts to interested investors who will share the risk and, hopefully, the profits.

COMMODITIES

Commodities future contracts are promises that the seller will deliver a specific amount and quality of a certain commodity on a predetermined future date—without regard to price changes, weather conditions, etc. The buyer of a future contract has a comparable commitment to accept delivery on that date. The only way to avoid giving or taking delivery of the stated commodity is to sell the contract prior to the delivery date. Since the producers want control of the commodities, they will readily buy back the contracts at current market value. By doing so, a producer can plan to make money through the future contract or the market price of the product, whichever is more favorable to obtain future ownership.

While commodities are traded through professional brokers who can assist their investors, the market is extremely volatile and the odds are generally against the amateur investor. Risks are very high, liquidity and safety of principal low. Commissions, however, on the purchase and sale of commodities are also modest. And, like many of the other investments discussed, there are mutual funds on the market that deal exclusively in commodity futures.

Throughout the centuries and around the world, gold has been a store of value. Therefore, despite the fact that it is essentially only another commodity, it is considered by some to be an important component of a good investment program. First, it is thought to be a hedge against financial chaos because of its longstanding use as a medium of exchange.[6] Second, it is viewed as a mirror image of the stock market, rising when stocks fall and vice versa.[7] Therefore, gold provides a logical alternative investment to stocks and bonds when these markets are depressed, so an investor can switch back and forth between them as economic conditions warrant. Third, even when viewed only as a commodity, gold can be traded on the futures market or at current values with greater understanding than most other commodities because you need only comprehend economic conditions rather than characteristics of a particular item in order to invest wisely.[8] Unlike most other commodities, gold can be purchased directly in bullion, coins, or jewelry; in common stock of gold mining firms; or in mutual funds.

GOLD

SELECTION CRITERIA

INDIVIDUAL
PRIORITIES

When analyzing investments in light of the primary variables of risk, liquidity, and rate of return, it is essential to establish priorities. What is most important to you—preservation of capital, convertibility to cash, or potential profits? The answer to that question will have a significant affect on your investment choices since no two types of investments carry the same orientation to these variables.

A very practical guideline for selection that allows for these individual differences and a rational approach is the investment pyramid. The base of the pyramid, which holds most of the available assets, is a group of conservative investments that offer good liquidity, safety, and a reasonable return. Included here are the emergency fund held in a savings institution, money market fund, etc.; bonds and other debt securities; and your home, if one is purchased. The midportion of the triangle, containing a smaller percentage of investable funds, includes somewhat higher risk, less liquid investments like high value stocks, and carefully selected real estate or business investments. The apex of the triangle contains a still smaller portion of investable funds used for higher risk investments in the hope of maximizing the return. These may include some stocks, commodities, certain types of real estate or business opportunities, etc.

In the broadest sense, anything you purchase with cash or credit is an investment. However, only certain items appreciate in value. Most possessions depreciate, thus reducing the return on the dollars spent. Therefore, the intelligent investor will routinely consider the difference in value generated over time of the various things she or he buys—from cars to shares of stock, etc.

Opportunity Costs.   Be sure to remain aware of the tradeoffs or opportunity costs involved in the selection. Goal achievement may be a good motivator to prioritize profits in your investment decision making. Do you understand that approach can also mean absorbing some losses of capital when your stock, real estate, or other profit-oriented investments don't always succeed—or do so within your time frame for goals attainment? Can you afford these losses and still reach your goal in time? Can you accept the concept of losing? Can you watch the value of your investment fluctuate as you read the daily news?

One often misunderstood area of opportunity costs relates to growth versus income-producing investments. *Growth investments* generally yield their greatest profits as increases in market value over time. *Income-producing investments* return profits primarily through dividends. Therefore, a common investment strategy has been to buy growth stocks during peak earning years and let profits multiply through reinvestment. When earning power is lower (in retirement, for example), strategies should be changed to supplement earnings with dividends and interest from income-producing investments while preserving the principal. Ironically though, under present-day inflation, this later philosophy could have a net negative effect.

Unless the yield from the income-oriented investments grows at a rate equal to inflation, the purchasing power of both income and principal will decline to a point where this investment cannot meet its intended purpose over time. However, if these same funds were invested to produce a rate of return greater than inflation, it would not matter if some profits were taken directly from the sum invested rather than from dividends and interest alone. This is because the principal plus reinvested profits would generate sufficient yield to meet investment goals.

To some investors, the psychological effects of annually "dipping into" the principal could be sufficiently disturbing to be inappropriate. Loss of purchasing power might actually be a more acceptable risk for them to encounter. In other cases, the acknowledgment of opportunity costs involved could help these investors overcome their anxiety and maximize investment potential.

Personality Factors.   While goal achievement should be the top consideration, personality factors also deserve attention. Some people are gamblers at heart and can accept the loss of spare funds if their attempt at big profits fails. Others cannot live with the risks involved. They prefer to accept purchasing power losses and know that their hard earned dollars will remain intact forever, if necessary.

Time and energy available to devote to investment management may also have an effect. Often, increased knowledge of investment vehicles decreases fear of losses through more careful selections and better timing of investment choices.

Public Opinion.   In our society, your home is a status symbol of your success, so some people will choose this investment vehicle for public image purposes. For comparable reasons, others "dabble" in the stock market, gold, etc., primarily for peer group acceptance, to be fashionable, etc. Yet some investment analysts have proven that following the crowd is not profitable. Contrary investments can produce a greater yield. Here is how the philosophy works:

> Since the future is largely unpredictable, an overwhelming consensus on where stock prices are heading usually ignores numerous uncertainties. Such a consensus is therefore likely to be wrong. In addition, a market trend that nearly everyone has been predicting isn't likely to occur because investors have already acted in anticipation of it, thereby changing market conditions. . . .[9]

When crowd psychology causes investors with limited as well as bountiful knowledge of market conditions to overwhelmingly favor a particular profit strategy, the logical person seeks out valid reasons for this choice. By the time the investment becomes this popular, its profitability may actually have passed. In those cases, it is wiser to look elsewhere for sound investments where profitability is based on fact, not fancy.

This means defying group pressures, "marching to a different drummer," etc. Not everyone can follow that investment strategy despite the consequences—and long-term prospects for profit. Even though it is common knowledge that investor attitudes affect stock and bond prices, few people will actually believe it is appropriate to counter a trend. Yet research during the 1970s has shown that this can, indeed, be true by following the logical investment strategy of buying undervalued assets and selling overvalued ones, despite crowd psychology about these decisions.[10]

ECONOMIC CONDITIONS

The best investments of the last decade may not be the best investments of the next decade. Therefore, an analysis of past, present, and future economic trends will be needed to help predict investment performance as an aid to decision making.

For the individual investor, that means learning to understand basic economic theories and their practical implications. While these principles will not be discussed here, they should be reviewed prior to investing, with a regular update of market conditions as an ongoing part of investment management.

COMMISSIONS AND OTHER COSTS

In the discussion of investment types, it was noted that there is usually a cost involved in entering or leaving a particular investment market. Most of these costs are levied in the form of commissions paid to the *broker,* or professional salesperson who negotiates the purchase or sale agreement for the buyer and seller. Brokers and their fees are virtually unavoidable in the stock, bond, real estate, and commodities markets.

There are, however, exceptions to this rule. Mutual fund investors in any of these areas can avoid direct brokerage fees via the purchase of no-load funds. U.S. government debt obligations can be purchased directly from the issuing Federal Reserve Banks. Commercial and residential real estate can legally be purchased without a broker as liaison between buyer and seller, but this decision is purely the seller's choice. To avoid the broker, a buyer would have to shop for real estate not presently under a brokerage contract.

In order to buy and sell stocks, bonds, and commodities, you have to have a seat on the appropriate exchange where trading in these securities takes place or be a licensed representative of a firm owning such a seat.

While anyone with sufficient financing and knowledge of the securities can buy a seat on an exchange when it becomes available, most investors find it far less costly to hire a broker or representative to perform their buy and sell transactions for them. An added benefit is the professional assistance available from many of these firms in researching wise investments and analyzing various future indicators of profit trends.

Some investments carry other direct costs as well. Real estate investments are most notable in this regard due to ongoing taxes and property maintenance. Direct business investment carries comparable costs plus the investments in inventory, labor, operations, and marketing before a profit can result. In some forms, gold will require an assay or professional appraisal to determine its value prior to purchase or sale. Antiques and collectibles may also require appraisal, as will most real estate. In addition, storage and insurance protection may be required for these investments.

To determine the true profits of any investment, all costs of purchase, ownership, and sale must be deducted from gross yield. When high costs are incurred during purchase or the early years of ownership, an investment may only prove profitable after long-term ownership—as in the case of some homes and most "load" mutual funds. Other investments, like commercial real estate, are most profitable in the early years of ownership because of the tax advantages of depreciation. Analyzing the timing of investment costs can, therefore, be crucial to maximizing the investment return.

Reduction. When most of the investments previously discussed are held for at least one full year prior to sale, the profits from that sale will be treated as a capital gain for federal income tax purposes. That means these profits will be taxed at 40 percent of their full value minus comparable long-term losses. Accordingly, while assets held less than one year will be taxed at full value, short-term losses can usually be deducted in full before the tax is calculated. That means profits of $1,000 received as a long-term capital gain will be taxed as though the profits were only $400. To a taxpayer in the 25 percent bracket, that would mean taxes due of $100 rather than $250. For a taxpayer in the 50 percent bracket, the savings would double to $300. To put it another way, that same taxpayer would pay 50 percent on $1,000 of wages or $500 in taxes versus 50 percent of $400 or $200 in taxes. That makes it fairly obvious that putting your money to work for you can be more profitable than working for more money—or stashing spare funds into a savings account the interest on which is also taxed at full value. (Since each state sets its rate of taxation on capital gains, some of these profits will be lower in those states that charge higher rates than the federal government.)

TAX CONSIDERATIONS

Avoidance.   Interest earned on state and local government bonds are tax free when computing federal income tax. In most cases, these profits are also exempt from state and local income taxes. In addition, while the interest paid on federal debt securities are fully taxable for federal income tax purposes, they are exempt from state and local income taxes.

Investments in some very risky business ventures also carry tax savings or *shelters* because the U.S. government perceives them to have the potential to produce social or economic benefits. Many of these center around real estate, oil and gas exploration, etc. Generally, these enterprises sell shares of ownership to limited partners who are allowed to deduct from their income a share of losses equal to their share of ownership. Since depreciation is a major factor, plus comparable special considerations given to various investments, losses are often more important to the limited partners than profits. The losses can actually total enough tax savings for high bracket taxpayers that they are reason enough to invest. But the failure rate of these ventures is high, too, so that limited partners can lose all or most of their investment. In addition, as Congress seeks to close tax loopholes, the tax benefits of these programs can be withdrawn, leaving investors without benefits unless the tax shelter selected has the ultimate potential for profitability.

Deferment.   The interest earned on Series E or EE savings bonds can be paid annually or deferred until the bonds are redeemed. Since these bonds have an interest-bearing life of at least thirty years, this can mean taxes are deferred until after retirement when many people fall into a lower income tax bracket. Tax deferral can also be attained by exchanging Series EE bonds for Series HH bonds within one year of their final maturity. The only interest then taxable is the amount paid semi-annually by the new HH bonds.

If the Series EE bonds are purchased in the name of a child with an adult beneficiary, all interest earned is exempt from taxes provided the child's earnings remain below the tax free limit per year. (However, gift taxes may become due if any one person gives the child more than $3,000 in bonds during one year.) While this investment strategy saves tax dollars, it gives the child full control of these bond funds upon reaching the age of eighteen. As the rightful owner, decisions on how to spend the bond proceeds will then be at her or his discretion.

Various forms of saving for retirement also offer tax advantages that serve to compound these funds because taxes are deferred until retirement when the money invested is withdrawn. The details of these programs will be discussed in Chapter 11. It is sufficient now to note that tax deferral means that all dollars invested (except load charges) are put to work to multiply profits without any annual drain on these profits to pay income taxes. So the profits can also multiply for many years to increase yields before taxes become due—and payable at the probably lower rates accompanying reduced retirement earnings.

Capital gains achieved through home ownership carry two tax deferral features generally associated with retirement. Capital gains made on the sale of a primary residence may be deferred as long as all profits from that sale are reinvested in another dwelling used as your primary residence (with certain time constraints). This process can continue until you no longer choose to own your residence. At that time, the accumulated capital gains are due and payable—except for the first $100,000 in profits which are now exempt from taxation for homeowners who sell their dwellings after they reach age fifty-five. For some people, this means tax deferment and lower rates of a retirement income bracket. For others, it means tax avoidance entirely—a strong incentive for home ownership, indeed!

LEVERAGE

In several instances during our discussion of investments, profits have been shown to reach higher levels through credit buying. Commonly practiced in real estate transactions, this means that a small down payment increases significantly over time because it is used to represent a much larger sum which is at the investor's disposal through his or her borrowing ability or *leverage*. The most easily understood use of leverage is in home ownership as presented earlier in this chapter. As you will recall, the purchase of a $60,000 house with $12,000 down payment yielded a gross profit of 40 percent. Had the same home been purchased for cash, the resulting yield would have been only 8 percent. Leverage made a real difference in profits, even after all probable costs were deducted. The leveraged investment yielded more than twice the cash investment.

The principle of credit buying can be used with the purchase of most securities as well as real estate, although there are strict requirements on the size of the down payment required which have been established by the federal government. These are often supplemented by the stock exchange and/or brokerage house you choose to handle your trades. Investors who meet all of these requirements are then allowed to buy securities "on margin" by using his or her broker's credit to purchase more shares than the investor's cash will buy alone. Interest rates for this service vary with economic conditions and brokerage houses. However, it is harder for small investors to buy profitably on margin because of the commission charges, finance costs, etc.

Leverage can be used in a similar manner in the bond market, commodities (including gold), or collectibles—but the prospect of increased profits can also mean increased losses. Both profits and losses are calculated on the sum of the down payment plus borrowed funds invested jointly. Profits are multiplied many times because of the small down payment actually invested. Accordingly, losses are calculated on the total sum invested. For many investors, that means the loss of their down payment plus additional dollars if the investment does poorly. Since few investors can afford to lose that much money, leveraging an investment must be used with great caution despite its potential for profitability.

Options.   There are, however, methods of leveraging your investments with a certain limitation on your losses. This is accomplished through the purchase of options that allow you to buy or sell securities at a predetermined future date and a predetermined price. Their greatest advantage over margin buying lies in losses limited to the cost of the option if the investment fails to perform as hoped.

Pyramiding.   This term is used to describe a method of accumulating wealth that is common to real estate but also applicable to other investment media. It begins with the use of leverage to purchase securities. As profits rise in these leveraged securities, they are used as loan collateral to buy more securities (or real estate). This is done repeatedly, utilizing all or most profits for reinvestment in order to maximize the number and quality of properties bought with the minimum realistic capital expenditure, or the maximum use of borrowed money.

The technique is useful to small and large investors alike, but it takes significant time and energy for the investor to manage these investments to maximize leverage returns. It also requires a thorough knowledge of the market for your chosen properties as well as credit costs and availability.

SPECULATION

At times throughout this chapter, investing has been viewed to include some gambling or taking chances that an anticipated outcome will be realized. While this is, indeed, a component of the broad field of investing, it is essential to clarify some points.

Investing is generally considered to be the commitment of money for the purchase of securities or other properties based on a careful analysis of anticipated risks and rewards over a period of time usually equal to one year or more. This implies the investor's acceptance of the fact that safety of principal and quick profits are not synonymous, nor is liquidity directly related to high yield. In other words, patience is an investor's virtue. She or he does substantial research to obtain moderate profits over time.

In contrast, the person who uses spare funds to reap quick profits based on impulsive action is a gambler. This is also a person who accepts big losses when the big winnings fail to materialize. She or he demands fast action as the priority, despite the consequences.

A compromise position to these extremes is *speculation*. With this approach, someone with spare funds carefully selects investment instruments that hopefully will yield substantial profits relatively quickly. Accordingly, he or she is also in a financial position to absorb the substantial losses that may occur when research efforts fail to yield the anticipated results.

In actuality, one person can utilize all three approaches in putting money to work. Doing so means starting with a sound and secure investment program geared toward goal achievement. Then as additional funds become available for investment purposes, more speculative, or higher risk, investments higher up on the investment pyramid can be added, if desired, in an attempt to increase total investment yield. But these additions can only be made if the funds used can afford to be lost or reduced without causing trauma to the speculator. Funds used for gambling are even more likely to be lost. So, if used in this manner, gambling money should be viewed as any other recreational expenditure with no real return anticipated, although it is always pleasantly accepted.

GUIDELINES FOR DECISION MAKING

The multitude of investment vehicles, coupled with the numerous criteria affecting selection, make investment decision making a real challenge. Moreover, there is no easy way to riches guaranteed to reduce the variables to a more manageable number. There is, however, a logical process of decision making that can help to reduce confusion and simplify complexities.

The process begins with seeking and analyzing relevant information about investment, market conditions, and your own goals. Professional help is available in this endeavor and should be considered as an aid in decision making. Once the investment choices become clearer, timing becomes the critical element to insure realistic profit margins and minimal losses in light of ever-changing market condition. For peace of mind, diversification is equally important, so one miscalculation does not eliminate all of your funds available for investing.

You, the Investor.   As in all other financial decisions, it is imperative to choose investments that "fit" comfortably. To do so, you must know your values and goals as well as your personality quirks. Why is this so impor-

INFORMATION
SOURCES

tant? Because the value of an investment is determined by a combination of its intrinsic worth, market conditions, and investor attitudes—factors that can produce daily changes in market price for many investments. If you are uncomfortable watching short-range price declines resulting from these factors, your attitude may pressure you into inappropriately timed changes in your portfolio in an effort to save shrinking principal that should be left alone to realize its potential profitability. Conversely, someone who always expects a rainbow after every rainstorm may have difficulty parting with nonproductive investments and fail to limit losses appropriately.

Current Periodicals.   National and international economic conditions and trends are newsworthy. Therefore, much mass media time and/or space is devoted to presenting this information to the public. All you have to do is listen to or read your favorite media to gain some insight into market conditions that could affect investor decision making. Since no media presentation can be totally free from bias, it is wise to review various sources of current information on market conditions to be sure the analysts agree, or find out why they disagree so you can form your own opinion on the matter.

It bears repeating that investor profits will depend on future trends, not past histories. There is no accurate crystal ball to predict what will really happen in the future. Decision making relies on the probability that someone's educated guess becomes reality. That means the investor must concentrate on selecting the analyst's predictions that will hold true—no small effort, indeed!

Some periodicals, like the *Wall Street Journal, Business Week,* and *Fortune,* concentrate on providing information to aid in investor decision making. Reviewing these publications regularly can provide a compilation of facts and opinions about economic and industrial or governmental conditions that can and do affect investment values. There is less extraneous news to distract the reader. The same is true of the Public Broadcasting System's show, "Wall Street Week," as opposed to a nightly news show.

In addition, the *Wall Street Journal* and other major daily newspapers offer daily price quotations on a vast array of stocks and bonds traded daily to help you follow changes in your current investment portfolio. As you will note in reviewing this information, the data provided varies with the market place for the stock and bond transactions. Stock traded on one of the major exchanges generally lists the high and low price of that stock over the last year; its dividend; yield; sales volume (in multiples of one hundred); high, low, and closing price for the day; and its net change. In addition, a figure is given for the stock's "P/E" or ratio of the closing price per share to current earnings. Many investors feel that this analysis offers helpful insight into the value of the stock.

The majority of stocks are traded "over-the-counter," or without the aid of a stock exchange facility that brings buyer and seller representatives together physically to negotiate a price. Instead, the stocks are bought and sold via telephone or telecommunications among dealers who buy and sell these securities professionally. Then other investors negotiate with the dealer to buy or sell these stocks from her or his inventory. This differs from trades made on the exchanges where the buy and sell transactions are made directly for the investor with a representative of the exchange acting merely as liaison to complete the transaction. The *Wall Street Journal* and some other papers publish a sampling of OTC trading activity. Information is provided by security dealers in the form of "bid" prices and "asked" prices rather than actual transactions made. Sales are also listed in multiples of one hundred, as is the net change from the last report.

Information on corporate bonds traded on a bond exchange is similar to that provided for stock exchange trades. This includes price changes during the year, volume in multiples of one hundred, closing prices, and net change. Current yield information is also given by dividing the interest rate by the closing price. Because one firm can have many bond issues outstanding, descriptive information including the stated interest rate on the bond and its date of maturity is given to aid in distinguishing among them.

Over-the-counter quotations are given on government debt securities. Interest rate and date of maturity are stated as well as bid and asked prices and net change. In addition, yield to maturity figures are calculated to incorporate additional profits or losses as a result of a purchase price different from par value.

In some newspapers, similar information is also available on stock options, mutual funds, and commodities futures. That makes it possible for an interested person to follow certain trends proposed by the media in the investment markets as an aid in evaluating analyst predictions. It also helps amateur investors "play" the securities market on paper to determine the profitability of their choices before risking any actual dollar losses due to inexperience or ignorance.

Indexes and Averages. Sometimes all you want to know is the trend of stock market investments in general. This information is readily available via a host of stock market indicators. Several stock exchanges and the OTC market publish indexes that tell you at a glance what the price trends are of a large group of stocks. Other indexes are also published indicating trends in specific types of stocks. Their usefulness is geared to comparative data. They can help you judge if your securities are yielding average or better profits. They can also help you compare profits in other investment to those in the stock and bond markets.

Prospectus.   In order to assure complete and accurate information for investor decision making, the federal government mandates that a *prospectus* be made available to all investors in new issues of all stocks and bonds. This document contains relevant details about the offering and the issuing company or agency so the investor has sufficient information for informed decision making. Some of the information in the prospectus includes the use of the proceeds for this offering, dividends and price range of the security, statement of earnings, report of independent accountants, and financial statements. Before this information is released as fact to the buying public, the Securities and Exchange Commission as agent of the U.S. government examines the information for accuracy and amends it as necessary. However, although they do *not* endorse or approve the new offering in any way.

Annual Report.   Similar in content to the prospectus, a corporate or government agency's annual report can also provide valuable information to prospective investors and current shareholders. By law, the annual report must be sent to all shareholders and corporate bondholders to keep these investors informed of corporate management and profitability. Municipal bondholders must request these reports since these are bearer bonds and the municipality does not know the identity of the bondholders.

Some of the helpful information now required as part of the corporate annual report includes:

1.   Breakdown of sales and earnings by type of business.
2.   Five-year statistical summary of operations.
3.   Management analysis of operation for the last two years.
4.   Quarterly high and low of stock prices for last two years.
5.   Quarterly dividends for last two years.
6.   Long-term lease commitments.
7.   Pension obligations.
8.   Auditor's report and opinion.
9.   Balance sheet of assets and liabilities.

If this list implies a mass of figures and statistics, seemingly unintelligible to nonaccountants, you are correct. Often the most significant gain from reading annual reports is in raising valid questions for which answers must be found prior to your investment decision making. These questions may be presented to the corporation directly or your investment broker. No money should be invested until you receive a satisfactory reply.

For the novice or expert investor, the real usefulness of annual reports is comparative analysis. How does this year differ from previous years for the same company? How does this company differ from competitors? Do the differences show positive future trends to encourage investment? While the annual report alone is insufficient information on which to base an investment decision, it is certainly a vital component.

Professionals. Many people make their living giving advice to others in investment decision making. Their training and expertise may vary as much as the fees they charge. Shopping for an investment advisor is critical to the appropriate selection of investments to meet your unique goals.

Professional investment advice is widely available through books and periodicals, investment brokers that help you execute buy and sell orders, and independent advisors that sell advice only. Each has some merits and some drawbacks.

Written information on investments is a good starting point to increase understanding of investment alternatives, costs, risks, etc. However, the time span between drafting, publication, and your access to them may be long enough to invalidate some of the advice.

An investment broker is capable of providing individualization of advice in keeping with diverse investor needs. He or she is also potentially capable of answering questions generated from the investor's research into various investment instruments. The big question is whether the broker chosen will take the time and effort to perform these services for clients. After all, the broker's earnings are based on commissions generated from each purchase or sale of securities, real estate, etc. Therefore, a selfish broker could concentrate on increasing trading volume rather than assisting clients in decision making.

A good broker will begin the client/counselor relationship by helping the investor ascertain investment readiness, tax considerations, appropriate risk levels, and profit standards. She or he will help the client understand why one type of investment or one company is more appropriate than another. The broker will also follow-up on client suggestions about investment choices, usually with the aid of brokerage house analysts whose role is to provide needed research into corporate and government stability and future prospects for stock and bond investors. Accordingly, a good securities broker will also cross-file your holdings by investor name and security name. Then if it comes time to sell a particular security, or buy more of it, the broker will be informed of all clients holding that security who should consider action, whether they own a small or large share in the venture.

Conflict of interest and limited knowledge are the major problems with broker advice. Frequent trading is more profitable to investment brokers than to many of their clients. Investors, therefore, have to analyze broker advice on each buy and sell transaction to determine the actual necessity for trading at a specific time. If the investor disagrees with the broker's advice, she or he should decline to act on it—at least without further information to support this view. Impulsive action is seldom profitable to anyone but the broker. That includes "hot tips" and other recommendations, unless the projected profitability is based on facts available for you to study if you choose.

Limited knowledge may stem from broker specialization. For example, a real estate broker is not likely to have sufficient breadth of knowledge to properly advise clients when to reduce real estate holdings for further investment in stocks and bonds (although the realtor may readily suggest the reverse to increase his or her personal profits). Accordingly, accountants, bankers, or insurance salespersons should not be asked for advice in areas beyond their expertise. Some securities dealers each specialize in stocks or bonds rather than keeping abreast of the important interchange between them with economic conditions. The ever-growing development of new securities opportunities, like the recently introduced money market mutual funds, also require constant professional updating by brokers. Not everyone is willing to devote the necessary study to these diverse investment vehicles; nor are all brokerage houses prepared with adequate research and support staff to handle the necessary analysis in all of these areas. You should comparison shop to find someone with whom you can place your trust as well as your investments.

The credentials of a broker and independent investment advisor may actually be quite similar. The major difference is that an independent advisor does not buy or sell investments for clients. The advisor's sole product is advice. Like brokers, the abilities of advisors to do the job can vary considerably. Investment brokers must be licensed to perform their trade. That assumes some level of knowledge required to enter the field. Investment advisors must also be registered. However, there is a growing group of people calling themselves "financial planners" who offer investment advice as part of a total financial package. At present, there are no specific regulations on these individuals. Therefore, their services must be even more carefully scrutinized to determine objectivity even when they propose to sell only advice. An informal study conducted in 1979 of financial planning services revealed questionable practices and some illogical advice from these professionals.[11] Buyer beware!

For the investor who prefers to rely on personal abilities in the selection of securities, etc., some purchase and sale costs can be reduced via the use of discount brokers. These licensed salespeople will act as your liaison in the purchase and sale of select investments for a lower fee than is usually set by traditional brokers. (Fixed fee-setting by these industries is illegal.) In order to do so, services to clients are reduced to simple execution of buy and sell orders. This can mean less time is devoted to obtaining the best possible price for clients. No advice is given, nor does the broker regularly review client accounts to propose improvements. All actions must be initiated by the investor. Discount brokers are available in the securities industry and real estate. They generally advertise their services locally. Again, comparative shopping is essential.

In order to reduce the risk of losses, it is imperative for investors to diversify their holdings or spread the dollars invested among several investment vehicles. Diversification can be interpreted to mean buying some common stocks and a few bonds to insure some benefits despite economic changes. It can also mean buying several different common stocks in case one company does not live up to its expectations, or selecting bonds that will mature at various dates in case a default does occur on one of them.

DIVERSIFICATION

While diversification can also mean lower profits if one among a group of investments yields unusual returns, it is a safety mechanism that should not be ignored. Diversification can also improve liquidity because one of the many investments held should be easily converted into cash at any given time.

Small investors must diversify carefully. Securities and many other investments are more liquid in common units of trading called *round lots*. One hundred shares of stock is a round lot, as are five bonds (valued at $1,000 each). If you cannot afford to buy round lots and diversify, you may be better off in other investments until you have more dollars available. Or you may prefer to gradually diversify with each additional round lot purchase. *Odd lots* or uncommon units of trading cost 1/8 more than round lots to buy and sell.

Today's economic conditions are changing rapidly and in new directions for which there is limited historical precedent on which to base investment decision making. Mrs. Beloin never imagined her nest egg could provide so poorly for her later years because the past history of American inflation is significantly lower than recent records.

TIMING

Stagflation is a new word, coined during the 1970s to describe an inflationary wage/price spiral despite otherwise recessionary conditions of rising unemployment and growing product inventories. Investors have been faced with real perplexities because traditional decision making philosophies did not quite fit.

The result of these and related economic variables has been controversy among the analysts about how to invest wisely today. The only consensus that has been clearly and uniformly upheld is the need for regular review and change in investment strategies in keeping with changing times. No longer is it realistic to buy and hold investments for decades, unless regular reviews show continued profitability with more of the same for the future. No investment is a sure thing indefinitely.

It takes time and energy to analyze market conditions and economic trends. The use of professional advisors does not eliminate that expenditure, although it can reduce it. The fees involved in buying and selling investment instruments may grow, too, if changes are made every two years, for example, instead of every ten years. Opportunity costs must also be considered. Which will produce a greater net return to you—increased efforts in investment analysis to increase yield, or moonlighting to increase the principal available for investing? How do taxes affect these alternatives? Can your time and energy be better spent to enjoy intangibles of companionship, etc., that have no inherent monetary value but contribute to the quality of life? Which orientation is more in keeping with your personality and household goals?

If your preference is to increase management efforts for investments, a valid beginning point is formal and informal study of today's economy, its history, and its future trends. Government intervention through monetary policy and taxation are vital components of this study, as are consumer attitudes and their impact on economic activities. The second step would be in-depth analysis of various investment instruments in relation to economic changes in order to better ascertain the proper timing of your decisions. Of course, information learned from these studies must be analyzed in light of personal goals to be most useful.

CONSUMER PROTECTION

The complexity and size of the investment market make it ripe for fraud and deception, especially with so many people hungry to make big profits with a modest investment of money and time.

LAWS

In order to reduce the probability of fraudulent practices, the state and federal governments have intervened in an effort to assure the provision of full and accurate information to investors for more informed decision making. These "Truth in Securities" laws were first passed at the state level to control information available to state residents about firms within that state. In 1934, Congress established the U.S. Securities and Exchange Commission with the following comparable responsibilities:

1. Companies that offer their securities for sale in "interstate commerce" must file with the Commission and make complete and accurate information available to investors.
2. Investors must be protected against misrepresentation and fraud in the issuance and sale of securities.

Through a series of related laws passed since the late 1930s, the federal government now regulates trading procedures on most American stock exchanges, the OTC market bond exchanges, and tax exempt markets. It requires the licensing and/or registration of all brokers and investment advisors and stipulates legal and illegal business practices in buy and sell transactions. While federal regulation is confined to regulations for interstate commerce, most states provide comparable regulations for intrastate securities dealings. In fact, some states have more stringent regulations than the federal government. Although federal regulations are limited to disclosure laws, some states have authority to ban the sale of "objectionable" securities within that state.

The Real Estate Commission at the state level provides regulations in this field. While there is no federal counterpart of this agency, the Department of Housing and Urban Development affords some protection to investors on interstate land sales, and so on.

INSURANCE

In 1970, Congress established a protection program for customers of investment brokerage houses. The newly created Securities Investors Protection Corporation is a nonprofit agency funded by essentially all broker/dealers in the industry. Its function is to protect investor losses due to the bankruptcy of a brokerage house. SIPC will pay $100,000 maximum per investor's claim. Reimbursable losses, though, are limited to those incurred by bankruptcy, not poor advice in selecting securities.

Some brokerage houses carry additional protection through private insurance against bankruptcy losses or theft of securities held in employees' possession. A common coverage per claimant is now $300,000. Since many investors leave stock certificates, bond coupons, etc., in their brokerage accounts for easier servicing, this type of protection is invaluable for safety of the securities. For bearer bonds, in particular, it can provide an unmatched protection otherwise unavailable to the bearer.

COMMON SENSE

Despite these safeguards developed by and for the investment industry, the best form of consumer protection remains *caveat emptor*. "Let the buyer beware" that there is no such thing as an easy road to fast profits. The time involved in investigating before you invest is always well spent. Con-artists rely on impulsive actions and get-rich-quick motivations to find easy prey for their fraudulent schemes. The wise investor must use common sense to avoid emotional entrapment into an unprofitable sham.

Part of this common sense approach means taking time to inquire about the facts on profits, company reputation, etc. What does the state or federal Securities Exchange Commission say about the firm's compliance with their regulations? What can your broker or investment advisor find out about the firm for you? After the facts are compiled, does it still appear to be a sound investment? Is the sales representative willing to wait out your investigation or is the offer too hot to last?

Sometimes just taking a day or two to think over the investment opportunity and evaluate it in light of current economic projections is enough to clarify decision making. Impulsive actions are seldom justified by hindsight. It is important to make decisions based on logic rather than dreams.

PROFESSIONAL GUIDELINES

Money management counselors who do not specialize in investment decision making can best serve their clients by knowing when such a referral is needed and how to help the client find a capable investment advisor. That is no small task. It can, however, become easier when the money management counselor has a basic knowledge of investments sufficient to discuss intelligently with the client and the investment advisor (if necessary).

The best use of resources can be for the money management counselor to help the client define her or his goals, and then calculate net worth, a workable spending plan, and some idea of acceptable levels of risk. This makes the client better prepared to discuss investment options with the investment advisor—or to conduct independent research in selecting appropriate investment instruments.

The money management counselor also plays an important role in helping clients to realistically evaluate investment readiness. In some cases, clients are investing dollars that can yield a better return by reducing personal indebtedness. In other cases, clients should consider using leverage to their investment advantage.

Equally important today, clients will need to understand the costs of investing, particularly in regard to wise management. It is essential to emphasize opportunity costs and the drain on total resources. If the money management counselor helps the client to fine-tune his or her decision making skills to carefully evaluate all of the variables unique to his or her own situation, this can then assist the investment counselor in steering the client toward profitable and appropriate investments.

A well informed money management counselor would be alert to broad-based timing factors and attitudinal changes that require review and possible revision in investment strategies. While it would generally be inappropriate to recommend specific changes without full information, it is always wise to inform clients of the need to review and reassess their position.

Of all the topics discussed in this book, investments are likely to require the most additional study for an effective level of understanding in order to make informed decisions. That additional study time can be most well spent when other financial concerns are under control and the motivation is there to put your money to work for you. The teachable moment is critical to properly training the money management counselor as well as her or his clients. The credit counselor is not as likely to feel the need for this training as will the adult educator in a wealthy suburban community. That is why only the rudiments of investment decision making are presented here, with the hope that self-motivation will help eager students expand on this knowledge base as needed.

ENDNOTES

1. Andrew Tobias, *The Only Investment Guide You'll Ever Need* (New York: Bantam Books, 1979), p. 29.
2. Howard Ruff, *How to Prosper During the Coming Bad Years* (New York: New York Times Books, 1979), pp. 14–16.
3. Harry Browne, *New Profits from the Monetary Crisis* (New York: William Morrow and Company, 1978), p. 50.
4. Roger Klein and William Wolman, *The Beat Inflation Strategy* (New York: Pocket Books, 1976), p. 12.
5. Michael Creedman, "A Franchise Is a Hard Way to Get Rich," *Money* (September 1973): 34.
6. Ruff, *How to Prosper,* p. 218.
7. Patricia A. Dreyfus, "Gold Goes Respectable," *Money* (October 1978): 48.
8. Browne, *New Profits,* p. 191.
9. "Investment Insights: Profiting from Contrariness," *Money* (March 1979): 82.
10. Klein and Wolman, *Beat Inflation Strategy,* p. 61.
11. Jeremy Main, "What Financial Planners Do and Don't Do," *Money* (April 1979): 77.

ELEVEN

Lifestyle Adaptations for Retirement and Estate Planning

As she walked to the bus stop, Jessica thought again about the people she had interviewed today. At age fifty-five, Emil Jacoby approached retirement enthusiastically. He was ready for a change from the working world in which he had participated for thirty long years. Free time looked wonderful—especially since he and his "bride" still had good health, companionship, productive hobbies to fill their leisure hours, and what seemed like enough money to relax and enjoy life for a while.

Those are the same preceptions of retirement that Angela Beloin had expressed about her later life. Now that she has survived over twenty-five years of retirement living, the world does not look as rosy. Her husband, Andrew, died a year to the day after retiring. The perceived joys of leisure diminished quickly for him as too much time suddenly became available for too few activities. Angela believes he actually died of boredom, although the death certificate said pneumonia.

Life alone for all of these years was far from Angela's goal, but it became reality. She had many friends. Yet the infirmities of old age took their toll, as did dwindling financial resources. Now Angela's children are expressing concern about her safety in the apartment alone and encouraging her to move to a nursing home.

As neighbors, Emil watched the effects time and inflation had on Angela's life. He was determined to avoid similar plight, and he was willing to work very hard at that goal. The perseverance was essential for goal achievement. Jessica and Emil both knew that. But Jessica still wondered if Emil was one of those fortunate people who could make it work for twenty-five or more years! In her observations as a social worker, careful planning only helped if the retiree followed through by implementing these plans and evaluating them in line with necessary adjustments to keep pace with the changing outside world.

LIFESTYLE ADJUSTMENTS

First of all, retirement changes your responsibilities. It is no longer essential to awake at 6:00 A.M. to go to work. Your wardrobe no longer needs to be planned around the regular business day, nor will your travel or shopping activities.

TIME

Suddenly the thirty-five or more hours per week that you devoted to work may now be used for other activities. That is a large chunk of time to have "on your hands" every week. To make this transition pleasant and productive, the retiree needs to find nonwork activities to constructively fill some of these hours—before they arrive, if possible. Hobbies and leisure time activities are a logical choice. But very often these pleasure-oriented activities must be started long before retirement if the interest and related skills are to be developed enough to enjoy them when time is plentiful. Emil is keenly aware of this. Angela was not and suffered the consequences.

Those people who have always lived under a strong work ethic may have difficulty adapting to a retirement that focuses only on pleasure. Instead, they may prefer to select income-producing hobbies or volunteer activities that reinforce these lifetime values. Other retirees prefer part-time work in their chosen profession or a related area for a few years so they can gradually ease into a retirement lifestyle.

MONEY

Compounding this change of focus for retirees is the related reduction in income that commonly coincides with retirement. Wages end when the job does. They are substituted with Social Security benefits, pensions, and those assets you have been accumulating throughout your lifetime. But these sources of retirement income are relatively fixed and often fail to keep up with inflation.

In addition, the division of assets to produce a comfortable level of living throughout your lifetime is tricky. No one ever knows just how long they will live. So if the retiree overspends in early years, or simply doesn't plan ahead, the last years of life can be spent in poverty. Or the retiree could pinch pennies for a lifetime only to die early, leaving thousands of unspent dollars that could have eased his or her retirement years.

Recent legislative changes further compound the variables in the retirement decision. It is now illegal to require mandatory retirement of most workers prior to age seventy. Nonmilitary federal workers cannot be forced to retire at any age. Exceptions do exist, but the coincidence of a sixty-fifth birthday and retirement can generally no longer be required.

Ironically, this legislation came at a time when demographic trends indicated a turn toward earlier retirement at about age sixty-two.[1] Projections for the immediate future are contradictory. Some experts reaffirm the present trend with less than 10 percent of the labor force over sixty-five choosing to continue their careers.[2] Others perceive that more highly educated professionals will opt to continue working because their jobs are such a vital portion of their lives.[3] The smaller working age population anticipated in the 1980s could encourage longer productive years in the future, just as today's bountiful work force provides an incentive to retire workers early. That means the incentives for working or retiring could change with market place needs. The person considering retirement in 1980 could have incentives weighted quite opposite from the person ready to retire in 1990. When job skills are needed and adequately compensated, alternatives to working have less appeal than when the job is boring, unchallenging, or physically draining.

Because of the growing multitude of variables affecting decision making about retirement and the negative image of old age and fixed incomes, more and more employers are attempting to help their employes cope better. The field of retirement counseling has emerged as a professional resolution to reduce employe anxieties and ease projected transition. The concept has excellent potential to aid in the required adaptation, but because the business is financially profitable it is subject to abuses by persons preferring to sell products and services rather than good advice.[4]

Therefore, an increased understanding of possibilities for retirement lifestyles can aid in evaluating the quality of professional counseling or completing your individual planning and implementation. An awareness of the costs of living during retirement plus an accurate assessment of potential annual income should aid in financial decision making. A basic knowledge of the related implications of these choices and methods of controlling them will also prove helpful.

COSTS OF LIVING IN RETIREMENT

Your retirement goals will play an important part in your cost of living during retirement. Do you want to maintain the status quo as much as possible—live in the same home, drive two cars, dine out regularly, etc.? Or do you want to make sacrifices earlier in life in order to enjoy a luxurious retirement (health permitting), full of travel to sunny climates and a chance to see the world?

GOALS

Begin by establishing your priorities and estimating their cost. If you choose to remain in the same home, will the mortgage be paid off before retirement? Can major repairs and remodeling also be completed before your income is reduced? Will you be able to handle necessary home maintenance chores? Is this residence comfortable for retirement living if you are troubled by the lesser mobility that can accompany aging?

If you prefer to move into a retirement home, investigate before you invest to rent or buy. Spend some preretirement vacation time in the new neighborhood to be sure it meets your expectations. Check the cost of food, transportation, medical supplies, and so on—and also check the prices of phone calls or visits home to see relatives or friends. Will you really be more comfortable in new surroundings? A little exploration of the proposed new environment will help make this decision more realistic.

COST PROJECTION

A general guideline suggested for figuring retirement costs is to estimate 75 percent of your preretirement needs. However, that figure is only workable if your retirement is pending immediately. If it's twenty years away, you must compute a substantial inflation factor. In addition, if your lifestyle will change sharply after retirement, your costs must be figured on the basis of these new priorities instead of the old ones.

Those expenses that hit retired people hardest are obviously the fixed costs. These include housing, utilities, taxes, etc.. Medical care costs generally rise at this time too, although government programs like Medicare and Medicaid can alleviate some of this cost. In addition, adding to your savings may become an impossible task. Clothing, transportation, and even food costs may drop with age and a simpler lifestyle. Spending on entertainment and recreation activities will vary with goals, income, and state of health, perhaps more so than other costs. Other expenses are highly individualized and are often adjusted with changes in income and health.

Expenses for taxation are commonly a heavy burden on retired persons. However, the size of this burden can differ significantly by state and locality of residence due to sales and property tax levies. Some forms of government have also initiated tax relief programs for the elderly. This is often available in relation to real or personal property taxes for persons over sixty-five years of age; however, it is not automatic. An application must be filed at the appropriate local government offices. When available, it may alternatively apply directly to reduce the tax portion of rent in nonsubsidized housing. There may also be income guidelines to qualify. In addition, IRS allows taxpayers over sixty-five years of age to claim an extra dependency allowance to reduce the total income tax burden for the elderly.

Begin by estimating retirement living expenses in relation to your values and goals. Compare this to your present spending plan so that you can orient yourself to the areas of potential change among spending priorities. Do they seem acceptable or in need of modification? Also remember to review your plans every few years to be sure you are working toward your retirement goals. As retirement draws closer it will be much easier to estimate expenses.

Obviously, an appropriate spending plan for retirement living plus adequate recordkeeping will help match income and outgo. When income may become fixed for the first time, the prospects of maintaining a chosen lifestyle for the rest of your life can appear dim—particularly with the increases in longevity which provide longer retirement years. That prospect has led many retirees to opt for "life care" arrangements that fix all or most costs for the remainder of their lives.
COST CONTROLS

In 1976, 240,000 retired Americans chose to use a significant portion of their assets to guarantee lifetime care in one of 900 communities established for this purpose.[5] These residential facilities for the elderly can provide everything from housing, housekeeping, medical care, food, and spending money for residents in exchange for a large entrance fee plus a relatively stable monthly fee. The entrance fee can equal the retiree's total assets, with monthly fees obtained by the resident assigning all Social Security and pension checks due to her or him. The concept has merits and demerits. Financial insolvency of the facility is the biggest problem coupled with calculating equitable refunds for persons who want to leave. In a carefully chosen life care community that reflects your retirement goals, the benefits can begin with peace of mind that you will have your needs met without significant additional effort. Careful selection, although time consuming, will be the key to a positive retirement experience.

SOURCES OF RETIREMENT INCOME

In 1935, Congress passed legislation creating the Social Security system to ease the financial burden of life for retirees, select dependents and survivors, and certain other disadvantaged workers and/or their families. Social Security was always intended "to augment your savings," not provide full support Yet for some retirees, it is the only source of income and,
SOCIAL SECURITY

therefore, meager in that regard. Because most American workers are eligible for some Social Security retirement benefits after age sixty-two, this is a logical starting point for analyzing anticipated income.

Full Social Security benefits are given to qualified persons who apply for them after sixty-five years of age. However, persons willing to accept a smaller monthly sum may apply for Social Security at age sixty-two. Benefits are not sent automatically. A nonworking spouse is eligible to start collecting benefits equal to 50 percent of the working spouse's benefits at age sixty-five. If the wage-earning spouse retires and receives benefits at age sixty-two, and the nonworking spouse likewise receives benefits at age sixty-two, the nonworking spouse's benefits will be less than 50 percent. If the wage-earning spouse receives retirement benefits at age sixty-two, but the nonworking spouse does not receive benefits until age sixty-five or more, her or his benefits will be larger than 50 percent. When both spouses have been wage earners and thus qualify individually for Social Security, each is entitled to draw her or his own benefits at full value. The individual with very low qualifying earnings can elect to take 50 percent of her or his spouse's benefits instead, if it is a larger sum.

Under certain conditions, retirees may continue to work full or part time and still continue to collect all or part of their Social Security benefits. In 1980, retirees can earn up to $5,000 worth of earned income (in wages and salary) before Social Security benefits will be reduced. That sum rises to $5,500 in 1981 and $6,000 in 1982. After that, increases will be contingent upon wage level rises. Nonexempt retired workers lose $1 in Social Security benefits for each $2 earned above these maximums. For some people, that is a strong deterrent against continued wage earning. However, those workers seventy years old or older in 1982 will be exempt from this earning limit—or free to earn any amount while continuing to receive full Social Security benefits. Until 1982, a worker must be seventy-two years of age or more to qualify for this exemption.

In addition, as of 1979, a divorced wife may now apply for benefits from her former husband if they were legally married for at least ten years. To further ease the financial problems of the elderly, Social Security recipients of survivor benefits, both of whom are over sixty, may now marry without suffering a reduction in benefits.

Calculations used for determining the amount of Social Security benefits to be paid are based on the number of quarters or 3-month periods of work the applicant has completed with earnings at or above a certain dollar minimum. For many years, that minimum has been $50 per quarter. In 1978, that figure was changed to $250 per quarter, with automatic increases as wages rise. While the number of work quarters required can vary with the age of the worker, anyone born in 1929 or after needs forty work quarters to be retirement insured.

Any earnings received over $250 per quarter affect the amount of Social Security benefits payable, not your eligibility to receive them. Generally a worker with regular, high earnings will receive higher Social Security benefits than someone with irregular, low earnings because of the various requirements to qualify for benefits. However, there are maximum benefits payable that cannot be exceeded despite the retiree's work record. Accordingly, Social Security contributions are only made by employees up to a certain annual salary limit. Any wages earned above that limit (subject to routine changes by law) are exempt from Social Security or FICA taxes.

The amount of Social Security benefits payable to qualified retired workers is established by law and subject to annual increases tied to the cost of living. Basic benefits are calculated on average annual earnings. For persons born after 1930, this calculation is made by assessing qualified earnings received annually from age twenty-two to retirement at sixty-two or older. The five years of lowest earnings are first deleted from this list. Then the sum of earnings is totalled and divided by the number of years worked (minus the five years already deleted). Minimum and maximum benefits have been established by law for calculating these benefits.

Obviously, accuracy of recordkeeping is critical to proper calculation of Social Security benefits. While this responsibility falls primarily on the Social Security Administration, it is wise to check their records every few years. To do so, you request a review of your earnings record through your local Social Security office. The review is to determine if the annual earnings reported are the same as those earned for the years listed. If not, now is the time to correct any discrepancies. The best proof of actual earnings are the withholding tax forms filed with your annual income tax return. So keep these until you retire in case a question occurs about your earnings record.

Persons nearing retirement age can also request an estimate of retirement benefits for which they will qualify at retirement age. This will be far less accurate to calculate for persons with several decades to work prior to retirement age because of the unknowns between now and then.

Benefits paid to the surviving spouse of a Social Security insured retiree may vary with the age of the spouse. In some cases, benefits will increase since a widow or widower can become eligible to receive the deceased spouse's full retirement benefit if it is larger than the survivor's present benefit as a retired worker or spouse. Although this addition is still a small sum in relation to need, it has helped Angela Beloin and others to cope a bit more easily. It is a point worth remembering in calculating retirement income needs.

PENSIONS

Employer Plans. Many companies also assist employes to meet retirement needs by providing a pension or retirement income to employes with a minimum or more number of years with the firm. Usually each employe is asked to contribute to the pension system during their wage-earning years, but it is possible that the company will pay full pension benefits. Pension benefits can vary enough that some people use this criteria for selecting an employer—and it's not a bad idea to do so.

Pensions come in many forms. To assure fair treatment to retirees, the federal government has passed regulations affecting their management and benefits program. The newest of these laws is the Employe Retirement Income Security Act of 1974 (ERISA).

Under this law, specific standards have been established for vesting (a guaranteed return from the plan). An employe is now 100 percent vested in benefits from his or her own contributions; the employe should always be able to withdraw these benefits no matter when or why he or she leaves the plan.

In addition, people who change jobs regularly will be eligible for some benefit from their employer's contribution to the pension program. Employers have three alternatives for establishing vesting of their shares of the pension program. These are:

1. *The ten-year rule.* Full vesting is required after an employe has ten years of service with the employer.
2. *The graded fifteen-year service plan.* Full vesting is not complete for fifteen years, buy partial vesting begins after five years of service. At that time, an employe becomes 25 percent vested, adding an additional 5 percent per year for the next five years and an additional 10 percent for each of the last five years.
3. *The rule of forty-five.* Vesting begins after five years of employment in this plan when the employe's age and total years of service total forty-five. Then each year of additional service adds another 10 percent of vesting until 100 percent vesting is achieved.

The law also requires employers to have enough money in their pension plans to pay out benefits as they come due. In addition, an employer who promises retirement benefits based on a variable rate of employee contributions must participate in an insurance program to guarantee basic pension benefits even if the employer's retirement plan fails.

Employee Plans. When there is no employer-sponsored pension plan available, any worker may establish an independent pension via an Individual Retirement Account (IRA). The qualified employee may contribute as much as 15 percent of her or his salary up to $1,500 annually in an IRA. The amount an employee contributes to the IRA annually is tax deductible on income tax. The sum becomes taxable as income only after the employe begins drawing money out of this plan after age fifty-nine and one-half. There is a choice of investments in which to keep these annual set asides to best meet retirement goals, provided the plan's sponsor has been approved by the Internal Revenue Service.

In addition, a worker qualified for this program with a nonwage-earning spouse may set aside an extra $250 per year to provide some benefits to support the dependent spouse. However, the working spouse cannot put a larger amount in the IRA on his or her own behalf than is contributed to the dependent spouse's IRA. So, if one spouse receives $250, the other spouse is only permitted $250. When both spouses are employed outside the home for firms that do not offer pensions, each spouse may establish a separate IRA in accord with legal maximums.

Self-employed people may establish a similar retirement program under the Keough plan, which allows tax free contributions of 15 percent of income up to $7,500 a year. This applies even to part-time earnings through self-employment. In fact, those people who earn $3,000 annually or less can open a mini-Keough with 25 percent of their earnings up to $750 per year. Like the IRA, taxes are not paid on these sums until they are withdrawn as retirement income.

A Compromise.   Employers may also choose to offer a Simplified Employee Pension as a method of increasing employe retirement benefits without the disclosure and other requirements of ERISA. This is accomplished by letting the employer contribute to an employe's IRA in sums up to 15 percent of her or his salary up to $7,500, whichever is less. In those cases where the employer contribution is lower than that allowed the employe, that worker may contribute the difference, up to the $1,500 annual limit.

SAVINGS AND INVESTMENT

After retirement it is generally no longer realistic to add regularly to the principal that is saved or otherwise invested. Yet these assets may become more important than ever because they may now be needed to meet survival needs and other retirement goals. Therefore, liquidity needs may change.

During retirement it is especially important to maintain an emergency fund which can easily be turned into cash when needed. For most people this is done through a combination of savings and checking accounts or government bonds. Usually the total assets held in this manner should equal four to six months' income.

Other investments can be less liquid to yield a higher return. However, because you may be dependent on these assets for retirement income, it is important that the dividends and/or interest paid on these investments be available to you as needed. If they yield a sufficient return, you may not need to draw on the principal for many years. Keep in mind, though, that the higher the return or yield, the greater the risk of loss. And remember that when the value of investment outpaces inflation, you can afford to draw on the growing principal amount in lieu of interest earnings without shrinking the original sum invested. (See Chapter 10 for details.)

Charting your retirement expenses versus income will help you determine if preretirement investments are the wisest choices for postretirement goals. Should changes be in order, it may be advisable to make them gradually to minimize taxes and/or losses. As with other investment decisions, you should consult a reputable investment counselor before liquidating or converting assets haphazardly.

LIFE INSURANCE AND ANNUITIES

After retirement you generally no longer need life insurance to protect your dependents against the loss of your earnings in the event of your death. Term insurance policyholders can simply cancel their coverage. Those persons who have carried cash value life insurance will find a sum of money accumulated in that policy that will vary with the size and type of policy, as well as the number of years it has been in effect.

You essentially have two choices of how you may choose to use this accumulated cash value:

1. Surrender the policy and take the cash value as a lump sum or in regular payments.
2. Keep the insurance protection to provide an inheritance to your chosen heirs (or cover funeral and probate costs, etc.), but convert the policy to paid up insurance.

Policyholders who choose to receive this cash value via regular payments may purchase an *annuity* with this sum in order to provide a guaranteed income for a specified period of time. Therefore, an annuity, which pays benefits to the policyholder while alive, is the opposite of life insurance, which pays benefits only after the policyholder's death. They are, however, both generally sold by the same companies. In fact, some people choose cash value life insurance because it is often convertible to an annuity upon retirement and is therefore a forced savings program purchased at any age, totally separate from life insurance. They are unique among investments because they can prevent an investor who lives longer than average from exhausting the principal before death. In some cases, though, an annuity can correspondingly reduce the investment yield if the policyholder dies early. This will vary with the type of annuity selected.

Annuity policies differ by the amount and nature of benefits provided and the cash value accumulated. The basic types include:

1. *Straight life.* Payments are made to the policyholder only until death. Despite the dollars invested, no return is made to the heirs of the policyholder.
2. *Installment certain.* Payments are made for a specified dollar amount and a specified number of years to the policyholder or the designated beneficiary if the policyholder dies during this period.
3. *Installment refund.* Payments are made to the policyholder as contracted with the lump sum remainder of the principal paid to the beneficiaries in installments (although these may differ from the payments received by the policyholder.)
4. *Cash refund.* Payments are made as contracted to the policyholder with the remainder of the principal paid in one lump sum to the designated beneficiary upon the policyholder's death.
5. *Joint and survivorship.* Payments are made as contracted to two or more persons who buy this annuity jointly. After one policyholder dies, the remaining joint owners share the benefits as long as any one of them remains alive.
6. *Variable.* The return from this annuity is not fixed like the others because the principal is invested (totally or in part) in the purchase of common stock in the hope that benefit increases will be possible equal to or greater than the cost of inflation.

Annuities can be purchased with a single lump sum payment or annual premiums over a number of years. Persons ready now for retirement may choose to liquidate other investments for a lump sum purchase of an annuity that will begin benefit payments immediately. Younger people may prefer to purchase the annuity from current salary for deferred coverage after retirement. As part of IRA and Keough pension plans and otherwise, annuities purchased for deferred coverage can have tax-sheltering advantages. Deferred coverage annuities can also be purchased with death benefits to a designated beneficiary if the policyholder dies before payments begin.

Other options that affect the purchase price of annuities include a cash surrender value, loan value, and dividend payments. Accordingly, immediate benefit annuities are cheaper for the older buyer while deferred payment annuities are a better buy for the younger buyer. In both cases, the return from annuities must be compared to other investments in order to determine the value of the purchase to meet individual goals. Family life span in relation to the average will also be a relevant factor since people who live longer can often derive more benefit from some type of annuities.

Although traditionally an instrument for retirement planning, annuities must also be analyzed for their investment potential. *Tax deferred annuities* (TDA) are of particular interest in this regard because of their unique ability to grow tax free until income is drawn from them during retirement. This significantly increases investment yield, especially for those in higher tax brackets. In addition, since TDA's can be purchased without sales commission from many investment brokers, their rate of return can be far above comparable instruments purchased directly from insurance companies.

ESTATE PLANNING

Unfortunately, not everyone lives long enough to spend all of their assets during retirement, nor does everyone want to do so. Some people hope to have enough money left over to provide a nest egg for their heirs. Therefore, it is imperative to plan ahead to be sure that your assets are distributed as you desire.

WILLS   The safest legally binding method for assuring the distribution of your assets according to your wishes is the making of a will or document directing this distribution. To be legally binding, the will must be unaltered in any way and signed by witnesses. It is also advisable to have this document drawn by an attorney, although it is not required by law.

If you die without leaving a will, the state in which you lived decides how your assets or estate will be divided. These laws of intestate, as they are called, vary from state to state. Therefore, if you choose to have your property distributed differently from the laws of intestate you must make a will to express your wishes. In addition, if the guardianship of minor children must be provided, or if you wish to control how certain heirs are to receive their share of your assets, you will need to do so by will.

To assure your wishes are properly carried out and/or the laws of intestate followed, the transfer of property after your death is supervised by the probate court in your district. That is the primary function of this special court. It is also the appropriate place of inquiry to determine the laws of intestate where you live. This court does not, however, intervene in the passage of property that automatically passes to a specified person after an individual's death, such as life insurance or jointly held property.

The degree of probate court involvement and cost varies with the existence of a valid will or lack thereof, as well as other vehicles for estate planning. Since the costs of settling an estate must be paid under probate court supervision before the property transfer is completed, it is important to plan adequately to provide enough liquid assets to cover expenses of the last illness, funeral, outstanding debts, taxes, and the cost of administering the estate. Federal estate taxes are due within nine months after death, and state inheritance taxes must also be paid. The lack of sufficient cash to cover these costs may result in the required sale of assets from the estate at an inopportune time from an investment perspective, or despite the wishes of the beneficiary to keep the property intact.

The transfer of property after death is taxable at the federal levels. Taxable property for this purpose usually includes everything of value that the deceased person owned, including life insurance policies, some jointly held property, and all individually owned property (although there are numerous exemptions that vary by state laws). The amount of money paid by your heirs in estate and inheritance taxes can be controlled through careful estate planning.

TAXES

Sometimes these taxes may be partially avoided or reduced if you choose to make gifts of your property while you are still alive. By law, you may give to any one person $3,000 in cash or property each year without paying gift taxes on it. You may make as many of these $3,000 gifts as you wish to different individuals. Under some circumstances, the exclusion is even higher if the gift is to your spouse. But if you give gifts above this limit, they are taxed at the same rate as the property in your estate. Gift taxes are charged to the giver, not the recipient. Estate taxes are paid under Probate Court supervision before any nonexempt inheritance is passed to the heirs.

However, under the 1976 Tax Reform Act, many people will be exempt from paying federal estate taxes by 1981 when this law is fully implemented. The reasons for this are:

1. A simple tax credit replaces the old estate and lifetime gift exemptions. After the five-year transition period, this will result in tax credits by 1981 equal to an exemption of $175,625.
2. Gifts and inheritances passed from one spouse to another are also protected from estate taxes by additional exemptions. The new law lets you leave one-half of your estate or $250,000, whichever is greater, to your surviving spouse, tax free. Additional gift tax exclusions can result in the tax free transfer of estates equal to $425,625 by 1981 (only passed by one spouse to another). The same benefits do *not* apply when the surviving spouse dies, leaving the total estate to their children or others.

The benefits from these revised tax laws do not negate the need for a properly drawn will and appropriate estate planning. Instead, they reinforce the need for these protections. Most specifically, the legal and tax consequences of ownership vary with the size of the estate. Acceptable practices for modest estates that fall below the new tax limits could prove costly to the heirs of a taxable estate. If the will and registrations of ownership of taxable assets do not coincide, more costly consequences can follow for the heirs.

The classic estate plan anticipates the death of the husband before the wife. In so doing, the will is drawn to maximize benefits of the marital deduction with remaining assets left in *trust* for children or other heirs. A trust is an arrangement whereby property is managed by an individual or bank for the benefit of someone else. It is a vehicle for tax savings and a means by which the trustmaker can influence how his or her funds will be used after his or her death. In the classic plan, funds held in trust are not taxable when the wife dies because these assets were never owned by the wife. Hence, more money is ultimately available to the children or other heirs. However, the assets held in trust can be used for the benefits of the wife during her lifetime, so she need not be deprived of any benefits this money could bring during her years of widowhood.

If the wife dies first, tax savings under the classic plan are lost. While the program can be drafted with the husband and wife in reverse roles, this type of estate plan is not reciprocal. In other words, the spouses must decide who they anticipate will die first and prepare the estate plan according. Statistically, the man more commonly dies first. However, unique circumstances could made the reverse situation more probable to justify reversing the role of spouses in the estate plan.

An "equalization of estate" plan would better allow for the uncertainties of which spouse will survive longer. However, it is only when the individual assets of each spouse are essentially equal in value (as a result of dual employment, etc.). Then the equalization of estate plan would establish a trust for the surviving spouse until her or his death. The trust would terminate at that time, with assets divided equally among the surviving heirs. No use would be made of the marital deduction.

State governments also tax the proceeds of an estate held by their citizens. This is called a *succession or inheritance tax* because it is computed at a graduate rate on the total value of property passing to the different types of heirs. For this purpose, heirs are classified by relationship to the deceased. Those classes of heirs most closely related have higher tax exemptions and lower rates of inheritance taxes due beyond this exemption. The dollar amounts are determined by the individual states. As a general rule, inheritance taxes begin to be due at levels far below the federal exemption limits and at lower rates.

The taxability of any asset for estate and inheritance taxes depends on ownership. If an asset is owned individually by a person at the time of death, it is clearly part of the taxable estate. However, most assets are jointly owned by two or more people. So, upon the death of one owner, a determination must be made about the portion of the jointly held property attributable to the deceased's estate. Some of that decision is based on the nature of the joint ownership. The three types of joint ownership include:

ASSET OWNERSHIP

1. *Joint tenancy with the right of survivorship.* The individuals own the property jointly during their lives. Upon death of one owner, the property becomes owned by the surviving joint owner unless this arrangement is negated by the deceased's will.
2. *Tenancy by the entirety.* Similar to above, this form of joint ownership is limited to husband and wife. Under some state laws it provides exemption from state inheritance taxes.
3. *Tenancy in common.* The individual owners hold separate and distinct interests in the property that are not necessarily equal.

Unless it can be proven that the surviving spouse actually purchased part of the jointly held assets with individually earned money, the full value of that asset is calculated into the estate of the deceased for tax purposes. While there are exceptions, particularly in regard to joint ownerships created after December 31, 1976, that is why joint ownership may be disadvantageous to persons with taxable estates. For persons with a far more modest estate, tax savings are not a concern. Then the simplicity of ownership transfer via joint ownership can work in their favor. Since all holders of jointly held property have full rights to use the property during their lifetime when one dies, the surviving owner(s) have the right to use or dispose of the property as they see fit. Therefore, most jointly held property passes outside probate.

Once a decision has been reached about how you wish to register the ownership of bank accounts, real estate, automobiles, etc., it is important to be sure your choices are consistent with the intent of your will. Estate planning to save taxes usually requires individual ownership of assets. Joint ownership with the right of survivorship could wipe out much of that savings. It would be wiser to maintain individual ownership of assets to avoid this problem. If most assets are already jointly owned, changing that form of ownership can result in gift taxes under some circumstances. It would, therefore, be wise to consult an attorney or tax counsel before making these changes. Be certain that any prescribed changes are made in both the will and registration of ownership.

Young people who are uncertain about whether they will ever accumulate the fortune sufficient to make their estate taxable should plan early to prevent future problems. They may find it wiser to own property individually with passage directed to appropriate heirs via a valid will instead of the possible entanglements of joint ownership. When joint ownership is preferred, tenancy in common may be the most appropriate registration to minimize the possible tax burden.

TRUSTS

Sometimes an individual wants to keep some control over the use of her or his assets by the named beneficiaries after her or his death. As stated earlier, this can be accomplished by the use of a trust, often developed simultaneously to save taxes, protect the interests of minors, etc. In so doing, you must draft a written agreement by which you authorize a responsible third party and/or institution to manage your inheritance for your beneficiaries according to your wishes. Both real and personal property may be placed in trust.

An important advantage of the trust is its flexibility. The trustee can be empowered to "sprinkle" trust property among beneficiaries as their respective needs may require. This feature recognizes the possible emergency situations that may arrive for medical bills, education, etc. In addition, the trustee may be given the power to use some of the principal held in trust when annual income is not enough to adequately provide for the beneficiaries. This procedure has clearly been a blessing for Angela Beloin since inflation has eaten away much of her husband's estate.

There are two basic kinds of trusts: *living* and *testamentary*. The first is created and effective while the trustmaker is living. The second is established under the provisions of the trustmaker's last will and testament. It does not become effective until the will has passed through probate. Since a testamentary trust does not go into effect until the death of the owner, there is no tax savings in the estate. However, the trust may be drafted to save estate taxes in the estates of the beneficiaries. For example, a husband may leave part of his estate or trust for his children, with the income payable to the wife during her life. The trust is not part of the wife's estate, thereby saving estate taxes since the children own the trust. When the heirs are minors or inexperienced in money matters, the trustee is also empowered to conduct financial affairs on their behalf as directed by the trustmaker in the trust agreement.

Trusts can also be *revocable* or *irrevocable*. The former can be terminated or altered by the trustmaker at any time. It offers no special estate tax advantage for the maker, although it can reduce the estate tax of beneficiaries. The revocable trust can eliminate the costs of probate of the trust property. This includes executor, attorney, court, and appraisal fees.

An irrevocable trust cannot be amended, altered, revoked, or terminated. Therefore, assets placed in an irrevocable trust are removed from the estate of the person creating it. That can reduce estate taxes for the trustmaker. However, the transfer of ownership from trustmaker to beneficiary can involve a gift tax which is now the same rate as estate taxes.

A *marital deduction trust* is a special type of trust to take advantage of estate tax laws. It is useful only between spouses. As explained earlier, it involves the establishment of two trusts. Part one, equal to the legal marital deduction, is given to the surviving spouse outright. Part two, encompasses the remainder of the estate held in trust for the children with lifetime use for the surviving spouse, thereby reducing estate taxes at the death of the surviving spouse.

A *life insurance trust* is another special type of trust that can be utilized to provide for payment of insurance proceeds to a trustee in a sum estimated to equal anticipated probate costs plus estate and inheritance taxes. By so doing, the principal within the estate can remain in tact for passage to the heirs without liquidation to pay these required costs. In some cases, this trust can also prevent beneficiaries from receiving lump sum payments which may be inappropriately handled by some individuals. However, this type of trust has an ongoing cost equivalent to the price of the life insurance policy used to achieve this goal. When paid-up life insurance is used for this purpose, that cost drops significantly. Since this generally involves cash value insurance, the policyholder must consider if the low investment return is offset by the anticipated benefits. The usefulness of this trust must also be figured from a cost/benefit analysis.

As you can observe, there are a multitude of choices in retirement and estate planning that are worth considering to plan wisely. This is especially important since each choice affects the next one. For example, you cannot consider an irrevocable living trust unless you are certain there are enough other funds available to provide for a comfortable retirement; nor can you give $3,000 away each year without the same information. Those persons with limited assets may have to make hard decisions about selling a home, etc., just to make ends meet during retirement, never mind leaving a nest egg for the next generation. While that can be a difficult decision for some people because of their values, it may be a reality that has to be considered.

This is why careful planning and study of the alternatives is essential for rational decision making. Experiment with several retirement lifestyles before you make a permanent commitment. Talk with several authorities in the field. Do the same with your estate planning to be sure you are up to date on all available options. Then be sure you and your family can live as comfortably as possible with your decisions so you can all relax and enjoy the pleasures of these later years!

PROFESSIONAL GUIDELINES

The uncertainties of the future and the complexities of legal and tax considerations make retirement and estate planning a difficult area in which to provide counsel and guidance. For anything beyond development of an awareness of areas of concern, the average money management professional must seek specialized training or referral sources. As mentioned earlier, retirement counseling as a career field is composed of persons with highly diverse levels of expertise. Therefore, referrals must be made with caution and advance screening, as well as client feedback.

The biggest decision facing clients is the question of meeting present versus future needs. What sacrifices, if any, will you make today to build assets for retirement? What sacrifices will you make early in retirement to preserve assets for later life or your heirs? Values play a vital role in making these decisions. Value clarification is an essential starting point, followed only by interpersonal communication among household members involved in these decisions. A good money management professional can help clients to understand and express themselves without ignoring the economic facts of life.

ENDNOTES

1. "When Retirement Can't Happen," *Business Week* (June 19, 1978): 73.
2. "What the New Retirement Law Says," *Changing Times* (October 1978): 15.
3. "When Retirement Can't Happen," p. 75.
4. "How Counselors Help Employees Manage Funds to Insure Comfortable, Carefree Retirement," *Wall Street Journal,* January 8, 1979, p. 30.
5. "Opting for a Lifetime of Care," *Money* (August 1976): 57.

TWELVE

A Word in Closing

Paycheck in hand, Jessica left the office with mixed emotions. This was her last day conducting the local Consumer Expenditure Survey. The work had been pleasant, the hours flexible, and the pay adequate. These facts she had anticipated. The surprising factor was how much she had learned about people and their interactions with money. As a social worker and graduate student, she had always perceived that money problems were unique to low income people. Now she had to acknowledge that she was wrong. Money strongly influences the lives of people regardless of income. Moreover, its wise management will yield a positive impact for anyone just as inadequate management will produce a comparable negative effect. Most importantly, each individual or household has the power to choose among these alternatives and allocate resources to meet their goals with money as a helping agent rather than a barrier.

Of course, acknowledging the importance of informed money management decision making and implementing it are two different things. The implementation takes work, including skills training and a conscious effort at cost/benefit analysis. With ever-changing economic conditions and a related adaptation in values, this is no small task. But Jessica knows it is a challenge she must accept, and she must help her future clients to do so as well—or they will all have to deal with the consequences of ill-informed choices in an increasingly complex world.

IDEOLOGIES CHALLENGED

As demonstrated throughout this book, the traditional guidelines for personal economic behavior are breaking down due to national and worldwide economic conditions never before experienced. No longer can we successfully follow the precepts of our forefathers to save for a rainy day, buy for cash, etc., without adapting these axioms to present market conditions. Inflation, in particular, is impacting so heavily on the needs and wants of the present generation that its projected effects must be calculated and evaluated in relation to any and all economic conditions. The coincidental effects of inflation on our values must also be given priority. Those Americans who have seen only spiraling costs throughout their lifetime evaluate economic choices differently from those who have experienced first hand the doom of the Great Depression. Traditional economic ideologies are questioned, and they are sometimes abandoned and sometimes modified. Yet, new theories cannot be embraced too quickly until they, too, can be evaluated and adjusted to the needs of the people choosing among them.

The one thing that remains unchanged and unchallenged is that money is merely a means to an end, a vehicle for achieving goal attainment. For mentally and emotionally healthy people, that is and should remain a top priority. That makes an increased knowledge of money management strategies essential for coping with the world. For those people whose goal is the achievement of affluence, it means understanding inflation and related economic factors to maximize their utility in goal attainment. If self-actualization is the goal, careful dollar management is equally important in order to reduce the actual dollars needed for survival and intellectual pursuits. Because of specialization of labor, as well as the legal and environmental demands on an American lifestyle, self-sufficiency from the uses and abuses of money is almost impossible. Dollar dependency can only be minimized rather than eliminated. Therefore, the most effective coping mechanism becomes good management.

REALITIES PERCEIVED

Stated simply, you must manage your money instead of letting your money manage you. That is easier said than done. Good management requires the utilization of resources toward that goal. It takes time, energy, and talent. Sometimes it even means devoting some money to skills training toward this goal; however, the end result is worthwhile because it increases your coping skills in dealing with the realities of a money world. When the values and goals of the individuals and groups involved are added to this cost/benefit analysis of economic choices, there is a far greater control over one's life than can otherwise be anticipated.

Opportunity costs are a vital concern in decision making. They cannot be ignored without increasing the probability of negative impact. Yet to be fully utilized, the widest possible range of choices must be found and evaluated. In the beginning, this can be very time consuming. Yet when application of the management process to plan, implement, and control your lifestyle choices becomes a norm for decision making, the time commitment shrinks. Making informed choices becomes easier and faster when the criteria for choosing are more clearly defined and the results of earlier selections have been implemented and evaluated. In other words, practice simplifies the process.

Accordingly, the good manager skilled in cost/benefit analysis will also be better able to separate household priorities from societal pressures to spend, save, or invest because the mass media says it is a good idea. Development of that ability alone can improve individual coping skills with money and reinforce its value as a means to an end. Then you are in charge and the money works as a useful tool in goal attainment—at last!

Glossary

Adjustable Life Insurance similar to modified whole life combining term and permanent insurance in one policy, with the amount of each purchased at the discretion of the policyholder; can allow policyholder to alter face value of policy while modified whole life does not.

Amortization a method of repaying an installment loan in equal monthly payments which cover accrued interest plus part of the principal, with interest calculated only on the unpaid balance.

Annuity a contract that provides an income for a specified number of years or life; the opposite of life insurance.

Assessment fair market value of real and/or personal property as calculated for tax purposes.

Assigned Risk Pool a composite of all auto insurers licensed to do business within a state whereby each company must accept a number of high risk drivers for coverage in proportion to the amount of business they conduct within that state.

Balloon Payment a large final payment due on an installment loan contract that is equal to two or more regular monthly payments.

Bankruptcy court-ordered sale of debtor assets to discharge total liabilities.

Beneficiary person(s) named in a life insurance, annuity, or pension contract to receive the proceeds of that plan upon death of the policyholder.

Bonds debt securities with an original maturity date of five or more years into the future.

Broker professional salesperson who negotiates the purchase or sale agreement for the buyer and seller of securities and many other investment instruments.

Capital Assets property you own or use for personal, pleasure, or investment purposes.

Cash Surrender Value the dollar portion of a permanent life insurance policy that is kept by the policyholder upon cancellation of that policy.

Cashier's Check a draft against the financial institution's own checking account purchased from the institution as a means of proving funds are available to cover payment.

Certificates of Deposit high interest time deposits at financial institutions for fixed terms up to eight years during which there can be no withdrawal without penalty.

Certified Check withdrawal notice to remove funds from your checking account presented to the bearer with a guarantee by the financial institution holding the account that there are sufficient funds in that account to cover payment.

Check Credit open-end credit available from many banks in the form of an automatic line of credit that offers borrowers an instant loan up to a stated amount by either writing an overdraft check on their regular checking account or using checks drawn to a separate account for this purpose.

Closed-End Credit all of the terms of the contract are fixed at the time of the signing; any changes in amount borrowed, etc., would require the signing of a second contract by both parties.

Closed-End Fund investment companies that sold a set number of shares in their corporation that could be traded in the market like stocks.

Closing Costs fees for professional services for the legal and financing arrangements involved in home ownership transfer.

Coinsurance provision of some insurance policies, especially major medical, whereby the policyholder agrees to pay a specified percentage of all claims filed up to certain limits on some or all claims.

Collateral security for a loan.

Collision a type of auto insurance providing protection against financial losses incurred because the insured vehicle was damaged by overturning or crashing with another object or vehicle.

Co-Makers or Co-Signers all persons who sign a credit contract along with the original applicant and are therefore equally responsible for its repayment.

Commodities Future Contracts promises that the seller will deliver a specific amount and quality of a certain commodity on a predetermined future date—without regard to price changes, weather conditions, etc.

Common Stock shares of ownership in a corporation and its profits without the promise of a fixed rate of return.

Compounding paying interest on money that has previously been earned as interest in a bank account, etc.

Comprehensive Insurance a type of auto insurance that provides protection against financial losses from theft or damage to the insured vehicle due to fire, vandalism, windstorm, hail, flood, smoke, falling objects, etc., other than collision or upset.

Condominiums Multiple-family dwelling units in which owners purchase and care for their individual apartment and a proportionate share of all common areas.

Confession of Judgment a contract clause whereby the buyer agrees to let the creditor take legal action to collect this account without first notifying the buyer of this action.

Consolidation Loan money borrowed from a financial institution for the purpose of paying off old bills of the borrower.

Conventional Mortgage   a long-term amortized installment loan offered to all creditworthy applicants by financial institutions.

Convertability   an available term life insurance rider which allows the policyholder to transfer coverage from term to permanent insurance without a medical exam.

Convertibles   preferred stock of some corporations that can be purchased with the option to exchange it for a predetermined number of shares of common stock at the stockholder's discretion; sometimes also possible with corporate bonds that can be exchanged for common stock.

Cooperatives   multiple-family dwelling units in which owners buy shares in a stock corporation that owns the building. The shares purchased equal the amount of private dwelling space assigned to that shareholder plus an equivalent percentage of common areas.

Coupon or Nominal Yield   the rate of return on a debt security calculated at par value.

Credit Bureau   a credit-reporting agency owned privately or cooperatively by local lenders which collects relevant financial information about local borrowers and sells it to properly identified member creditors and select others.

Credit Life Insurance   Decreasing term life insurance equal to the outstanding balance on a mortgage or other credit contract so this debt will be paid in full in the event the debtor dies before full payment is rendered.

Credit Record   individual or joint file of credit history maintained at a credit bureau.

Credit Scoring   method of assigning various point values to selected characteristics of the potential borrower, as provided on the credit application; the sum total is compared to a minimum company standard for good credit risks.

Credit Unions   banking "cooperatives" in which members pool their savings in order to provide the funds necessary to meet most of the members' lending needs.

Cross-Collateral   a clause allowing the seller to retain ownership (title) to all goods purchased under a single installment contract until the last item is paid for in full.

Current Yield   interest paid on a bond expressed as a percentage of the present market price thereby considering purchase discount or premium.

Debit Cards   plastic cards carrying personal ID and an account number which can be used for purchases at properly equipped retail stores in lieu of checks for withdrawal against your checking account.

Debt Poolers   commercial prorate firms who make a business of establishing and administering debt adjustment programs for financially distressed clients.

Debt Proration   a debt adjustment program whereby installment obligations, usually already in default, are repaid to creditors at a percentage of the original installment payments for a longer contract period in order to achieve full repayment.

Deductible   a predetermined sum of money specified in an insurance policy which the insured agrees to pay out-of-pocket before the insurer begins benefit payments under this contract.

Default   when the borrower fails to make payments according to the terms of credit contract.

Deficiency Judgment   a clause allowing the creditor to collect from the buyer the balance owed on the contract after sale of the repossessed goods.

Demand Deposit   funds on deposit with a financial institution that can be withdrawn immediately (or on demand) by writing a check or negotiable order of withdrawal.

Depreciation   the loss of value of the automobile, etc., during ownership due to passage of time, and/or mechanical and physical condition.

At Discount   to purchase or sell an investment instrument below its face value or original price when marketed.

Diversification   spreading the dollars invested by an individual among several investment vehicles in an attempt to limit possible losses without sacrificing profitability.

Dividends   a share of the profits of a corporation paid regularly to shareholders.

Double or Triple Indemnity   riders that can be purchased on life insurance policies to pay the beneficiaries two or three times the face value of the policy if the insured dies due to accidental causes.

Electronic Funds Transfer System (EFTS)   the application of computer technology to transfer funds via electronic impulse from the purchaser's bank account to the seller's account—without real money being handled by human hands or paper transactions.

Endorsements   amendments or changes added to an insurance policy to modify its terms to better meet unique needs; usually calculated at extra cost to the policyholder.

Endowment Insurance   a form of life insurance emphasizing the savings component so much that the face value of the policy is paid in a specified number of years whether the insured lives or dies.

Estate Taxes   federal taxes paid (after exemptions are taken) from the assets left by the deceased prior to the transfer of these assets to legal heirs.

Face Value   dollar amount of insurance purchased under one policy.

Fair Market Value   the price at which you could sell a piece of property today without taking advantage of buyer or seller.

Family Policies   a package of life insurance protection purchased to cover all family members under one policy.

Finance Charge   total dollar cost of borrowing.

Fixed Expenses   those which remain stable for relatively long periods of time, such as installment obligations, taxes, housing, etc.

Fixed Return Investment   one with a predetermined yield which is promised to the holder at the time of purchase and will not change if the investment instrument is held to maturity.

Flexible Expenses   those that fluctuate continuously such as food, clothing, gifts, recreation, etc.

Float   time lag between a purchase made by check and the deduction of that sum from your checking account.

Franchising   a marketing method that joins a large corporation with buying power and management experience with a small investor willing to trade dollars and sweat equity for a share of corporate profits.

Gambling   using money in an attempt to reap quick profits based on impulsive actions.

Gift Taxes   federal taxes paid by the giver on gifts of over $3,000 made to one individual in any one year, with some greater exemptions between spouses.

Graduated Payment Mortgage   borrowers make interest only payments on the mortgage at the beginning of the loan with periodic increases in the monthly payment through the years until the unpaid principal is repaid as well; monthly payments change but the rate of interest repaid remains constant.

Guaranteed Insurability   rider available on permanent life insurance that the insured may purchase additional permanent insurance coverage at specified times during his or her life without medical exam.

Guaranteed Renewability   a rider available to health insurance and term life insurance policies that promises that the insured will definitely be allowed to buy successive policies, despite health conditions, although the rate to reflect these changes may rise.

Holder-In-Due-Course   a third party creditor who buys credit contracts at discount from the original creditor and collects full payments from the borrower via assignment of the credit contract.

Home Service Insurance   permanent life insurance purchased from door-to-door salespeople in small amounts to cover burial costs; includes industrial insurance with premiums collected weekly and monthly debit ordinary with premiums collected monthly.

Indemnity Policy   health insurance benefits paid on the basis of a flat fee for services regardless of actual cost.

Inflation Guard Endorsement   amendment to a residential insurance policy that automatically increases the policy coverage by a predetermined rate each year, in an effort to keep coverage in line with inflation's effect.

Inheritance taxes state succession taxes on the proceeds of an estate left by citizens of that state to their heirs.

Installment Loan a contract between borrower and lender that stipulates that the loan will be repaid in fractions at regular intervals over specified period with each fractional payment representing the repayment of a portion of both principal and interest.

Interest cost of borrowing figured as a percentage of the amount borrowed or as a dollar amount (finance charge).

Intestate laws by which the state government decides the distribution of assets to heirs of persons who die without a valid will.

Investing the commitment of money for the purchase of securities or other properties based on a careful analysis of anticipated risks and rewards over a period of time usually equal to one year or more.

Investment Companies corporations that operate for the purpose of investing other people's money at a profit to be shared by the investors and the corporation.

Irrevocable Trust a trust which cannot be amended, altered, revoked or terminated by the trustmaker; this trust essentially removes the assets included herein from the estate of the trustmaker thereby possibly reducing estate taxes.

Joint Tenancy individuals own the property together during their lives, with rights of survivorship bringing sole ownership of the total property to the joint tenant that lives longer, unless negated by the deceased tenant's will.

Late Charges an extra fee charged on each installment loan payment made more than the contractually agreed number of days beyond the due date.

Lease a contract to rent property (often a dwelling or car) for a specified period of time, usually from several months to several years.

Leverage using credit to maximize an investment return far beyond what could be expected if the investment was paid in full with cash.

Liability legal responsibility for property damage or injury to others.

Life Insurance Trust a special trust used to provide for payment of anticipated probate costs, estate, and inheritance taxes from a life insurance policy purchased for this purpose.

Limited Payment Life a permanent insurance policy with payments condensed to be made over a short number of years, usually during peak earnings periods.

Liquid easily converted to cash.

Liquid Assets things you own that can easily be converted into cash.

Living Trust a trust created and effective while the trustmaker is living.

Load the salescharge if any on the purchase of mutual fund shares.

Loan Value the portion of some life insurance and annuity policies that can be borrowed under conditions specified in the contract.

Margin Accounts credit accounts established by a brokerage house to allow interested and qualified investors to purchase more securities than that investor's cash will allow.

Marital Deduction Trust a special trust usable only between spouses for the purpose of maximizing benefits under present federal estate tax laws (and reducing estate taxes).

Medicaid a health insurance program sponsored by state and federal governments to help qualified low income people of all ages obtain sufficient health care that they could not afford to buy privately.

Medicare a federal government program providing mandatory and supplemental voluntary medical insurance for most Americans age sixty-five or over.

Medigap Insurance health insurance coverage sold by private companies to fill in some of the voids in Medicare coverage, especially the deductible and coinsurance provisions.

Mill one thousandth of a dollar; equivalent in tax assessment to "___ dollars per thousand."

Modified Whole Life a graduated payment plan for life insurance coverage whereby the premiums start low with a majority of coverage provided by term insurance and increases in a predetermined number of years to provide full coverage with permanent insurance after the policyholder is assumed to have increased earnings to more easily afford higher costs.

Money Market Funds mutual funds that invest in short-term debt securities of governments and/or corporations.

Moratorium temporary suspension of debt repayment until the debtor's financial circumstances stabilize.

Mortgage long-term installment loan made on real estate with the dwelling and land used as security for the loan.

Mutual Funds investment company that sells shares of ownership in itself, the total number of which can be increased or decreased to meet investor demand and redeemed directly by the company.

Net Worth the difference between all you own (your assets) and all you owe (your liabilities).

Nonparticipating Life Insurance all policies that do not pay dividends.

NOW accounts demand deposit accounts that pay interest on the funds remaining on deposit.

Odd Lots uncommon units of trading in securities.

Open-End Credit revolving credit agreement that allows fluctuating charges and payments at the borrower's option in line with contract terms for an unlimited time period; often a maximum credit limit is also imposed.

Opportunity costs sacrifices that must be made when you allocate finite resources to a specific end use and therefore no longer have that resource available to meet other goals.

Options a contract to buy or sell securities at a predetermined future date and a predetermined price.

At Par purchase or sale of an investment instrument at face value.

Partial Disability the ability to return to work part time only or to perform only some of your predisability job related tasks.

Participating Life Insurance policies that pay dividends to policyholders to reflect difference between premiums charged and actual experience.

Passbook Loans using a sum already in your savings account at a financial institution as security for borrowing an equal amount from that institution.

Pension retirement income paid by the employer or union to a retired worker for the rest of his or her life, the amount of which is calculated on a formula considering salary and years of service.

Pension Accrual Benefits a provision of some long-term disability insurance policies whereby company retirement benefits will be calculated as though the insured person worked during the years of her or his disability.

Permanent Life Insurance continuous life insurance protection provided until the policyholder cancels the policy orders; includes a combination of savings and insurance protection; also called "whole life" or "straight life."

Personal Property Floaters amendments to the residential insurance policy that provides compensation for loss or damage to select, expensive valuables like jewelry or silverware not otherwise fully covered by the policy.

Points A fee equal to 1 percent of the home mortgage and charged as a one-time fee payable when the loan is granted.

Preexisting Conditions sickness or physical defects which were known prior to taking out the medical insurance policy.

Preferred Stocks shares of ownership in a corporation that resemble bonds in that they pay a predetermined dividend as set by the Board of Directors of the corporation.

Premium rate charged to purchase an insurance policy.

At Premium to purchase or sell an investment instrument above its face value or original price when marketed.

Prepayment Penalty   a clause contained in some credit contracts that requires a borrower who chooses to repay the loan ahead of schedule to be charged a specified fee for costs incurred by the lender to alter the original contract.

Principal   original dollars invested before interest, dividends, or other profits are added.

Probate Court   judicial authority in each state that supervises the transfer of property either by will or laws of intestate to heirs after a resident's death.

Prospectus   written information available to stock and bond investors of new issues to provide relevant details of the offering and the issuer, so the investor has sufficient information for informed decision making.

Pyramiding   the method of profitmaking based on the purchase of leveraged securities, the equity of which is used as collateral to buy more leveraged securities and increase profits.

Quit Claim Deed   title to property in which the seller agrees to give up any interest he or she has in the property, without regard to anyone else's claim upon it.

Repossession   action that occurs when lender under a secured credit contract take the property purchased with the loan or other security away from the borrower after her or his default in order to recoup losses resulting from that default.

Reverse Annuity Mortgages   a long-term installment loan that allows qualified homeowners to borrow the equity accumulated in their homes without selling the dwelling; they pay interest only at conventional mortgage rates while drawing on monthly reduction of principal for personal use.

Revocable Trust   a trust that can be terminated or altered by the trustmaker at any time.

Rider   additional provision added to an insurance policy to provide greater protection to the policyholder for selected provisions.

Round Lots   common units of securities trading, like 100 shares of stock, etc.

Second Mortgage   closed-end installment loans available through many financial institutions as a means by which homeowners can raise money by borrowing the equity in their homes.

Security   a property that you own which you would allow the lender to take away from you if you fail to keep your promise to repay the loan as agreed.

Service Benefit Policy   a type of medical insurance policy, the benefits of which pay in full for covered services to the policyholder regardless of actual cost.

Settlement Options   choices in how life insurance benefits will be paid to the beneficiary.

Single Payment Note   contractual agreement that specifies the borrower will repay principal plus interest in one lump sum on a specific date.

Social Security   an insurance program of the U.S. government that provides pension benefits to qualified workers upon retirement and/or death benefits to their qualified surviving dependents as well as long-term disability payments under certain circumstances.

Speculating   carefully selecting investment instruments that will hopefully yield substantial profits relatively quickly.

Stock   shares of ownership in a corporation.

"Stop Gap" Health Insurance   nonrenewable basic medical policies with coverage effective immediately but limited to 60 to 180 days and modest dollar benefits.

Tax Credits   reduction in tax liability subtracted directly from the amount of taxes you owe or have paid.

Tax Deductions   reductions in taxable income that shrink total tax liability.

Tax Exemption   reduction in taxes due because certain portions of income or property are rendered nontaxable.

Tenancy in Common   the individual owners hold separate and distinct interests in the property that are not necessarily equal.

Tenancy by the Entirety   joint tenancy with tax advantages in some states because it is limited to husband and wife only.

Tenancy for a Fixed Period   tenancy for a mutually agreeable time period as specified in the lease.

Tenancy at Will   continues tenancy until either landlord or tenant chooses to change the lease agreement under which this tenancy was established.

Term Insurance   life insurance protection provided to the policyholder for a limited period of time—one, five, ten, or twenty years.

Testamentary Trust   a trust established under the provisions of the trustmaker's last will and testament, becoming effective only after the will has passed through probate.

Time Deposits   savings accounts at financial institutions.

Total Disability   the inability to work in any gainful employment.

Trust   an arrangement whereby property is managed by an individual or bank for the benefit of someone else.

Unsecured loan   a credit contract backed only by the borrower's promise to repay the loan.

Variable Life Insurance   a permanent life insurance policy that provides a guaranteed minimum benefit to the beneficiary plus the possibility of additional monies resulting from company investment in common stock with a portion of premium dollars.

Variable Rate Mortgages   Long-term installment loans offering flexible interest rates to the borrower modified on a predetermined schedule based on market fluctuation; monthly payments can rise and fall as a result as can the total interest paid on the loan.

Vesting   a guaranteed return from a pension plan at least equal to the full employe contribution even when the worker leaves the firm prior to retirement.

Wage Assignment   a credit contract condition that allows the creditor to collect payments on a delinquent account directly from the debtor's wages via a payroll deduction by his or her employer—without first notifying the debtor.

Wage Continuation Plans   short-term disability policies that pay most or all of your income during a set period of disability, usually on a short-term basis; also called "sick leave" plans.

Wage Garnishment   a court order asking a debtor's employer to pay the debtor's past due bill for her or him in installments deducted directly from wages before they are paid to the debtor.

Waiver of Premium   a rider available on some life insurance policies whereby the insurance company will keep an existing policy in effect without further payment of premiums by the policyholder under certain conditions such as disability of the policyholder.

Warranty Deed   title to property that carries a written warranty by the seller that he or she legally owns the property and has the right to dispose of it because no one else has any claim to it.

Will   legal document directing the distribution of your assets to your heirs as you prescribe.

Worker's Compensation   disability coverage required by law for persons suffering job-related sickness or accident.

Writ of Attachment   a court order allowing a sheriff to take specified items of a debtor's personal property which are owned outright to his or her creditor for sale in full or partial payment of a defaulted debt.

Yield   the rate of return on an investment.

Yield to Maturity   the rate of return on a debt security that considers present market price of the bond, coupon yield, years to maturity, and par value.

Index

Activity checking account, 211
"Add on" interest, 111
Adjustable life insurance, 198
Adjusted payments in debt, 139
Adjustments to income, 42–44
Affordable indebtedness, 137
Age discrimination in granting credit, 118
Alternate dwellings, 56
Alternate lifestyle needs, 22–24
Alternative mortgage instruments, 73
Alternatives in transportation, 98–99
Amendment to Truth in Lending Law, 113
American National Standards Institute, 59
Amortization, 72
Annual percentage rate, 111–112
Annuity, 268–269
Apartments, 57–58
Appeals in taxation, 38
Applying for credit, 113–120
    credit reporting services, 114–116
    credit scoring, 116–117
    equal credit opportunities, 117–120

Assessment of debt, 138–141
Assessment of property taxes, 35–36
Assets, 17–18
    ownership taxation, 273–274
"Assigned risk pool," 178
Assignment of credit contract, 130–131
Assuming a mortgage, 75
Attitudes toward debt, 136–137
Audit, in taxes, 46–47
AUTOCAP, 97
Automatic payroll deduction program, 199
Automobile
    bill paying, 30
    insurance. See Motor vehicle insurance
    loans, 107
    registration fee, 90
    titling tax, 91
    transportation, 86–87

Balloon payment contracts, 141–142
Banking. See also Financial institutions

cooperatives, 207
institutions, types of, 206–208
by mail, 212, 221
Bankruptcy, 148, 230
    avoiding, 162–163
    definition of, 5
Bankruptcy Act, 149
Bartering, 2
Beneficiaries, 109, 196
Best's Insurance Reports, 169
Bicycle transportation, 82–86, 89, 98, 174, 175
Billing errors, 30
    in credit card statements, 132
Bills, definition of, 230
"Blue book" value, 36
Bodily injury liability insurance, 175
Bonds, definition of, 230
Borrower/creditor public relations, 143
Breaking a housing contract, 69–70
Breaking a lease, 64
Bribing with money, effects of, 6
Broker, definition of, 242

Brokerage agreement, 71–72. *See also* Realtors
Bureau of Labor Statistics, 21
Buses as transportation, 87–88, 98
Business Week, 248
Buying an automobile, 93–95
Buying housing, 65–76. *See also* Housing

Calendar/payday chart for recordkeeping, 27–28
Canceling life insurance policy, 197
Capital assets, 43
Capital gain/loss, 43–44, 243, 245
Carpooling, 83, 87, 96, 139
Cash vs. credit auto financing, 90
Cash surrender value of a policy, 197
Cashless/checkless society, 29
Ceiling limits in taxation, 37
Certificates of deposit, 215–216, 218, 229, 235
Changing insurance policies, 203
Changing lifestyles, 11, 88, 98, 136, 195
    for estate planning, 270–275
    for retirement, 259–270
Changing Times, 169
Chapter 13, 158–160
Charge accounts, 106
Charitable contributions, 139
Charters in banking, 208
Checking accounts, 211–215, 227
    credit, 110–111
    fees, 211
    for recordkeeping, 27
    services, 214–215
Child care services, 23, 46, 195
    expenses, 7
Childless couples, spending plans for, 7, 22–23
Children, insurance for, 195–196, 202
Children and money management, 6, 9, 23–24
Christmas/vacation clubs, 218
Claim procedures for medical insurance, 184
Clearinghouses, 114, 155
Closed-end credit, 106–107, 111, 127
Closed-end funds, 234

Closed-end installment loan, 110
    contract, 120–130
Closing costs when buying housing, 65, 68
Coinsurance, 184–185
Collateral on a loan, 74
Collectibles as investment, 238
Collection accounts, 116
    past due, 141–149
Collection agency, 143
Collection costs in loan contract, 126
Collection practices for loans, 110
College students, 17
College years and money management, 8, 192
Collision insurance, 175
Co-makers, 159
    definition of, 126–127
Commercial banks, 74, 206
Commissions in investments, 242–243
Commodities, 239, 242
Common stock, 233–234
Community resources in coping with debt, 138–139
Community transportation systems, 80
Commuting, 81, 83, 87, 139
Comparison shopping
    automobiles, 92–93
    housing, 61–62
    insurance, 168
    medical insurance, 182–183
    mortgages, 72–73
    transportation, 92–93
Compounding, definition of, 216–217
"Comprehensive" insurance, 176
Computer technology, 29
Condominiums, 67, 70, 71
    insurance, 173
Confession of judgment, definition of, 141
Consolidation loans, 110, 154
Construction standards, 61, 68–69
"Consumer Credit Counseling Services," 158, 159
Consumer Expenditure Survey, 53
Consumer Leasing Act, 91
Consumer Price Index, 22

Consumer protection
    agencies, 92, 97
    laws, 208, 254–255
Consumer Reports, 92, 169
Contracts
    automobile, buying, 92
    credit agreement, 120–130
    housing, 69–72
        apartments, 57
        renting, 63–64
Contributions, 45
Controlling finances, 9–10
Conventional mortgage, 74. *See also* Mortgage
"Convertibility" riders, 201
Convertibles, stock and bonds, 234
"Cooling off period," 170
Cooperative Extension Service, 21
Cooperative housing, 70
Cooperatives, 67
Corporate bonds, 231
Correcting credit records, 115
Cosigner, 119
Cost-of-living index, 22, 224
Costs
    borrowing, 107
    housing, 53
        selling, 66
    insurance, auto, 177–178
    loans, 74, 111–113
    retirement, 261–263
    transportation, 82–83
Counseling in money management, 10, 12, 21, 220–221
    investments, 251–253
    retirement, 261
Coupon books for loan repayment, 106
Credit
    applying for, 113–120
    arrangements, 109–111
    availability, 30
    contracts, 71–72, 120–130
    cost comparisons, 111–113
    disadvantages of, 104–105
    files, 115–116
    granting, 72, 208
    histories, 114, 120
    post-transaction activities, 130–133
    scoring, 116–117

sources, 107–109
in taxing, 46
trends in usage, 102–104
types of, 105–107
Credit bureaus, 114, 120
Credit cards, 28, 102, 108, 113
agreements, 127–130
charges, verifying, 132
errors in billing, 132
Credit reporting services, 114–116
Credit unions, 107, 207, 208, 213,
216, 218, 227
Credit worthiness, 112–113
Creditor/debtor communication, 139
Creditors' rights, 141–142
Cross collateral, definition of, 141

Damage to insured vehicle, 176
Debit cards, 219
Debt, 18, 135–164
assessment of, 138–141
attitudes toward, 136–137
collection of past-due accounts,
141–149
court action, 142
danger signals, 137–138
instruments, 229–232
load, 225–226
management alternatives, 149–163
securities, 249
"Debt poolers," 157
Debtors' rights, 147–149
Decisions concerning investments,
247–254
Decisions concerning spending, 11–12
Decreasing term insurance, 196
"Deductible" insurance, 176,
184–185
Deductions for depreciation, 65
Deductions in taxes, itemizing, 44
Defaulting, 126, 128
definition of, 125
Deferment of taxes by investment,
244–245
Deficiency judgment, definition of,
141
Delivery of goods and/or credit
cards, 131–132
"Demand deposit," 211
Dental coverage, 180

Department of Housing and Urban
Development, 255
Dependents exempt from taxation,
42
Deposit on housing, 56
Deposit insurance in banking,
208–210
Depreciation
of autos, 87, 89–90, 91, 94
of real estate, 238
Designated percentage of fair market
value, 37
"Discount" interest, 111
Discrimination in granting credit,
117–120
Disposable personal income, 53, 87
Double/triple indemnity riders, 200
Down payments, 72, 75
Direct business investment, 236–237
Disability
definition of, 188–189
income protection insurance,
187–190
Discretionary money, 5
Diversification in investments, 253
Division of work and home
responsibilities, 23
Driving expenses, 42
Dual income families, 7

Early retirement, 261
Earnings, loss of, 43
Economic conditions in selecting
investment, 242
Economy in group insurance,
171–172
Effective annual yield of interest, 216
Effective date of deposit, 217
Efficiency apartments, 57
Electronic funds transfer systems,
29–30, 219–220
Eligibility for tax benefits, 48
Emergency fund, 9, 17, 227, 267
Emotional aspects of money, 1, 3, 10
Emotional stress of moving, 53
Emotions ruling housing choices, 54
Employee benefits, cash value of, 17
Employee Retirement Income
Security Act, 266, 267
Employee travel, 42

Employer-based credit unions, 107
Employer-paid sick leave benefits,
187–188
Employment fringe benefits, 180
Employment reports in credit
bureaus, 115
"Enabling Declaration," 70
Endowment insurance, 199
Energy costs, 61
Energy usage in transportation, 83
Envelope method of recordkeeping,
26–27
Environment influencing money
management, 10
Equal credit opportunity, 117–120
Equal Credit Opportunity Act, 117,
119, 120
"Equalization of estate" plan, 272
Equity in housing, 65, 73
Estate planning, 270–275
Evaluating borrowers, 113
Excise taxes, 35
Exemptions in taxes, 42, 47
Extension Home Economists, 155

Face value, definition of, 196
Fair Credit Billing Act, 129, 130,
162–163
Fair Credit Reporting Act, 115, 116
Fair market value
definition of, 35
of real estate, 17
False sense of affluence, 128
Families and money management,
7–8
Family life insurance policies, 202
Farmers Home Administration, 74
Fault vs. "No-fault" insurance, 177
Federal Communications
Commission Act, 144
Federal Deposit Insurance
Corporation, 209, 235
Federal Fair Debt Collection
Practices Act, 145
Federal Highway Administration, 87
Federal Home Loan Bank Board,
208
Federal Housing Administration, 75
Federal income tax, 65
Federal Reserve Banks, 208, 230, 242

Federal Reserve Board, 208
Federal Savings and Loan Insurance, 209
Federal Trade Commission, 94, 131, 144, 145, 170, 237
FIFO, 217
Filing health insurance claim, 184
Filing requirements in income taxes, 40–41
Finance charges, 110–111, 112, 128, 154
Financial counseling, 220–221
Financial disasters, protection against, 165–202
   disability insurance, 178–187
   life insurance, 190–202
   medical insurance, 178–187
   principles, 166–172
   property insurance, 172–178
Financial institutions, 205–222
   banks, 206–207
   for loans, 107–108
   safety precautions, 208–210
   services available, 210–221
"Financial planners," 252
Financial planning, 15–31, 55
   alternate lifestyle needs, 22–24
   flexibility, 103–104
   future trends, 29–30
   net worth, 16–18
   recordkeeping choices, 24–28
   spending plan, 18–22
   tips of the trade, 29
Financing
   automobiles, 90
   controlling, 9–10
   housing, 55–56, 60, 72–76
Fire insurance, 172
Fixed expenses, 7, 27, 77
   definition of, 20
   flexible, 55
Fixed fee setting, 252
Fixed return investment, 229–232
Flexibility in financial planning, 9, 12, 103–104
Flexible expenses, 27
   definition of, 20
Float, definition of, 219
Floaters, 173
Flood insurance, 168

Forced savings, 65, 103, 227
Fortune, 248
Franchising, 236–237
Fraudulent car repairs, 97
Fraudulent debts, 161
Free checking accounts, 212
Frozen interest charges, 153
Fuel usage, 61
Full-service banking, 206
Funeral expenses, 176, 195, 271
Future income, 3–4
Future trends in money management, 5, 29–30

Gift/inheritance taxes, 47, 244, 271
Goals, 11, 18–19, 20
   self-discipline in achieving, 29
Gold as investment, 239
Government programs
   disability insurance, 190
   life insurance, 193–194
   medical insurance, 185–187
Government spending, 34
Government supervision in banking, 208
Grace period, 111, 124, 128, 129, 219
Graduated payment mortgages, 73
"Grand List," 37, 38
Group considerations in spending, 11–12
Group vs. individual money needs, 9–10
Group insurance policies, 171–172, 181–183, 189, 196, 199–200
Growth investments, 240
Guaranteed renewable insurance policies, 183
Guaranteed renewable riders, 201

Handicaps in transportation, 83–84
Harassment by collection agencies, 144–145
Health maintenance organizations, 185
High pressure insurance sales, 170–171
High risk drivers, 178
Home economists, 21, 157
Home ownership. *See* Housing
Home service insurance, 201–202

Hospital room and board, 179
"House slaves," 53
Housing, 51–78
   buying, 65–76
      construction, 68–69
      contracts, 69–72
      financing, 72–76
      options, 67–68
   costs, 8, 53
   finances, 55–56
   inspection services, 69
   needs, 54–55
   renting, 62–64
   shopping for, 61–62

Illegal lender, 109
Impulse buying, 104
Income adjustments, 42–44
Income, increasing, 19, 139
Income-producing investments, 36, 240
Income sources in credit application, 118–119
Income sources for retirement income, 263–270
Income taxes, 39–47, 53, 65
   deductions, 211
Indebtedness. *See* Debt
Indemity, 182
Independent insurance agents, 169
Index of price change, 22
Indexes and averages, stocks, 249
Individual vs. group insurance policies, 182–183, 189, 199–200
Individual vs. group money needs, 9–10
Individual Retirement Account, 44, 220, 266, 269
Industrial insurance, 201
Inequity of taxation system, 38, 40–41
Inflation, 22, 53, 66, 103, 189, 192, 224
Inflation guard insurance endorsement, 174
Information sources for investments, 247–253
Inheritance taxes, 271–272
Inspection services for housing, 69

Installment loan, 105–106
Installment vs. single payment credit, 105–106, 108, 128
"Insured saving plan," 199
Insurance, 20, 168–169. *See also* Financial disasters, protection against
Insuring children, 195–196, 202
Insuring homemakers, 195
Interest-bearing checking accounts, 213–214
Interest payments, 45, 109
Interest rates, 72, 74, 107, 108, 210, 216
Internal Revenue Service, 35, 40, 41, 267
International Franchise Association, 237
Inventory of possessions, 174
Inventory of wealth and spending, 16–17
Investment, 223–257
  consumer protection, 254–256
  decisions, 247–254
  readiness, 224–228
  after retirement, 267–268
  selection criteria, 240–247
  types of, 229–239
    collectibles, 238
    commodities, 239
    debt instruments, 229–232
    direct business investments, 236–237
    gold, 239
    investment companies, 234–236
    real estate, 237–238
    shares of ownership, 232–234
    variables, 228–229
Investment pyramid, 240
Irregular payments clause in loan contract, 126
Irrevocable trusts, 274–275
Itemized vs. standard deductions in taxation, 44–46

Job transfer, 7, 23, 66
Joint tenacy, 273

Keough Plan, 44, 220, 267, 269

Landlord-tenant law, 64
Late charges, 124–125, 141, 142
Leasing apartments, 63–64
Leasing automobiles, 91
Legal remedies to bankruptcy, 158–162
Leverage, definition of, 245
Liabilities, 17–18
  coverage, 175–176
"Life care" arrangements after retirement, 263
Life cycles and money management, 6–9
Life insurance, 17, 74, 112, 169, 190–202
  from banks, 220
  basic policies, 196–199
    endowment, 199
    permanent, 197–199
    term, 196–197
  needs, 190–196
    fringe benefits, 194
    government benefits, 193–194
    net supplemental protection, 194–196
    net worth, 192–193
  purchasing options, 199–201
  after retirement, 268–270
  special policies, 201–203
  trusts, 275
Lifestyle costs when determining amount of life insurance, 191–192
LIFO, 217
"Limited payment life" insurance, 197
Liquid assets, definition of, 17
Liquidation, 192
Liquidity, 230, 235
  of funds or deposit, 210
  of investments, 228–229
Living trusts, 274
"Load" fund, definition of, 235
"Load" mutual funds, 243
Loan repayment, 105–106
Local debt management and counseling services, 156
Long-term borrowing, 111
Long-term disability protection, 188

Long-term gain, 65
  definition of, 43
Long-term loans, 90
Long-term sickness, 179–180
Loopholes in taxes, 39, 244
Loss of credit cards, 129
Loss of earnings, 43
Lots in shares of stock, 253

Macro impact of money, 3–4
Mail-order companies for medical insurance, 183–184
Major medical coverage, 179–180
  insurance, 183
Mandatory retirement, 261
Marital deduction trust, 275
Marital status, discrimination in granting credit, 118
Marketability, definition of, 229
Marriage penalty in taxation, 41, 44
Mass transit, 83, 87–88, 89, 175
Medicaid, 139, 168, 186–187, 262
Medical insurance, 45, 178–187
  exam, 180
  exclusions/limitations, 180–181
  expenses, 45
Medicare, 139, 168, 186–187, 262
"Medigap" policies, 186–187
Mental illness, 179
Micro impact of money, 2–3
Mill rate in taxes, 37
Minimum balance in checking account, 211
Mobile homes, 59–60
"Modified whole life" insurance, 197–198
Modular housing, 60–61
Money, 1–12
  definition of, 2
  leaks, 11, 20
  management problems, 10–11
  market funds, 235
Monthly spending plan, 20
Moody's Investor Service, 231
Moonlighting, 139
Mopeds as transportation, 86
Mortgage, 17, 18, 20, 65, 72, 75, 230
  interest rates, 72, 226
  loans, 107
Moratorium of debt repayment, 153

Motor vehicle insurance, 174–178
Motorcycles as transportation, 86
Moving
  emotional stress of, 53
  expenses, 42
Multi-family dwelling, 56–59, 65, 66, 67
Municipal bonds, 231–232
Mutual funds, 234–236, 238
  investors, 242

National Conference of Commissioners on Uniform State Laws, 64
National Credit Union Administration, 209
National Fire Protection Association, 59
National Foundation for Consumer Credit, 158
National Institute for Automobile Service Excellence, 97
National Mobile Home Construction and State Safety Standards Act, 59
Nationality discrimination in granting credit, 118
Negative net worth, 18
Negligence insurance, 172
Net supplemental life insurance protection, 194–196
Net worth, 16–18, 168
  determining life insurance, 192–193
  statement, definition of, 17
"No-fault" vs. fault insurance, 177
"No-growth" position, 18
"No-load" funds, def of, 235
Nominal rate of interest, 216
Noncancellable insurance policies, 183
Noncontractual collection efforts, 142–146
"Nonparticipating life insurance," 200
Nonprofit cooperative, 67
Notes, definition of, 230
Notice accounts, 215
NOW account, 214, 227
Nursing homes, 181

Official tax roll for community, 37
One-parent family life insurance plans, 202
Open-end credit, 108, 127
  vs. closed-end credit, 106–107
Operating costs of automobile, 96–98
Optimism in spending, 4–5
Options in transportation, 84–88
Out-of-pocket costs
  of automobiles, 87
  of home ownership, 226
  medical expenses, 169, 182
  of real estate, 237
Overdrafting checks, 110
  privileges, 212
Overdrawing checking account, 212
Overpayment of taxes, 40, 46
Overspending, 19, 26, 104
  habitual, 22
  on housing, 66
Over-the-counter stocks, 249, 255
Overtime work, 139

Partial disability, definition of, 189
"Participating life insurance," 200
Passbook loans, 109
Pay-by-phone banking, 219
Payroll deduction plans, 107, 199, 207
Pensions, 194, 260, 263, 266–267
Periodicals to consult for investing, 248–249
Permanent life insurance, 197–199
Personal financial life cycle, 6–9
Personal liability automobile coverage, 90
Personal loans, 107
"Personal property floaters," 173
Personal property taxes, 35
Personality factors in selecting investment, 241
"Plain language" insurance policies, 170
Point values in credit application, 117
Points on a loan, definition of, 75
Post-transaction activities in credit/loans, 130–133
Preexisting conditions in medical insurance coverage, 180

Preferred stock, 233, 235
Prepaid benefits, medical insurance, 185
Prepayment penalty clause, 74
Prepayment of whole note, 123–124
Principles of insurance, 166–172
Professional guidelines, 12, 31, 48–49, 77, 99–100, 133–134, 163–164, 203–204, 221–222, 256–257, 276
Progressive tax, 39
Prompt repayment discount, 130
Property damage liability insurance, 175
Property insurance, 168, 172–178
Property reassessment, 37–38
Property taxes, 35–39, 62, 65
  appeals, 38
  assessments, 35–36
  consequences, 39
  rates, 36–37
  uniformity, 37–38
Proration of debts, 157
Protection for dependents when investing, 226–227
Psychiatric treatment, 181
Public opinion in selecting investment, 241–242
Purchase/sales agreement, 70
Purchasing options
  in disability insurance, 188–190
  in housing, 67–68
  in life insurance, 199–201
  in medical insurance, 181–185
  in transportation, 89–99
Pyramiding, 246

Qualifications for borrowing, 107
Quit-claim deed, 71

Race discrimination in granting credit, 118
Rate of return on investment, 229
Rating systems of bonds, 231, 233
Real estate
  fair market value, 17
  investing in, 237–238
Real Estate Settlement Procedures Act, 76

Real property, 43
  taxes, 35
Realtor fees/commissions, 68, 71
Receipts, 18, 30
Recordkeeping, 16-19, 24-28, 45, 46,
    98, 132, 174, 211, 263
  calendar/payday chart, 27-28
  checking account, 27
  envelope method, 26-27
  rubber budget, 25-26
Reducing financial losses, 167
Reducing payments on "pro rata"
    basis, 150
Reducing taxes by investing, 243-244
Regional differences in housing, 58
Religious discrimination in granting
    credit, 118
Rent raising, 63
Renting an automobile, 91
Renting housing, 62-64
Repayment discount, 130
Repayment schedule for loans,
    109
Replacement value insurance, 173
Repossession, 161
  property, 126, 147
Request for Statement of Earnings,
    194
Resale values of automobiles, 90
Residential insurance, 172-174
Retail Installment Sales Act, 142
Retirement, 8, 259-270
  counseling, 261
  programs in banking, 220
Reverse annuity mortgages, 73
Revised credit contract in
    bankruptcy, 153
Revocable trusts, 274-275
Revolving charge accounts, 107,
    119
Revolving credit, 110
Rewarding with money, effects of, 6
Riders, definition of, 200
Rights of privacy in money
    management, 30
Risk vs. safety in investing, 228
Rooming houses, 56-57
Row houses, 58-59
Rubber budget, 25-26
"Rule of 78," 124, 126, 154

Safe deposit boxes, 218-219, 228
Safety factors in transportation, 81,
    82, 84-85
Safety vs. risk in investing, 228
Sales taxes, 34-35
Sample letter to creditors requesting
    reduced payments, 151-152
Savings accounts, 215-218
Savings banks, 73-74, 206-207, 216
  life insurance, 202
Savings bonds, 218, 232
Savings certifications, 215-216
Savings and loan associations, 73-74,
    108, 207, 216
Savings after retirement, 267-268
Second mortgages, 110
Secured credit agreement, 121-127
  sample of. 121-213
Securities and Exchange
    Commission, 250, 255
Securities Investors Protection
    Corporation, 255
Security agreements, 132-133
Security deposit, 56, 62, 64
Security on a loan, 74, 125
Selection insurance coverages,
    169-172
Self-employed persons, 43
Self-help programs for debtors,
    149-155
Service benefits vs. indemnity, 182
Service charge in checking account,
    211
Services available in financial
    institutions, 210-221
Sex discrimination in granting credit,
    118
Share draft accounts, 214
Shareholders of cooperations, 67-68
Shares of ownership, 232-234
Sheahy, Gail, 8
Shelter. See Housing
Short-term gains, definition of, 43
Short-term loans, 90, 119
Sick leave, 187-188
Simplified Employee Pension, 267
Single-family dwelling, 66, 67. See
    also Housing
Single individuals, spending plans
    for, 7, 8, 10, 22-23

Single-parent families, 23
Single payment vs. installment credit,
    105-106
Single payment loans, 111
Single payment notes, 107
  definition of, 105
Skipped payments, 139
Slush fund, 26
Small Business Administration,
    236
Small Loan Act, 142
Social insurance programs, 5
Social Security, 139, 190, 193,
    263-265
  benefits, 260
  life insurance, 268-270
  pensions, 266-267
  savings/investments, 267-268
Social Security Act, 186
Social Security Administration, 265
Soldiers' and Sailors' Civil Relief
    Act, 163
Sources of credit, 107-109
Specialists in debt management and
    counseling, 157-158
"Specific performance," doctrine of,
    69
Speculation in investments, 246-247
Spending chart, 28
Spending guidelines, 11
Spending inventory, 16-17
Spending plan, 18-22
Stagflation, definition of, 253
Standard vs. itemized deductions in
    taxation, 44-46
Standard and Poor's Corporation,
    231, 233
State Department of Insurance, 169,
    183
State income tax, 65
State-sponsored disability insurance,
    190
Statistical aids, 21-22
Status, 54, 63, 65-66, 241
Stocks and bonds, 17, 43, 242
"Stop gap" health insurance, 180
Stop-payment orders, 212, 213
Straight bankruptcy, 160-162
"Straight life" insurance, 197
Subsidized housing, 55

"Sum of the Digits," 124
Survival needs budget, 138

Tax Reform Act, 271
Taxes, 19–20, 33–49, 65
    audit, 46–47
    credits, 46
    deferral, 244–245, 270
    estate, 271–272
    gift/inheritance, 47, 271–272
    income, 39–47
    investments, 243–245
    liens, 116
    property, 35–39
    rates, 36–37
        increases, 237
    reform legislation, 46
    refunds, 40
    relief programs, 139, 262–263
    sales, 34–35
    shelters, 244
Technological influences of money,
    4–6
Teenagers and money management,
    6–7
Telephone banking, 219
Temporary insurance, 196
"Tenacy at will," definition of, 63
Tenant complaints, 64
Term insurance, 196–197, 268
Terms of repayment of loan, 123
Testamentary trusts, 274
Theft insurance, 172

Thrift accounts, 218
Time deposits, 215
Title insurance, 71
Townhouses, 58–59
Trains as transportation, 87–88
Transportation, 79–100
    handicaps, 83–84
    needs, 80–84
    options, 84–88
    purchasing options
        comparison shopping, 92–93
        decisions, 98–99
        operating costs, 96–98
        savings, 93–95
Trusts, 274–277
    definition of, 272
    and estate planning, 220
Truth in Lending Law, 111, 112,
        113, 123, 127, 128, 129, 146
Truth in Securities laws, 254
Two-parent families with children,
        7–8, 23–24

Unemployment, 5, 7, 23
Unexpected expenses, 17
Unfair sales techniques, 147
Uniform Commercial Code, 125, 132
Uniform Residential Landlord and
        Tenant Act, 64
Uniformity of taxes, 37–38
Uninsured banking institutions, 209
Uninsured motorist protection, 176
Unsecured credit agreement, 127

Valuation in taxing, 37
Variable rate mortgages, 73
Veteran's Administration, 75
Veteran's insurance, 190

Wage assignment, definition of,
    142
Wage continuation plans, 187–188
"Wage Earner Plan," 158
Wage garnishment, 146
Wage and property attachments,
    146–147
"Waiver of premium" riders, 201
Walking as transportation, 84–85,
    89
Wall Street Journal, 248, 249
Warranty deed, 71
Warranty programs, housing, 69
Wealth inventory, 16–17
Week-end marriage, 23
"Whole life" insurance, 197
"Widow's void," 194
Wills, 270–271
Withholding taxes, 40
Worker's compensation, 181, 188,
    194
Writ of attachment, 147

Yield, definition of, 229

Zero bracket, 44, 225
Zoning ordinances for mobile homes,
    60